KU-483-047

ASTRAL
TRAVEL

ELIZABETH BAINES

SALT

CROMER

PUBLISHED BY SALT PUBLISHING 2020

2 4 6 8 10 9 7 5 3 1

Copyright © Elizabeth Baines 2020

Elizabeth Baines has asserted her right under the Copyright, Designs
and Patents Act 1988 to be identified as the author of this work.

This book is sold subject to the condition that it shall not, by way of
trade or otherwise, be lent, resold, hired out, or otherwise circulated
without the publisher's prior consent in any form of binding or cover
other than that in which it is published and without a similar condition
including this condition being imposed on the subsequent publisher.

This book is a work of fiction. Any references to historical events, real
people or real places are used fictitiously. Other names, characters, places
and events are products of the author's imagination, and any resemblance to
actual events or places or persons, living or dead, is entirely coincidental.

First published in Great Britain in 2020 by
Salt Publishing Ltd
12 NORWICH ROAD, CROMER NR27 0AX UNITED KINGDOM

www.saltpublishing.com

Salt Publishing Limited Reg. No. 5293401

A CIP catalogue record for this book is available from the British Library

ISBN 978 1 78463 219 9 (Paperback edition)
ISBN 978 1 78463 220 5 (Electronic edition)

Typeset in Neacademia by Salt Publishing

Printed and bound in Great Britain by Clays Ltd, Elcograf S.p.A

NORTHAMPTONSHIRE LIBRARIES & INFORMATION SERVICES	
80003724442	
Askews & Holts	
DX	

CONTENTS

PART THREE
In which I ponder some further mysteries

PART FOUR
In which I get a revelation

PART FIVE
In which the book is judged by others

PART SIX
*In which, although the book is written,
further conundrums arise*

PART SEVEN
In which I conduct some research

PART EIGHT
In which my mother makes an even more stunning revelation

PART NINE
In which everything is thrown in the air

ASTRAL TRAVEL

AFTER AND BEFORE

I T WAS THE winter I discovered I had a cyst in my belly, grown all without my knowing, and my sister's heart started banging as if it wanted the hell out of there *now*.

I went over on the train to the hospital she'd been taken to and rushed down the corridor and into the ward. She was sitting up, dark curls on end, still hooked to the monitor, but they'd given her a shot and her heart rate was back to normal. She was scowling, reminding me of our father, because they wouldn't let her out of bed and she badly needed to pee.

There was a bed pan on the cover near the bottom of the bed. I said, 'Use it, I'll draw the curtains.' She said, 'You're joking! *Here?*' and looked around in horror at the drugged or sleeping patients each side and the curtains drawn on the bed opposite.

It's a small town, of course, the one she still lives in, where our parents settled at long last when we were in our teens, and where she's been a librarian all her adult life. She has her mystique to keep up.

The nurse came along and said my sister was OK now, her heartbeat had been normal for four hours, she could ring her husband to come back from his work to fetch her. As she took off the last plug my sister jumped from the leash and fled to the lavatory near the nurses' station, slamming the door with a sound that rang round the ward.

I didn't tell her about the cyst. And of course, the heart-thumping matter of the novel I had written, the novel about our family, wasn't mentioned. By then the subject was completely avoided.

❧

When I was six and my sister was four, she came down with scarlet fever, the one other time she was ever in hospital, carted off to an isolation hospital in the north Welsh hills.

We had only just moved from south Wales, the first of what would be several moves.

I sat outside the hospital in the car with my father, our baby brother asleep in the back in the carrycot, while our mother went in to visit her. Someone held her up at a hospital window for me to see her, but what I saw didn't look like my sister, like Cathy: we were too far away and the window seemed to be frosted; all I could see was a pink thing that made me think of a shrimp. I guess we must have gone at bath time and they were in the bathroom.

For years afterwards Cathy would recount the horror of that time, considering it one of her major childhood traumas: the enforced baths in Dettol; the compulsory drink of sickly Ovaltine at bedtime; being made to march beforehand down the central aisle with the other children, with their various strange accents, singing a song she didn't know in which you claimed to be something called an Ovalteenie, although she had no idea what that was.

Knowing nothing of this, cut off from my sister for the first time since I crawled across my mother's exhausted body to look at her newborn face and exclaim in wonder, 'Is she *ours?*', I felt a new bleakness and sense of loss. The hills outside the car window were alien and bare, and my father was broody and silent beside me, which was how he had been since we'd moved here.

And there was something that had recently come to me, a disappointing realisation. I wanted to ask my father about it.

He'd seen fairies, he'd said, in Ireland where he was born, and even here in north Wales. He insisted upon it. I'd looked and looked, desperate to see them myself, but never had. And now I had read that they didn't exist.

'Daddy?'

He didn't respond in the way he would have done once, with a languid, crooked-toothed, teasing grin. He didn't turn to me. His eagle-nosed profile was a stony sculpture against the car window. He was smoking, of course.

'Hm?' He sounded faraway, abstract.

'Daddy, fairies don't exist, do they, really?'

He didn't answer.

I persisted. 'Well, it's like Father Christmas, isn't it?'

He had gone completely still, and I knew what I'd done. I'd forgotten that he didn't even know I knew about Father Christmas. My mother had said better not tell him, he'd be disappointed.

'Daddy?' He was still silent.

Finally he said, 'No,' with such frozen shock and, yes, such flat disappointment, that I was filled with guilt and dismay. And a sense that things between me and my father would never be the same again.

Well, that's how I remember it. But what do I know? Things

3

get lost, memory can be muddled. As I say, by then, by the time we sat outside the hospital in the hills, my father had already changed. He was no longer the father who took me with him on his insurance rounds, rattling in the little Austin Seven down the flickering country lanes of south Wales, zooming up to the hump-back bridges with a grin, fag in the one hand on the wheel or stuck behind his ear, laughing his head off as I left the leather seat and squealed with delight. By this time, probably, he'd starting hitting us.

And it wasn't as if I went on not believing in fairies. I *wanted* to believe in them, or rather I didn't want *not* to. After that day, on Sunday outings to those hills I'd take a bag of silver charms I'd cut from the tobacco-smelling silver paper from my father's cigarette packets, hearts and flowers, bows and stars and sickle moons. I'd scatter them in the gorse, an offering and a plea for the fairies to appear and prove themselves.

As I begged for the silver paper and he handed it over, my father would snigger.

And a lot of what I remember is not the same as what the others remember, which was partly what caused the trouble when I tried to write a novel about it all.

PART ONE

*In which, against all previous likelihood, I begin
to try to write a book about my father*

PATRICK

MY FATHER HAD been dead ten years before I thought of writing about him. I surprised myself: there was a time when it was the last thing I'd have thought of doing. I'd put my father behind me for good, or so I thought.

It was the first of January, the first day of the new millennium. My kids had left home and I'd given up editing and publishing a literary magazine (twelve hours a day, in those days before you could publish at the press of a button). A fresh start, it seemed, a time to hope naively that all the conflicts of the old century were behind us, men against women, races and religions against one another, Manchester rebuilt after the IRA bomb. And Patrick Jackson, my volatile, contradictory and entirely unfathomable father, around whom we'd always had to tiptoe, long scattered on the spot in the narrow field above the sea in south Wales where he and my mother had first started courting.

I came back from the millennium parade in the city centre and sat down at my desk, and what popped into my head was the night my father died and the moments after he'd gone.

I was sitting then on the floor beside his bed and his newly dead body. I closed my eyes and behind my lids stars rushed towards me, as they did on the computer screensavers they had in those days. And then the ground rushed up, and I was zooming, flying low over a peat bog, rising and dipping with the subtle contours, towards the cottage I'd never seen but somehow knew, in which my father was born.

Of course I was dreaming – he had died in the early hours and we were all exhausted – but, still, I was spooked. I opened my eyes sharpish and stood up.

But now that sensation came back to me, and almost without thinking, I picked up my pen and wrote this:

He is falling, falling once more, this time through the legendary tunnel, out of the life he clung to against all the odds.

A light at the end, and he's gobbed, spat out, and lands in a heap. He sits up, looks around. He can't see much, the quality of light is strange, too bright yet somehow shadowed. There's a sound, a huge hiss, some kind of breathless pressure, like steam . . .

It comes to him, he understands: it's the sound of a water heater. He's in a transport caff, one of those shacks on the trunk roads he travelled all those years. Slowly things come into focus: the rickety tables, the chequered oilcloths, the greasy bottles of vinegar and HP sauce and tomato ketchup.

It was like automatic writing.

I was half shocked by the way the scene had surfaced in my mind unbidden, the somatic sense that had come to me of my father idling in transport caffs all the times in my childhood when he'd been out or away, when we'd felt him only as a black absence.

I was now gripped by the fluid way the writing had emerged. Next day I went out and, for the second time only in my life on my own behalf, bought a packet of cigarettes, and laid them on my desk as a visual and olfactory aid.

The smell of cigarettes. The smell of my father.

8

I picked up my pen again and it seemed to go on along the page as if independent of me:

In this heaven, or hell, Patrick gets to his feet. He's awkward and stiff, but all the pain of the last few weeks is gone.

The place is empty apart from one other man, a gnarled stringy feller like one of those men he once managed on the power-station sites, in a filthy tweed jacket and Fair Isle sweater, with wild dark hair and big bad teeth he's showing in a grin. He waves Patrick over.

Patrick is suspicious. He's hail-fellow-well-met, Patrick, but he's also a snob. 'Do I know you?' he asks – matey, of course: always cover your back, that's Patrick.

The feller doesn't answer. He sniggers as if it's a really good joke, and Patrick's a bit unsettled. But the urge for a fag overcomes him. 'You don't have a cig, do you, pal?'

With a nod and a wink the guy pats his chest and pulls out a packet, and flicks it open, and there's the row of orange-beige filters, pushed up like the pipes of an organ about to burst into glorious music. As the guy digs for his lighter, Patrick draws the silky stick under his nose, breathing in the perfume-clinical smell. And then, after all those weeks of dying, the smoke is curling down his bronchioles again, the cool clean burn steadying his shaken limbs.

A cup of tea appears in front of him, just as he always liked it, the colour of old leather. The guy pushes the sugar bowl towards him, the crystals caked and coloured caramel where others have pushed in wet spoons.

It's a damn good cuppa.

'So where are we?' Patrick asks, snapping the cup back on the saucer.

9

The feller doesn't answer. He bounces his bird's nest eyebrows and there's a sneaky look in his eyes, and this is when Patrick decides he can't be trusted.

He has to get out of here.

He downs the cuppa. He stands. The chair scrapes with an aching sound, the air gels in a sunbeam slicing the room. In the gloom beyond, the thin arm of the waitress drops like a broken wing.

'So long!' Patrick calls to the waitress, and he's through the door and out in a car park on windswept moors.

But the feller's right behind him. And there's nothing in the car park but the feller's vehicle, an old Ford Escort. Not Patrick's Rover, nor any of the vehicles he left in car parks like this down the years, the bright-blue sixties Ford Anglia, the motorbikes and vans, the Austin Sevens with their wooden dashboards drenched in the sun of stolen afternoons.

The feller unlocks his Escort and twitches his head for Patrick to hop in. 'Where to?' he asks Patrick, his tone magnanimous, as if he's offering a ride in a chariot not a boneshaker, dashboard covered in dust, sweet packets and tissues and cans littering the floor. And ironic: because, of course, for the first time ever, Patrick doesn't know where there is to go.

'You're the boss,' Patrick tells the feller grimly, and the guy turns the key.

The engine coughs, whines, then peters out.

Patrick might have known.

He tries again; the engine whimpers, expires again.

Now Patrick is stranded, unless he breaks his lifetime promise to himself and gets his hands dirty for someone else.

There's nothing for it. He tells the guy to release the

bonnet and gets out. Wouldn't you know it: distributor leads touching.

The leads are separated. Patrick tucks the rag back in its corner. He straightens. He reels. Maybe bending just after dying wasn't so clever. He steadies. He looks around. He's no longer on the moor. There are trees, oak leaves spilling dapples of shadow. He's in the garage at Ballymoyne, aged fifteen, wiping his hands on a rag and vowing to get away as soon as he can and never get his hands dirty for a living again.

I stopped writing. I knew where this last had come from. It was one of the tales we grew up with, my sister and I, Cathy and Jo Jackson, the tale of our father in the garage at Ballymoyne.

When we first moved to north Wales, when we were six and four, our mother started telling us stories of the past. Plucked summarily for our father's work from rural Llanfair in south Wales and transported to the seaside town of Prestatyn, we were homesick, the three of us, Cathy and I and our mother. We longed for the fields, fringed with creamy primroses in spring, for the lanes pungent with cow dung, the stroke of grey road leading down to the Bristol Channel and the quiet beach with its bank of clean-washed pebbles. Above all, Nanny and Grampa, our mother's parents, in their pink thatched cottage down the hill from the village, tucked beneath towering elms and the high ivy-covered walls of the farm and the manor house nearby. Our minds went back there constantly, and after lunch on Saturdays, in the poky kitchen of our flat above the office of the insurance company our father worked for, our father out on his rounds, our mother would push aside the greasy egg-and-chip plates and the dishes smeared with jam and semolina, and while the baby slept in the gloom beyond the sunbeam, she'd tell us stories of her childhood and youth there, and of the time she met our father and was first married to him.

By contrast, our father never talked about his past, but when he first met our mother he had told her a bit about his childhood in Ireland, which he'd wanted to escape, and did, and she passed these stories on to us.

He was the eldest of six children, she told us, in a one-room cottage at a crossroads, with a dirt floor.

'A dirt floor?!' I cried, the first time she told us.

There was just a tiny alcove off, where he said a mad aunt and a couple of his sisters slept. Our father, for a long time the only boy, slept in a truckle-bed pulled out of a cupboard beside the peat fire.

The fact that he went barefoot, even in winter.

'Barefoot? Even in winter . . . ?!' We couldn't imagine it.

'Yes,' Mummy nodded. 'I was shocked when he first told me, I found it hard to believe. And although he was clever, for a while he didn't even go to school.'

It was too many miles off, and his mother needed him to help with things like fetching water, so she taught him to read and write herself. But then, one day when he was seven, just as he was bringing the bucket back from the well, the schoolmaster happened to pass by the cottage.

'How old is that boy?' the master asked his mother. And there and then in the road he tested our father, Patrick, on his spelling, and our father got every single word right, including the last and most difficult, the word for a female sheep, *ewe*.

'This boy,' the master pronounced, 'is too clever not be at

school. Bring him in September. But get him some good tough shoes and cut his hair.'

His hair, our mother explained, was down to his shoulders, and blond, white-blond, though nowadays it was a crinkled dirty yellow. It was my father from whom I'd got my strange albino-blond hair, so different from our mother's and Cathy's and the baby's.

I would think of the scene: my seven-year-old father, just a bit older than I was now, standing staring through the flying silver wires of hair, staring and scowling the way I was always being told not to, his skin dark from the sun the way mine and Cathy's went too, dust from the road between his bare toes.

By the time he was ten the cottage at the crossroads was so overcrowded he was sent to sleep at his grandfather's house two miles off in the village, but every day after school he had to go back and work in the vegetable plot behind the cottage or fish in the lake for the family's meals.

'He was a bit of a terror, though,' she would say, wryly laughing. When he was ten or so, he and another boy caught a goose and put it in a sack and climbed onto a roof and pushed it down the chimney to terrify the old man sitting by the fire below.

He was a terror, still, or, rather, he had been when we lived in Llanfair in south Wales. Once in Llanfair I'd watched a young woman run screaming from our garden with earwigs down her back, while our father, the practical joker, bent over double at the gatepost laughing. And as for climbing a roof, well, I knew he'd have no trouble: there were pictures of him in the air force doing handstands on the backs of chairs or holding up another man standing on his shoulders.

He was slimmer then, but he still had those big rounded muscles: he went to weightlifting now in Prestatyn. They were iron-hard, his muscles, I knew: I'd dared to touch them when he lay on the living-room floor doing what he called his yoga, which he said he'd learned in the RAF.

The first time, I thought he was dead. He lay flat on his back, bare muscly arms spread and palms upturned, corrugated hair spilling on the brown-and-beige carpet with the orange flowers and stripes in the corners, eagle nose pointing upwards, long nostrils vertical. He didn't seem to be breathing. I ran to our mother. She laughed and told us that the first time she saw it she'd thought that, too, and she'd actually fainted.

So I dared to creep back and touch those muscles. I had to make myself do it, in a way I wouldn't have done once: I put my finger out carefully and gingerly pressed. And the skin didn't yield, didn't feel like flesh at all.

So yes, Mummy went on, that schoolmaster saw our father's ability and promise, and so he went to school. But then, once he left, what was there for a boy from a poor family to do but work as a menial mechanic in a garage? And so he made his vow of escape.

One night when he was sixteen, he put a small tin of treasures – a round pebble, a Stone Age flint and a blackbird's egg – deep in the yew hedge in front of the cottage, for the day in the future when he'd return triumphant, driving a Rolls. And next day he was on the boat for England with his cardboard suitcase.

He went to stay with one of his mother's two sisters who lived in Birkenhead in little red-brick terraces near the docks. The first night there, our mother told us laughing, he climbed out of the window and down the drainpipe to wee in the yard, because all they'd had in rural Ireland was a pit in the field, he'd never used a proper toilet before.

We wondered at that, and laughed too, yet I'd think of how nervous or puzzled and embarrassed he must have been.

I could now see a plan for what I was writing: my father forced in the afterlife to revisit the scenes of his life.

I went on:

Patrick hears footsteps behind him in the garage at Ballymoyne. Alert and taking no chances, he's slammed down the bonnet and is into the car. And there's his wild-haired companion beside him, and he's on the moors in the afterlife again.

'What the hell *is* this?' he demands. 'Bloody time travel?'

The feller opens up his palms. 'Not exactly. The past is all around you here. You've got to make an effort, though, to see it properly.'

Well, that's all right, then, thinks Patrick. It's not an effort you'd catch him making. Never look back, that's Patrick.

The guy is leaning on the wheel now, looking out at the near horizon with its mounds of heather like a heaving sea. He turns his head towards Patrick, almost underarm, his dark pupils burning in the hot white of his eyes, and suddenly Patrick knows where he's seen him before.

He was on the boat from Ireland that day in 1932. Patrick was leaning on the rails. Gold and silver coins of sun on the water, the Wicklow hills sinking away as the ship reached the open possibilities of sea, the smoke from the funnel scoring a fading marker down the route it had come. He looked up and straight into the eyes of a wild-haired feller standing beside him, staring almost underarm. He had a moment's unease. And then he dismissed it, discounted the stranger.

And now here he is in the afterlife, the feller, and Patrick's stuck with him.

The guy is starting the engine, and this time it surges into life. They nose out of the car park and up the brow of the hill. Patrick cheers up. He's always loved travel, was always up for adventure, and he's looking forward to a new, panoramic view. But when they get to the top there's another rise beyond and on the right the black wall of a pine plantation. The road forks, upwards on the left and on the right into the trees.

'Which way?' the guy asks, shrugging and ironic.

No contest: it's the open road for Patrick. 'Left.'

'Oh, that's another thing,' the guy says. 'If you won't make an effort you can be forced.'

With that he swings right and into the forest, and as soon as they're in, the road plunges downhill. He puts his foot down, and they're plummeting, sun strobing through the tree-tops; they hit a rock and Patrick's thrown, he's falling, falling through bright air into the shadow of a high metal cliff, the side of a ship –

꩜

This was another story our mother told us, the story of our father falling down the side of a ship into the water.

After working for some months on the Birkenhead docks, she said, he went as a deckhand on a ship that called in at Sydney, Australia, which happened to be where another aunt, his father's sister, lived. This aunt, Aunt Lizzie, had come up in the world: she'd once had a love affair with a famous

16

matinee idol who'd bought her a whole string of businesses in Sydney. Well, of course our father wanted to impress her, but when he stepped on the gang-plank in Sydney harbour, wearing a new suit with big brown windowpane checks that he didn't know was no longer in fashion, he slipped and went over the side into the water, the first of many falls.

As I wrote, I described it the way I had always imagined it: the glittering harbour, the high Australian sun, my father in his wide-checked suit looking like Charlie Chaplin. As a child I'd seen photos of the young Charlie Chaplin, and he looked like my young father: that crinkly hair, those deep-set eyes – except that, actually, I thought, my father was more handsome. The jacket plucked from his back as he falls, the baggy trousers lifted from his calves. And then, down between the ship and the harbour wall, his check shoulders and the almost-empty cardboard suitcase bobbing.

And on the quay his Aunt Lizzie. I always pictured her as stately yet cosy, elegant yet comfortable, in a plum-coloured dress, the thirties colour that my Nanny and great aunts in Llanfair still wore, shoes with little buttons, and a cloche hat on her head. I imagined her seeing my father for the first time and marvelling. She was stricken at once, our mother told us, with the handsome son of her brother, albeit wearing a ridiculous suit and dripping. I imaged him seeing her ad-miration, expecting it by now; by now, aged nineteen, he'd be fully aware of the power of his good looks and charm. I imagined the sleek black car I thought she must have been driving, her delighted glances at him sideways as she drove, rich childless spinster with a long-lost lover, desperate for someone on whom to lavish attention and affection, to treat like a son. The more fashionable suit she took him to buy and paid for, and the final scene our mother had always described:

Days later his ship is leaving; she is sad, devastated even, to see him go. On the morning before he sails she takes him to stand in front of one of her businesses and tells him that if he comes back and settles in Sydney, then that business, and all her others, will one day be his.

I saw it as I'd seen it all my life (though it has to be said that for many years I never gave it a thought, when my father was something I'd put from my mind), and the words flowed from my pen:

He's hurtling again, on to 1938, speeding on a bike down the hill at Llanfair, twenty-one years old, an airman recently arrived at the training camp nearby, about to meet Gwen for the very first time.

My mother, Gwen. As the years went by I would see this scene opening out from the centre like an early film: my father, skimming in the dusk down the hill (it's late October), the dark elms flicking each side, the double headlights on his bike – already in the camp he's famous for his madcap excesses – carving a double scoop of light down the deep-shadowed lane. They score the stone-walled curve at the bottom, gulp over the crossroad where the cottage and the cowshed nestle beneath the canopy of trees, swing right and flash in tandem round the farm-building bends, then fly out on the open straight road to the sea.

It's lighter out there. Ahead in the dusk there's a knot of people walking seawards. Two airmen he knows, with two girls.

It was my mother who would tell us this tale, of course, but it was only at this point that I would see it from her perspective: hear him screech to a stop just behind, turn to see the two skewed headlamp eyes, watch him alight, his feet seeming hardly to touch the ground.

I would hold that moment, a moment pregnant with consequence, imagining bats flitting through the dusk, the sea beyond the hedge and the narrow field breathing as if alive.

'Hey Jack!' the other two airmen cried. *Jack*, he had them call him in the air force, our mother told us: he wouldn't have them call him *Paddy*. When he got to know our mother he asked her to correct him if he came out with what he called any Irishisms – not that he ever lost his accent, or stopped saying *filum*.

'Show us your handstand, Jack!' the other airmen cried. And our father, Patrick, set off running with his bike, one hand on the saddle and the other on the handlebar, and then flipped up his legs and balanced on his hands on the moving bike.

'I thought he was a madman!' Mummy would say, dipping in and out of the sunbeam in the gloomy kitchen as she laughed. But of course it was impressive, I took it for granted she'd be impressed and attracted. It surprised me therefore, and unsettled me, to learn that it wasn't Mummy our father first starting *courting*, as she called it, but her sister Molly, two years older, the other girl on the road that night.

Of course, I realised as I grew, my mother was really then just a child. Now, all these years later as I sat at my desk, I saw her as I guessed he'd have seen her then, as I'd seen in photos of her taken at the time: fourteen years old and small and underdeveloped for her age, her straight black hair cut in a shingle and held back with a schoolgirl clip. It was Molly, a busty sixteen, working as a maid in the Manor, whom our father walked his bike beside as they all went back up the road. He probably didn't even notice my mother, lagging behind (as she told us), playing a childish game with one of the other airmen, tossing his cap ahead in the air and running to be the one to catch it.

But perhaps later, years later, after all that happened, he'd look back at that moment and see a look on my mother's face at once shy and brazen, that mixture of impulses that I came to see as typical of her: a yielding politeness shot through now and then with a contradictory critical appraisal.

And so, in the novel I was writing, in the fall from the afterlife into that moment, that was how I made him see her, prefiguring all that would come after.

And then he joined up with Molly, the bike chain ticking in the darkness. And they reached the knot of buildings at the top, the velvety foliage and high stone walls closing round with the certainty of a long-established and intimate community that must have been balm to my father, I always thought, a young man far from home, who'd grown up in straitened circumstances.

The pink-washed cottage beyond the crossroads, glowing, floating in the dark like the ship its Tudor beams had been taken from, two hydrangea bushes moored each side of the little wicket gate. The step down to the door – they invited the airmen in – and beyond the little porch, the flags of the one big room flickering with firelight. Gwen's mother, plump Nanny, her hair coiled in the two earphone plaits she still sometimes wore when I was a small child, rising from where she'd been knitting beside the big range, holding out her palms the way she always did, in comfortable surprise and welcome. And Grampa, our beloved Grampa, Gwen's father, in his braces and rolled shirtsleeves, the spike of bristly hair sticking up on his head. And from behind the range, the sound of crickets, a ticking heartbeat in the cottage walls.

PATRICK AND GWEN

RIGHT FROM THE start, before they even started courting, our mother said, she and our father quarrelled. She always laughed as she told us. In those early days we'd laugh too, but later, privately, ironically, we'd tell ourselves and each other it was no surprise.

'Well, you know your father,' she'd laugh (a laugh that got tighter and grimmer down the years). 'He could argue the hind legs off a donkey! He'll argue black is white and left is right!'

'People warned me not to marry him!' she'd say, laughing.

They first quarrelled, she said, about the principle of torque, which our father had learnt as a trainee airman fitter but which our mother had never heard of in grammar-school science: the idea that no object can exert a force on another without having the other exert a force on it in turn, making a nonsense of everyday notions of *push* and *pull*. Our mother thought *that* was nonsense, and I could always imagine her: a cocky schoolgirl whose best subjects, she said, were science, absolutely sure of her view, consciously pricking his airy-fairy bubble, just as throughout our childhood, in spite of telling me not to spill about the fairies, she did.

She had the backing of a stable, respectable village community; she was a Sunday-school teacher, from the age of thirteen she'd been the chapel organist; she was getting a grammar-school education. So maybe right away he felt resentful towards her. But I also suspect he felt superior, too:

not only was he eight years older, he had special skills. She could read music, and he couldn't, but he had the magical talent of picking up any instrument and playing by ear; he could diagnose a plane's engine simply by putting his ear to the metal frame; he had his athletic skills. He could lift my schoolgirl mother one-handed over his head, palm under her belly, and, held on high like that, she told us, she'd spread her limbs in a star-shape like a circus artiste.

But of course my mother quickly grew up, and of course she found him attractive. Of course in the end they were mutually attracted, I took that for granted, in spite of, or even because of, the challenge they gave to each other.

It was my father, though, once things had petered out with Molly, who fell head over heels in love. Always the more pragmatic, my mother had her eye on her studies and a career, and, besides, our father would soon be moved on with his unit.

The morning they moved on, she said, milling with their backpacks on the little leafy station, she was there too, waiting for her own train to grammar school in her uniform, the adjustable gymslip with the buttons on the shoulders, that had to just touch the floor when she kneeled, the straw boater and black thick stockings.

Our father had promised, though she hadn't asked or expected him to, that every time he was moved on he'd write and tell her, so she'd always know where he was. As soon as he arrived at the new base he did just that, making a point of telling her that all the airmen on the train who'd crowded behind him at the window as he waved goodbye had declared her *a peach*.

She wrote back, ironically flirtatious: 'It must have been the black stockings!' but she didn't write again.

He kept his promise, though. Every time he moved on he wrote to let her know, letters to which, since she hadn't agreed to receive them, she never replied. She turned her mind to her coming Matric. And now that the war had begun, there were dances for the service people every Saturday in the village hall, or up at the air force and army camps. She loved to dance. (And one thing about our father was that, in spite of his graceful athleticism, he'd never learnt to dance.) She was never short of partners, or, as a matter of fact, she would tell us with a laugh, offers of marriage.

Well, of course. Once she grew up, my mother looked like the actress in *Gone with the Wind*, only, actually, I thought, prettier. I would sit beside her in my parents' Prestatyn bedroom looking at our two reflections in the dressing-table mirror as she applied her wisps of makeup: a dab of powder, a quick spit of mascara, a flick of red lipstick. Me on one side with my fuzzy-but-straight albino hair, my square flat face, my sticking-out teeth (I sucked my thumb) and specs (by the age of seven I was short-sighted), and my mother on the other, with her heart-shaped face, her stark black hair swept back in waves, the winged eyebrows, the plump lips.

Well, anyway, she told us: it all backfired. She passed her Matric with flying colours and the school announced she was university material, but Nanny and Grampa had decided that with all this dancing and so many young men competing to woo her, she'd soon be married. They wouldn't let her stay on. She had to leave, and went to work at a chemist's in the next village instead.

By the age of six or seven I understood that people of Nanny and Grampa's generation had an old-fashioned view that women shouldn't have ambitions, and that, though she never sounded bitter, our mother had suffered for that. And she'd tell us as we grew – smiling ironically – how her brother Gwilym, our Uncle Gwilym who still lived with Nanny and Grampa and whom we loved almost as much, would come in from the farm before taking off his coat and drop husks and grain all over the flags. And Nanny would tell our mother or Molly to go and sweep them up, ignoring our mother's complaints. And how, once they started work, both Molly and our mother were expected to contribute to the household income, but Gwilym wasn't, since he was a *boy* and would have to save up to buy his own farm.

However, Nanny and Grampa's decision was a self-fulfilling prophecy: our mother went and fell in love with an airman, a man called Arnold Hitchins, and, since university now seemed a far-off dream, she agreed to marry him.

Arnold Hitchins. A name that sounded through our childhood, though never mentioned in front of our father. He had come as a lay preacher to the village chapel. She was very religious in those days, our mother, and it was the thing they had in common, which she and our father hadn't. Religion, in fact, was one of the big things that she and our father, brought up Catholic, had quarrelled bitterly about. He got upset, she would tell us, when she criticised his religion for the way it always let you off scot-free, left you free to sin because you knew you could confess. And by the time we were about nine and seven, we knew all too well our father's view of our mother's religion: as moralistic, uptight and hypocritical.

Well, she and Arnold Hitchins had agreed they would eventually marry, and our mother had gone with him more than once on his leave to his parents' house in Nottingham.

But she didn't want to get officially engaged: she hadn't entirely given up on her hopes for a career. The chemist she worked for had promised to make her his apprentice, which could pave the way to study Pharmacy at college after the war. She didn't want to scotch her chances, as you would have done in those days, by getting engaged.

She had still been getting letters from our father and ignoring them, but now she did reply, thinking it only proper and fair to let him know that she was promised to someone else, and to ask him to stop.

One evening in March not long after, she was coming home from work in the dusk to the empty cottage – Nanny and Grampa had gone to the pictures in town, Molly was on duty in the Manor and Gwilym busy with the lambs – and she rounded the bend by the cattle shed and there was a man sitting on the low cottage wall. Her heart turned over in fright – in those days, in the war, you had to watch out for strangers in the lane. The man stood up, and she saw it was our father: he had come to claim her back.

I wrote it all down, and, since that was the form I'd hit on, I made my father relive it from heaven. But even in those early days when my mother told the story, I would see it that way, from his point of view. For didn't I know that aching hiraeth for Llanfair? Didn't I live it every day since we'd left? And didn't I know that sense of relief and anticipation as you returned, stepped from the station at the top of the hill, the ancient branches roofing the road, hazels sprouting in the hedges, the earthy, ferny smell. The crossroad on the bend at the bottom, the cottage about to swing into view with honey-coloured light leaking from the windows and porch.

This night, the house is in darkness. At first my father thinks it must be the blackout curtains, but then he understands the cottage is empty – something I'd never known, and the thought of which made my stomach hollow. He sits on the wall. The dusk gathers. Across the way in the barn the cattle move unconcerned through the straw. Above and unseen in the dense dark trees, a bird shrugs off from a branch with an indifferent rustle. In the field beyond the trees the sound of a horse grazing systematically rips the dusk. The cold seeps from the stone through the wool of his RAF uniform. It's almost dark when Gwen's light footsteps approach and she rounds the bend.

Perhaps he didn't feel like that. Perhaps he was excited, sure of his success. Perhaps I was simply seeing the scene through its outcome.

She told him outright that he was wasting his time. I imagined the adamant air she could turn on sometimes. She'd meant what she said in her letter, she told him, she was promised to someone else. And next morning, after a night spent on the sofa, he had to trail up the hill to the station again, and watch from the train as the silver marshes slid by and away for what, it seemed, was the very last time.

I wrote:

His squadron's on the move again. They're piling onto the trucks. Ahead is the flat grey land they must cross to the base where Gwen will now never know or care that he has gone. He pulls himself up onto a truck; the truck moves, sets him adrift.

They pass through the barrier. The sentry salutes, and catches his eye. Grins, knowing. A gnarled dark face beneath the field cap. Teeth yellow and long. Patrick remembers with a thud that this is a replay; the thud becomes an almighty slam, and he's falling again, wheeling through the air, hit from behind by a car.

He was hit from behind by a pilot officer drunk as a lord and racing his open-topped Bentley round the bend in the country lane where our father was walking.

Our father was not expected to live. He was in a coma. His skull was cracked, all four limbs and several ribs were broken.

He had terrible scars. A white worm wiggled from his forehead into his hairline, his shins were deeply pitted. Sometimes, when we were small, if he lay on the floor on his belly and we were playing nearby, he'd say, 'Give us a scratch,' and lift up his shirt and we'd see the scar on his shoulder, a deep puckered dent.

Before we got to be too afraid, we'd creep up when he was doing his yoga, and gingerly lift the wide bottoms of his trousers and gaze at the blue pits reaching into the bones of his shins. Until the time, that is, when I'd carefully lowered them back, stood as quietly as I could and turned to go, and something vicious bit my ankle: his hand. I struggled to turn – he was holding my ankle so tight it hurt – and met his blue eyes, sharp with cold mocking triumph.

We knew he'd had other accidents, too. Twice in Llanfair he'd had motorbike crashes. I had a memory of one of those times, when his brakes failed on a hill and he crashed through a plate-glass shop window at the bottom. I remembered the moment he came back from the hospital. I was five. I remembered the greeny, acrid electric light as he stepped through the door, his face dotted all over with what looked like grey metal studs, a glittering sliding look in his eyes.

I ran from the room. My mother called out that the things on his face were just scabs, they'd heal, but this didn't dispel my feeling: a sweeping feeling of dismay, of something lost for good.

I probably got over it, he probably took me bouncing over bridges and laughing again, but that was the moment, at the age of five, that I first felt an aching desolation somehow connected to my father.

Of course, after being mown down on the road, he did live, he pulled through. And once he'd regained consciousness he asked a nurse to write down a letter he dictated to our mother – he couldn't write it himself; both his arms were in slings – telling her what had happened.

Our mother didn't think she ought to reply. Nanny thought she was hard-hearted. Poor boy, Nanny said, so ill and far away from his family, but our mother didn't think it right to give him false hope. So she closed herself up in the way we would come to discover she sometimes could: so positive and smiley so much of the time and then, out of the blue, surprisingly firm.

She was eighteen by now, and no longer working at the chemist's. She'd had a bad blow: the chemist had failed to keep his promise; his son had finished school and he'd given him the apprenticeship instead. Six and four, seven and five, we consciously absorbed the lesson: another instance of the unfair practice of boys being put before girls. She'd left the chemist's in disgust and dismay, and now she was working up at the station, filling in for the ticket clerk who'd been called up.

All her chances of college seemed to be gone, and Arnold Hitchins was starting to be insistent about getting engaged.

He was about to be moved on with his unit, and he wanted to make things official before he left. Our mother thought this ridiculous: why did they need to prove their love to others? They didn't need a ring or a public announcement to keep them faithful to each other! Besides which, she loved dancing, and she didn't want to have to stop going to the dances – the way it was in the village, once you were officially engaged, you couldn't go to the dances without your fiancé without being considered *loose*.

So they didn't get engaged. And instead of a ring, Arnold gave her a little Bible in purple leather, to think of him by.

Three days after he'd gone, she got a letter from him telling her this: the night before writing – two days after leaving! – he'd gone to a dance and met somebody else!

I suppose, looking at it now, he must have decided before he even left that she wasn't committed, and maybe she wasn't, because when she received another letter from our father – 'He would never take no for an answer!' she would laugh, and the older we got the more grimly we'd think, How true – she gave in and wrote back.

She had been in Hull, staying with her uncle, a Baptist minister, to whom Nanny had sent her because the letter from Arnold Hitchins had caused her a deep crisis of faith. The hypocrisy of Arnold! Supposed to be so in love with her! So insistent on getting engaged . . . And the letter was so formal, so cold . . . No expression of regret, or any thought for her feelings . . . So un-Christian. And him so pious – a lay preacher, even! So much for pious Christians and Christianity!

Her uncle had talked her through it. She shouldn't blame Christianity, he reminded her, quoting from the Bible, but false Christians. *Beware of false prophets which come to you in sheep's clothing but inwardly they are ravening wolves.*

When she got back, our father's letter was waiting. Arnold had been a wolf in sheep's clothing; it was Patrick, our father, who'd stayed faithful, after all that time and in spite of all the rejections.

So she and our father started courting again. Previously whenever he got leave he'd go to his aunts and cousins in Birkenhead, but now he'd come down to Llanfair. And it wasn't long before they got engaged: she had no doubts now.

That is, not until a fortnight before they were due to be married in mid-August.

The banns had been called in the chapel, she had given in her notice at the station, and our father had organised a married billet outside the camp in Shropshire where he was based. She had been to town to buy her wedding outfit, a woollen dress she always described to us in detail: powder-blue, knee-length, with short sleeves and Peter-Pan collar.

But a fortnight before the wedding a terrible thought came to her: that she was marrying our father on the rebound. And if she had any doubt, she knew, she shouldn't be doing it . . .

She knew then what she had to do. She got on a train to Shropshire.

She had sent a telegram to say she was coming. I always imagined him cycling, unsuspecting, to the station to meet her. I imagined the blur of blue vetch in the verge as he sped, the quiet of the station as he parked his bike against the wall, the song of a blackbird spilling through the hot afternoon. Then the rails beginning to hum as the train approaches, the station filled with the long harsh cough of steam, and our mother stepping down with her terrible news.

She said he broke down. Not far from the station he leaned

on a farm gate and bent over and sobbed, on and on.

And so she gave in.

She said seeing him so desperate made her so upset too that she knew she loved him. Whatever the odds, whatever anyone said – *People warned me not to marry him!* – she had to be with him.

And so they were married.

She always kept the wedding photo in pride of place on their bedroom wall. I would study it closely. There they were, in black and white, standing in front of a curtain as if on a stage. My mother, twenty years old, not wearing the blue dress she'd bought after all, but a bias-silk wedding dress someone had lent her at the last minute, slimline and spilling in a circle on the floor all around, so she looked like a fairy queen. A spiky tiara in her dark waved hair, from which dropped a diaphanous veil edged with embroidered ferns, and in her hands a frothy tumble of moss and pale roses that she told us were pink. And there was our father beside her, eight years older, handsome in his uniform, holding his folded cap and showing his crooked teeth in a smile. Happy, I would think. He looked happy. And on his other side, Gwilym, our mother's brother, Uncle Gwilym, his best man, hair slicked down in a way we never saw it as a rule, making his ears stick out even further, and on the far side of Mummy, Aunty Molly, taller and bigger altogether, looking like an Amazon in a long, wide, stiff dress with huge shoulders.

But because our mother had said, that day she went to see him, that she was afraid she was on the rebound, our father, she said, was afterwards constantly jealous. I'd think: Well, she was so pretty – even the young minister who married them had been in love with her, she'd told us. A week after they were married, they went to a dance at the camp and our mother accepted a pilot officer's invitation to dance, and our father, who of course didn't dance, was furious!

They were billeted with a spinster, a retired schoolmistress, down a country lane in a slate-roofed cottage with an orchard, beside a track where our father kept his first car, an Austin Seven. When we were small we loved to hear the tales of that time because they were funny. Miss Protheroe was a very proper lady, aristocratic-looking, tall and thin with a long hooked nose and her hair in a steel-grey bun at the nape of her neck, and a real stickler. But she doted on our father, just like his aunt in Australia, just like all the old ladies, in fact, and all women, really. Round about then our mother and father cycled all the way from Shropshire to see his aunts and cousins in Birkenhead, and our mother could see that all the women there adored him – turned out that when he'd lived there he'd even had a fling with one of his girl cousins. When he'd left to join the RAF, the aunt he'd lived with had told him, just like Aunt Lizzie in Australia, that he'd always have a home with her if he wanted, and had always kept his room ready and intact, the little cardboard case sitting on top of the wardrobe where he'd left it and his dressing-gown hanging on the back of the door.

Miss Protheroe was very deaf, and used an old-fashioned hearing trumpet, like the ones we'd seen in Victorian illustrations, but it hardly ever worked. So our mother learned some sign language, but our terror of a father wouldn't. He would sit at the breakfast table eating the eggs it was our mother's task to collect each morning, and say to our mother, through the side of his mouth away from Miss Protheroe, 'We'll go for a run in the car this evening, but we're not taking the old bitch.' 'What did he say?' Miss Protheroe would ask our mother, and our mother would tell her: 'He says we'll all go for a run this evening,' and our father would kick our mother under the table while Miss Protheroe smiled a smile of great satisfaction and patted his hand and indulgently passed him more toast and home-made jam.

She was so innocent, Miss Protheroe, in spite of having been a teacher, that the first time they took her out and she saw the cats' eyes on the road, she asked from the back, 'Who lights them up?' 'The fairies, you daft old bat,' said our father, knowing she couldn't hear him, and our mother had to struggle to keep a straight face as she turned back to explain. When we were teenagers and old enough, she would tell us how when they took her to the pictures at the aerodrome and the camera panned discreetly away from a romantic scene to a train entering a tunnel or a foaming stream, Miss Protheroe would shout in her loud deaf-person's voice: 'What's happening? What are they doing now?' and lift up her trumpet for our mother to shout her answer, and the whole cinema would erupt in laughter.

But by the time I was eight or nine, the tale of living with Miss Protheroe had become for us darker. Although our mother laughed as she recounted it, we felt on her behalf the resentment we'd have felt ourselves at being treated the way Miss Protheroe treated her.

In that place the war was distant. Our father was working on a base where planes were sent for overhaul; he had risen in the ranks now and was an Acting Warrant Officer, overseeing several workshops. But there was no work for our mother – no war work, even: she'd been sent with an official letter to a nearby cheese factory, but they didn't need her and sent her away again. She had to stay home and help Miss Protheroe, who was very strict when it came to housework. Every doily to be kept in line on every surface, every cupboard to be emptied and cleaned out monthly, the potatoes for tea to be put on the stove at five-thirty prompt every afternoon. Clearly, we could see as we got older, though our mother never suggested it, she was jealous of our mother and was keeping her in line. And it was in this story that first surfaced the dark question that sat, a tense knot, at the heart of our childhood and beyond: the question of money and our father's profligacy, and the poverty that ensued.

THE QUESTION OF MONEY

A S SOON AS we got to Prestatyn we started being poor.
I knew my mother loved clothes; I knew that when she
was young she had made herself things, I'd seen them in the
photos: lacy puff-sleeved jumpers and dresses with tucks, a
tweed suit with kick pleats. But though she managed somehow
to make just enough clothes for me and Cathy, there wasn't
enough for material for clothes for herself. And so one of her
aunties, the fashionable wife of a Cardiff policeman, took pity
and sent her some cast-offs. Six years old, I sat and watched
as they spilled from the brown-paper parcel, and something
else, intangible, spilling with them: shame. Two coats and a
dress, all with huge wide skirts, which my mother said were
New Look, although, it was pretty clear, they weren't a new
look any more for Aunt Flo. The dress shivered as she lifted it
up, crepey synthetic silk, grey-blue with little maroon sprigs
of flowers, and was cold to the touch. When she wore it and
I walked beside her on the prom after school, my hand on the
icy steel handle of the pram, the skirt would lift and stay suspended in the breeze, undulating like water, then dip suddenly,
almost violently, as if snatching something, some meaning I'd
almost grasped, away.

Then there were the strange baby bags from Australia. Our
father's aunt in Australia, who had never stopped expecting
him to go back there, regularly sent him parcels of books and
comics and chocolate and tobacco. When Cathy was born

she'd sent these weird baby garments: rectangular flannel bags with straps to go over the baby's shoulders, hand-embroidered with flowers in cruder stitches and brighter colours than the fine embroidery our mother did (though at the moment she was pushed to buy the cloth and silks). So weird did our mother find these bags, she didn't use them then, for Cathy, she put them away. But now, in Prestatyn, she had no choice but to put them on David, the baby. He would kick up his legs in the carrycot and the corners of the bags would flick up like ears. He'd stretch his toes into the corners and I'd grab them and make him grin his gummy grin, and the rough French knots grazed on my palms, little blue forget-me-not flowers like knotty conundrums.

He wasn't a well baby. He had strange turns, his face going greasy and grey, and his eyes rolling up into his head. It was part of the darkness that had descended on our life, along with the poverty and our father's new moods, since we'd come to Prestatyn.

Our father was over-generous, that was how our mother put it in telling the tale of their time with Miss Protheroe, though the older we grew the clearer we were that he simply couldn't resist spending money. Time and again in our childhood he'd come back with antiques he'd bought from some second-hand dealer he'd been schmoozing, when our mother was struggling to provide egg and chips for tea. He'd had generous RAF compensation for his accident, but by the time they lived with Miss Protheroe he'd 'pissed it up against a wall', as she'd later tell us he said, admitting it freely. The thing was, she said, he liked to entertain. To put it another way, as we soon worked out for ourselves, he liked to be the generous guy that everyone loved. One time in Prestatyn we had to take in bed-and-breakfast guests (and retreat to the attic to sleep), and he'd entertain them in the evenings, a whole room of enchanted young people, many of whom came from Liverpool and Manchester and had Irish backgrounds too, talking about Ireland and playing Irish tunes on his flute. 'Make us all some sandwiches, will yeh, Gwen?' he would call. Sandwiches in the evening were no part of the deal for the guests, and, aged eight, I would cringe for my mother as she went with a bright but brittle smile to make the sandwiches with ingredients meant for next day's tea.

One constant expense, our mother told us, was our father's practice of sending money back to his parents in Ireland: in Ireland, she explained, it was considered the duty of the eldest son. Now and then his mother would write and ask for extra, for seeds for the field, or to mend the roof, for instance. Well, one day at Miss Protheroe's there came a letter from his mother asking for money to buy the ring and habit for his youngest sister, Cathleen, who at fifteen years old was preparing to take her vows. Because he'd spent his compensation, our father simply didn't have the money, and in order to get it – to save his face, we realised later – our mother had to sell her bike.

All our childhood, all our lives, she did that: save his face. And for much of our childhood she was tense with frustration about it.

And his evasions, and half-truths, and the goings behind her back.

The war ended, and our mother was looking forward to our father's being demobbed and to getting away from Miss Protheroe. But then it turned out he'd been offered a commission – and he hadn't even told her! He wouldn't be leaving the RAF after all. She was shocked. She had never expected that, and she didn't want it: a life permanently attached to the RAF, forever living in married quarters, constantly moving around. If they were going to have a family, which they'd agreed, they needed to settle down and make a home of their own. (Ironic, of course, in view of the way things did turn out.)

So our father agreed to leave the RAF. But then – would you believe it? – it turned out that he took for granted that they'd go to Australia where his aunt was waiting with her fortune – another thing he'd never mentioned: his demob address was in fact his aunt's!

If our mother had only known, she'd have made it clear from the start that she'd never want to go to the other side of the world, so far from her family and all she knew. And she had to tell him that now.

So he was stumped. He'd no idea what he could do in civvy street in England. In the RAF he'd been a supervising engineer, but his training of course was specialist, in planes, and the last thing he wanted was to break his vow and go back to working on cars and getting his hands dirty for a living.

And then Miss Protheroe decided to come to his rescue.

He may not have wanted to work on cars for a living, but he didn't mind doing it for himself or as a sideline, and all the time they'd been living there, he'd tinkered with the Austin in the lane beside the cottage, and he and another airman had been doing up cars in someone else's garage. All along, Miss Protheroe had cooed about how clever he was, and kept saying that if he and our mother would only go on living with her after the war, she'd give him some space at the bottom of the orchard to build his own garage and start his own business. Our mother, horrified by the very idea of staying on with Miss Protheroe, had told her: the last thing he wanted was to do it for a living.

But now, late one summer afternoon, Miss Protheroe sent her away on an errand. She had to take a crochet pattern to a friend of Miss Protheroe's in a nearby village, a three-mile walk and back again since she no longer had her bike. I would picture it: the dappled shadows of the trees, the slate roof of the cottage sinking behind the hedge as she set off down the lane in her war-time forties dress, unsuspecting, or maybe fully suspecting she was being got rid of and so feeling troubled or annoyed, even anxious, but with her Methodist training in politeness and amenability, unable to refuse.

With our mother well out of the way, as soon as our father got back from the base, Miss Protheroe told him to sit down at the table. Once he was seated she went upstairs and came down with a metal box with a lock and the key. She laid it in front of him and gave him the key and told him to open it. It was filled to the brim with pound notes. She told him to take it out and count it. Three hundred pounds. It was all his, she told him, to build a garage at the bottom of her orchard, big enough to employ a mechanic so he wouldn't need to get his own hands dirty again.

And he wanted to accept. Our mother had a devil of a job, she said, to persuade him against it, to make him see that they couldn't spend their married life in thrall to Miss Protheroe (Miss Protheroe who didn't like her and bullied her).

She did persuade him in the end, and they set off to seek their luck, as our father would have it, in London.

I wrote all this down as our mother had told us, but from my father's point of view, which by the time I was a teenager constantly exposed to his bad temper I couldn't help but know. The frustration he would have felt at her Methodist caution regarding Australia, which her schoolgirl ambition had maybe belied. His contempt of it, even. His feeling perhaps of being tricked. His resentment at the way, in spite of her chapel timidity, she put her foot down.

But then, as our mother said, he had faith in his luck. His Irish luck. If something went wrong, it was because for the moment his Irish luck had failed him. (Though as a teenager I would think his chief resentment towards my mother stemmed from the fact that it was she who had kept frustrating his luck.) His luck had brought him the schoolmaster happening down the lane to discover his genius; it had brought him his aunt in Australia and Miss Protheroe's offer. And now, lo and behold, it seemed to bring him another: another airman, a wheeler-dealer who, during the war, had been able to supply silk stockings, and, like so many others, was very taken with our father. This man was going back to his job running a floor in a department store in London, where he offered to get our father a job. So he and our mother set out for London with this man, and stayed a night with his parents while he went to the store. But when he came back he'd been sacked on the spot for running his wartime clothing-coupon scams.

Now our father's luck seemed to have deserted him altogether. There were he and our mother jobless in a bombed-out London, searching for digs past the No-Blacks-No-Dogs-No-Irish signs. In the end they found a place, a bedsit, with a hole in the wall right through to the next lodgers' room, which they had to fill with cardboard, and a geyser in the bathroom that kept exploding. The day they moved in, the landlady said the last couple had had to leave because the wife got pregnant, and pointedly looked at our mother's stomach in warning. They did get work, our mother sorting ration coupons at the Ministry of Food, and our father, well, he ended up doing what he vowed he never would, working as a mechanic in a garage.

It was as we got older that our mother added the following element to the story:

She had always saved her money. Right from when she began work at the chemist's, every week she would put some into a Post Office savings account, saving at the start for her career, and then when she got involved with Arnold Hitchins for her bottom drawer, and finally for the house that she and our father would one day have together.

She didn't really mind that our father didn't save, she said – he went on spending money, going drinking with the other mechanic who worked at the garage, buying a motorbike in addition to the car. His money, she reasoned, was his to do with as he liked. But by the same token, her money was hers, and what she wanted was to keep it where it was, in a private account of her own. He didn't like that, he saw it as a lack of marital commitment; in fact, it upset him so much that in the end she gave in and she took it out of the Post Office and they used it to open a joint bank account.

The other mechanic at the garage was a Welshman, de-mobbed from the army, and our father brought him home, expecting our mother to welcome him with open arms as a fellow countryman. She didn't like him. He struck her as sly. I knew, as a teenager, how my father would react to that: my mother was mean-spirited, he'd think; I knew what he'd call her, we'd heard him do it often enough: typical uptight Methodist witch.

And then, all without her knowing, he agreed to go in with this chap Dai and start a garage of their own, and, all without her knowing, emptied out the joint account – *her* money, he hadn't put any in – and gave it to Dai to buy the equipment.

They had rented a garage, but there were jobs to finish in the place they'd been working, so while Dai went off to set up the new place, our father stayed on to complete them. After a week he'd heard nothing from Dai, so one evening he drove round to the new garage. To his surprise, he found it all shut up. He tried his key and it didn't work.

He drove round to Dai's lodgings. Dai opened the door only a crack. What's going on? our father wanted to know. 'I've decided to run the business on my own,' Dai told him. But he couldn't do that, our father protested. What about the equipment our father had paid for? What about the contract?

'Have you *seen* the contract?' Dai asked him, sarcastic.

'You've been had, mate,' he told our father and shut the door in his face.

I always found this story deeply unsettling. In so many ways our father was intuitively clever, sussing out the faintest vibrations in an engine, picking up in others the slightest hint of hypocrisy and pretension (though needless, to say, he had his own). Yet, on this occasion, and others, he could misjudge so badly, be so easily duped. As we knew to our cost, he was domineering, yet this time, according to our mother, he so meekly gave in.

Now, writing my novel, I worked to imagined myself into his

state of mind in those moments. I wrote:

Patrick comes down the steps from Dai's lodging, the lucky charmer, everyone's friend and hero, done the dirty on for once. The guy with the sure instincts, for once proved wrong.

It's an evening in early summer, growing dusk.

There's someone leaning on the bonnet of his car. Hunched, bedraggled. Waiting.

The whites of his eyes show through the dusk as he slews them at Patrick.

He's the man on the boat coming over from Ireland. He's Patrick's afterlife tormentor.

Patrick brushes past him. 'Look, mate,' he says, 'enough's enough.' He's damned if he's going to be made to relive his past uncharacteristic failures. He's done the living, he's done the bloody dying, and he wants to move on now.

He's in the car, he slams the door and turns the key – what the hell? The bugger's already in the passenger seat, grinning.

'Sorry, pal,' he tells Patrick, 'but there's somewhere else you need to go now.'

And Patrick's driving, and it's no longer evening, it's five months on from that sorry episode, one of those late-October days when the sun is a cloth of gold dropped across the fields. It's Gwen who's in the car beside him, and they're travelling north out of London, replaying a journey that Patrick didn't even want to make at the time.

A MYSTERY

A LETTER HAD come from his Aunt Lizzie in Australia. For once he showed it to our mother – our father rarely showed her Aunt Lizzie's letters, she told us, although they were always addressed to them both.

This time Aunt Lizzie was writing with serious news.

One of our father's sisters, it had turned out, lived just north of London, though she and our father were not in contact, which our mother found strange, coming from such a close-knit family herself. However, Aunt Lizzie was asking him to contact her now: her immortal soul was in danger; she was about to get divorced. On behalf of their devastated mother, Aunt Lizzie begged our father to go and see his sister and dissuade her from this terrible course.

'Why couldn't Daddy's mother ask him herself?' we asked, the first time she told us.

Mummy shrugged. She didn't know. She didn't know much about Daddy's mother; he didn't often show her his mother's letters either, and when he did they always began with the odd and unwelcoming *Dear Patrick and Mrs Jackson*.

He didn't seem at all keen on carrying out this task, she told us.

'Why?' I wanted to know at six years old.

Well, she explained, he wouldn't want to interfere – not, she was implying, in the personal life of a sister he hardly knew any more, over a religion he no longer even practised. But as the story unfolded it was clear that she was guessing, because he wouldn't discuss it with her.

He went – out of filial and brotherly duty, she implied – taking her with him. And what happened when they got there was very strange indeed.

The sister wasn't at her lodgings, the address Aunt Lizzie had given them; she was round at her boyfriend's where the landlady directed them.

They knocked on the door. There was no reply.

I would always imagine it: my mother and father standing on the path of a red-brick semi, the paintwork faded and the garden neglected from absence in the war and abandonment by a wife, crows calling perhaps in the trees nearby. My mother bewildered and curious, but my father with his sure instinct knowing that they were in there hiding, and marching straight down the side of the house. (Our mother would tell that bit with relish.) And lo and behold, there they were in the kitchen behind the frosted glass of the door on which my father rapped.

Except now, in this seemingly peripheral tale, my father droops uncharacteristically, becomes a clown.

The door opened just a little and there in the gap was the boyfriend, a bit of a spiv, with a little black moustache, and looking not at all friendly.

Was his sister there? our father asked, all his matey confidence gone.

'Who wants to know?' the man demanded coldly, without opening the door any wider.

'Her brother,' my father told him meekly.

A woman's voice came from behind the man. 'Leave this to me, Dick.'

Dick stood back and there was our father's sister, staring coolly down at them. A really beautiful woman, our mother said: white white skin and black black hair tumbling in curls down her back, and turquoise-coloured eyes. She wore a tight black dress, her nails and lips were painted red, and she had a cigarette in a long black holder which she held like *this* – and in the dark Prestatyn kitchen our mother crossed one arm under her soft breasts (she couldn't afford decent bras) and propped her other elbow on top of her hand.

The sister stared, she said, as if they'd crawled out from under a stone, and our father seemed completely tongue-tied.

He found his voice at last and introduced Gwen, our mother. His sister merely gave her the curtest of nods. With cold reluctance she said, 'You'd better come in.'

They stepped up into the kitchen. The man had disappeared. She seated herself on a high stool at the breakfast bar, leaving them standing.

'Well?' she demanded down her nose.

Standing there near the door, looking foolish, our father said his piece: that he'd come on behalf of their mother at Aunt Lizzie's request.

She listened in silence, puffing on her cigarette and picking a piece of fluff off her dress. When he'd finished, trailing off, she was silent. Finally, frostily: 'Well, you can tell Aunt Lizzie it's none of her business.' She paused and turned her icy turquoise eyes full on our father. 'And it's most certainly none of *yours*.'

She got down from the stool and opened the door for them to leave. They stepped out, and the door closed before they'd both reached the bottom.

On the journey back our father was silent. Of course our

mother wanted to know, as we did, listening to the story: what was going on, why had his sister behaved so strangely? He wouldn't answer. He wouldn't talk about it then, or ever again.

It was a familiar mechanism in our childhood. Our father would do something unaccountable, or frustratingly extravagant, and refuse to discuss it, even to be questioned, *nagged*, as he called it. He'd grow silent and grim, or say she was like a bloody dog with a bone. And then there'd be the danger sign, the rippling of his cheek which meant he was grinding his teeth, and woe betide me and Cathy if we crossed him. And in the end our mother would have no option but to bite her tongue.

So, in the end, driving back from the encounter with his sister, whom they never saw or heard from again, my mother bit her tongue, and was never any wiser.

So I got to this scene in the novel and was stumped. I was writing it from my father's viewpoint but, as so often in his life, I didn't have the facts to know what would have been going on his head.

THE KNOTTY MATTER
OF RELIGION

WHEN I WAS seven my father decided to be Jewish. This was strange. If Daddy was anything, he was Catholic. Though actually he seemed the opposite of religious, the way he scowled and sneered and blasphemed. Mummy had told us that his mother had wanted him to be priest, it was the bargain she made when he went to school: the Church would give her son an education and in return she would give him to the Church. The very thought of it had made us laugh.

We knew that when I was born his mother had written asking to be reassured that he would bring me up Catholic. He'd written back and explained that because he and Mummy were of different religions, they'd decided to let their children choose their religion for themselves when they were old enough. When Cathy was born another letter came, this time from Aunt Lizzie in Australia, interceding again, begging him on his mother's behalf to reconsider his decision, but he wrote back and explained again.

Now Mummy told us something else: some months later another letter from Aunt Lizzie had regretfully informed them that, as a result, he'd been excommunicated from the Catholic Church in his absence. He was very upset, Mummy said. He'd turned round and pronounced: 'Well, I may as well be Jewish, then.' And then he told her something he'd previously never mentioned: that the grandfather he'd gone to live with was Jewish, and had cooked him Jewish food, potato cakes he called *latkes*, and had taken him to the synagogue in Dublin.

And now, in Prestatyn, he decided to put it into action. He had made friends with the Jewish family who owned the carpet shop over the road, and he began spending Friday evenings celebrating the Sabbath at their house. He started taking the *Jewish Chronicle*, and refusing bacon sandwiches (his favourite up till now) and banned all pork from the house. He bought our mother a Jewish cookbook, from which, from now on, he wanted her to cook. The stews and scones, it turned out, were no different from what she'd been making before, but when she tried the mazos everyone gagged, including Daddy.

By the time I was seven, religion was to me a thing of ambiguity: comforting yet also troubling; soft, yet hard like a knot too tight to unravel. We said our prayers kneeling beside the bed at night with Mummy, and there was peace in that, in the feeling that through all the strangeness of that brash seaside town, through the tensions of Daddy's ever-worsening moods and the constant fear of punishment, God would keep us safe as long as we asked. Yet, in spite of having been a Sunday-School teacher and chapel organist, Mummy had long ago stopped going to chapel for good.

She told us how and why.

It was after they moved back from London to Llanfair. In London she'd become pregnant with me, so they'd had to leave the lodgings, and just as they were despairing of finding anywhere else with her in that condition, Nanny wrote to say that a cottage owned by Nanny's father had become vacant up in the village. And so they went back to Llanfair. Once they were back our mother took it for granted she'd go to the chapel in which she'd previously been so involved, where some of her uncles and great-uncles were elders, and where of course our parents had been married. But our jealous father just couldn't stand her being there in that place where she'd met and been wooed by Arnold Hitchins – or indeed, where the minister who'd married them had been in love with her, though he too had long gone, in the way of Methodist ministers, to another Circuit.

Once or twice Nanny took me and Cathy to that chapel.

All year Cathy and I would long for our visits back to Llanfair with Mummy and the baby, for the cottage beneath the elms where the jackdaws made their homely sound like crockery chinking, for waking in the mornings in the deep old-fashioned feather bed, a sea of green through the tiny deep-silled window, swallows rustling in the thatch above. And for Grampa. For walking the lanes with him in the evenings, each holding a hand, and sitting on his knee by the fire as the crickets ticked behind the range, turning over his bare forearms and marvelling at the softness of the skin above the brown pleated muscles. We'd make calendars beforehand, obsessively knocking off the days.

And once or twice when we were there we went with Nanny to chapel, a small red-brick Victorian building with a step straight onto the road on a blind corner of the village where lorries thundered round, which made a panicky strategy of entering, and coming out downright dangerous. But our mother didn't come; she was sticking to the decision she'd had to make when she and our father came back from London.

As we grew older, she would tell us that at that time he was altogether miserable. The only work he could get was the kind he'd vowed to avoid, digging foundations for new houses with other navvies, in the driving sleet and snow of the terrible winter of the year I was born, a job to which he had to drive many miles. Years more later she would tell me: sometimes he couldn't get himself out of bed, he failed to go to work altogether, and she had to borrow money from her mother.

A familiar sight in the daytime on a Sunday in my childhood: my father a mound beneath the bedclothes glimpsed through the partly-open bedroom door, around him the dark bedroom suite our mother had told us she'd had to borrow money from Nanny to buy (money which down the years failed to be paid back), veneered with a pattern like clouds or waves that as a child I always felt could make meaningful shapes if only I could see them.

Before our mother stopped going to chapel, she said, the chapel had been bought a new harmonium and our mother had agreed to take the old one into the cottage. By now I had been born. I was a dreadfully crying baby, she said. Her labour had been long, and by the time I was born I was dehydrated and distressed, my skin red and raw and cracked all over. In fact, at the sight of me my father had cried, 'She's like a skinned rabbit!' Even after my skin had healed I went on crying, and the only way our mother could get me to sleep in the evenings was by playing the harmonium. But she had to stop: it made our father so mad that one night he chased her round the table with the gun Grampa had given him for shooting ducks!

In any case, the elders came to rescue the harmonium from this heathen household. They were angry with our mother for stopping going to chapel. They marched up in a body, two of our mother's great-uncles among them, and banged on the door. Stony-faced, they brushed past her and without a word hefted the harmonium between them and took it away. And the next day one of her uncles, another elder, cut her dead on the village road.

Though in a Methodist version of the pressure from our father's mother, the minister did keep calling, to try and persuade our mother to have me baptised. She told him precisely what our father had told his mother, but he persisted. He was still coming two years later, after Cathy was born. 'If your children die they will have to be buried in unconsecrated ground,' was what he kept saying, which she thought was a horrible blackmailing tactic to take, and thoroughly un-Christian.

So it was clear to our mother, and to us when we were small, that worshipping God was not necessarily the same as organised religion, that the most pious-seeming people could behave with unthinking coldness, or even cruelty.

As we got older, our mother filled in the emotional dimension of that time. The way her uncles were behaving didn't improve our father's mood. He began to hate the place – which at first shocked us: the place we so loved! The place where they'd met and courted, where my mother had had her idyllic childhood and would have been glad to spend the rest of the days, near to her parents. Where in the evenings they walked the lanes swinging their baby, me, in a sling between them, odd moments, she would later tell me, that gave her hope. But he still couldn't find decent work. One day, to her utter dismay, he decided he would have to go to sea: with his RAF qualifications, he thought, he could get work as a ship's engineer.

They were sitting one evening in the narrow field above the sea when he told her, she said. I would picture it, the gorse flaring all round, me on my mother's knee, my white hair lifting in the breeze as I'd seen in the photos, the sun making a broken path across the sea. My mother smiling a brittle smile and trying not to cry . . .

But the shipping company he applied to didn't find his training appropriate, and offered him instead the job of ordinary seaman, a job he'd had at the age of seventeen. There was nothing for it, he said, he'd just have to go back into the RAF, and this time, because he was so unhappy, she didn't object. But now, in peacetime, it turned out, he could be taken on only as a sergeant mechanic. Insulted and proud, rather than accept demotion within the force, he took a job back at the aerodrome as a civilian mechanic instead. He only lasted a week: the non-commissioned officers, he said, went to town sneering at his comedown and jumping at the chance to push him about, and one afternoon he threw down his tools and walked out. Swallowing his pride, he went straight to the garage opposite the cottage, the owner of which had been offering him a job ever since they moved in.

It wasn't just the matter of the menial work that prevented him accepting it beforehand. The owner of the garage had a haulage business, and during the war had collected from the station where our mother worked in the ticket office. At the time he'd kept offering her better wages to go and work for him instead, and our jealous father had concluded that he must be in love with her, and so had refused to have anything to do with him till now. He was the same, our mother told us, with her old schoolfriend who lived next door with his mother in the terrace of thatched cottages: he wouldn't speak to him, and whenever he came across them chatting in the garden, would fall into a black mood that lasted for days.

Desperate now, though, he accepted the job in the garage, and at last was on a steady wage.

At this point I would nod. One of my earliest memories was standing in the garden of the cottage opposite and watching the huge folding doors of the garage open to reveal my father with his crinkly hair and brown overalls.

But he still wasn't happy, our mother told us. And things got worse with her relations. Her crippled grandfather who owned the cottage was another church elder. When they'd first moved in, the place had been in a terrible state – windows letting in the rain, plaster falling off the walls and getting stuck on the limestone flags of the floor, the staircase so rotten it was downright dangerous. Our father had been disgusted. How could a so-called Christian – a pillar of the church! – rent out a house in that state? he wanted to know. Good God, they had hovels better than that in Ireland! In the weeks before he found work he had spent time doing it up, the materials for which took all that our mother had managed to save after the London garage disaster. But the thatch was rotten, and rain kept leaking in and spoiling everything he'd done. Each time, our mother's grandfather merely sent round a man with a bucket of straw to patch up the hole, and the thatch became crazily dotted with bright-yellow patches which soon began leaking all over again.

One day, when they had a toddler, me, running about and our mother was heavily pregnant with Cathy, the rain came running down the wall dangerously close to the electricity meter, and our father lost patience altogether. He got on his motorbike and gunned into town and put down their name for one of the new council houses just built in the village. Miraculously, somehow, he got us immediately rehoused.

Then she found out how. One afternoon her skinny spinster Aunt Beth, Nanny's sister who still lived with our mother's grandfather, stood at the door looking thunderous and clasping a letter from the council. Our father had declared the cottage unfit for human habitation, and the council had sent warning that unless it was reroofed and a bathroom installed it would have to be demolished – none of which our mother's grandfather was prepared to pay for. Furious with our mother's chapel-going relations, our father had neither cared about the consequences for them (maybe, I would think when I was older, he was even vengeful) nor about our mother's relationship with them. She loved her grandfather, she cherished her memories of playing in his orchard, but now he cooled towards her, and she was more or less shunned by the other, more religious relatives on her mother's side. Not long after we moved into the council house, her grandfather died, and when she went to the funeral in the chapel, she told us, they didn't speak to her. They made a point of sitting on the opposite side of the aisle, and stood away from her at the grave as her grandfather was buried.

When we were older she would tell us something she'd previously omitted from her tale of the jaunt that she and our father, newly married, made on their bikes from Shropshire to Birkenhead. Our father was upset, she said, because the aunt with whom he'd lived, who'd been keeping his things safe, turned out to have recently thrown them away, explaining rather stiffly that she'd assumed he didn't need them now he was married. Which wasn't logical, of course, unless you wanted to dismiss a person and their things once they'd married someone from a different religion . . .

Religion, I decided, as I went on writing about my dead father, must have been behind that strange encounter with his cold divorcing sister. She must have thought it a nerve: a man who'd strayed from their religion (and behaved like a heathen) coming and pleading in the name of that religion ('It's most certainly none of yours').

With his eye on the main chance, I supposed: for another bombshell dropped for my mother.

By this time my father had left the garage and started working for the insurance company. At the garage he'd worked on the car of a man who worked for the company, a spivvy type who like so many others had been taken with our father's matey charm, and had offered him a job. Now our father spent his days swinging down the lanes on his motorbike or in the Austin Seven selling insurance and making collections, clean-handed at last and master of his own time. He seemed at last to have settled. Until, one day after Cathy was born, another letter came from Aunt Lizzie.

She had bought our boat tickets out to Australia.

She had rented a garage in Sydney for our father to run before he inherited her businesses, and she had bought a bungalow for us to live in.

All along, our mother said she realised, our father been keeping his options open. Or scheming behind her back, I would think. Expecting her to capitulate when presented with a *fait accompli*. No wonder he hadn't shown her all Aunt Lizzie's letters.

As I contemplated it all for my novel, I thought: no wonder he wouldn't discuss with her why, in spite of his reluctance, he did Aunt Lizzie's bidding and visited his sister. He'd be keeping in with Aunt Lizzie, keeping up his image in her eyes. Protecting his future fortune.

Our mother didn't capitulate. She made him write back and say they weren't going. At which Aunt Lizzie booked a passage back for herself in order to come and persuade them. She never made it: before she could sail she fell ill and died in a Catholic hospice.

And here was the joke, our mother would say, laughing: her fortune disappeared. One of the Birkenhead relatives went out to Australia to investigate but apparently found out nothing. All that was left was a single ring, which went not to my father but someone else.

Another mystery. I came unstuck in my novel.

I rang my mother to ask her about it.

'What do you think happened to Aunt Lizzie's fortune?'

My mother laughed, remembering it. 'I've no idea.'

All these years later she no longer seemed particularly interested.

I persisted. 'Do you think it went to the Church when she went into the hospice?'

'I suppose it might have . . .' It had obviously never occurred to her. 'Why?'

'Because I'm putting it in a novel. Novels need reasons, explanations. You can't leave things up in the air.'

'You're writing a novel about *that*?'

'Well, no, about Dad, really . . .'

'You're writing a novel about your *father*?'

My mother was amazed, and inordinately pleased.

PART TWO

In which I trace the deterioration of my relationship with my father

CHANGES FOR THE WORSE

F OR ALL OF my adult life my mother had been trying in vain to repair the long-standing breach between me and my father. Before that, even: long before.

'Your Daddy loves you really,' she would tell us after a beating, as far back as the early days in Prestatyn.

We wanted to believe it, but in Prestatyn we were so frightened whenever we'd been naughty and he was due home. We'd listen out in panic for cars turning into the side street down below the flat, and whenever we heard one, jump in terror to the window. Finally there would be his Austin, a black square bomb beside the pavement. The slam of the outside door, the sound of his footsteps coming up the stairs through the building, approaching on the brown-lino corridor below, past the insurance office, to the door of our flat at the bottom of the inner flight of stairs. And then the punishment.

He would lift a chair with his weightlifter's hand, easily, as if it were a feather, and place it in the centre of the carpet. He'd seat himself on it, his huge muscular thighs splayed. 'Line up!' he would command (although there were only the two of us). There would be a struggle as we each tried not to be first. He would choose for us: the elder, the ringleader, me. And then the tip over his thighs, your lungs jamming in your throat, and the huge slam and sting of his hand on your behind. And then the sight of it coming down on Cathy's plump little bum.

Afterwards, as we sobbed, our chests juddering, Mummy, desperate to create harmony, would tell us – there was no point, clearly, in telling *him* – 'Go to Daddy, go and say sorry for being naughty.' Ever hopeful, I suppose, that it would do the magic trick.

'Sorry, Daddy,' we would shudder.

He'd look up from the table where he was working – writing in his ledgers or reading the musty books he bought from secondhand shops – raise his head slowly, coming back from somewhere faraway, as if he'd forgotten about us altogether, his ice-blue eyes glazed. And then he would focus: 'I should bloody well think so. You mend your ways, or as sure as bloody little apples you'll get it worse next time!'

And we'd feel terror all over again, because, since we'd moved from Llanfair to Prestatyn, we somehow couldn't stop being naughty all the time.

Though on Friday evenings, his pay day, he'd bring us each a packet of Rolos, or a secondhand book, and say with a snigger, 'Put that in your pipe and smoke it!' and we'd think: *He does love us, really.*

But then again there was the Children's Home.

Some Sunday afternoons he would drive us out to the hills, Mummy in the front with the baby on her knee, me and Cathy in the back, Cathy's legs sticking straight out on the ribbed leather seat. Sometimes he would sing (he always liked adventure, and he liked to drive). But going home his mood would darken. The car would be filled with his smoke, the hedges would slap by like irritable hands, and I'd start to feel sick and fidget. 'You bloody kick me in the back of my seat once more while I'm driving, and I'll clip you round the ear!' he would bawl, his dangerous smoke-yellowed hand moving on the wheel.

One Sunday we came down a steep hill among trees, and there at the bottom behind a high wall was a gaunt grey-stone building, tall but sprawling, with wings and turrets and blank-looking windows.

Instantly I was afraid. 'What is it?' I whispered in fear.

'It's a children's home,' my father answered. 'And if you don't start behaving better, it's where you'll be going.'

The way he was with us now made me believe him. From then on, whatever I was doing, playing with Cathy on the landing with our sixpenny Woolworth's plastic figures, down the alleyway behind the flat sorting into piles the different-coloured bottle tops from the pub opposite, or walking on my own to school (Cathy went to nursery, taken by our mother at a different hour), the thought of the children's home was always hovering, its black-roofed turrets, its blank eyes deflecting the sun.

I was becoming frightened, in a way I never had been when I was younger, in Llanfair.

For one thing, there was a ghost.

Down the years, our mother would recall it:

One night very soon after we arrived in Prestatyn, Cathy and I were falling asleep in our double bed when I felt the bedclothes lifting. I opened my eyes. No one was there. The room was empty, the door closed; just the empty room yellow with the sunlight of an early summer evening coming through the thin curtains. I suppose I imagined it; with all the changes that were happening I must have been in a state of heightened nervousness. If hysteria it was, though, it was shared: Cathy remembers too the bed dipping between us, making us tip towards the centre, as if something invisible had settled there between us. We both set up screaming.

Our parents came running. 'Must have been a mouse,' said Daddy, but no mouse could have done those things, and it was obvious that both he and Mummy were spooked.

After that we were afraid to be in our bed alone, and our mother would have to lie with us until we were asleep. Our room was separate from the rest of the flat, on a half-turn near the top of the staircase that rose up from the flat door. One night, as our mother lay beside us she fell asleep too. The three of us were woken by a crash just outside the door, followed by a tumbling, splintering and banging down the stairs, and finally an explosion against the door at the bottom, and a ringing like a gong that gradually faded. My mother was sure that the grandmother clock that hung on the little half-landing had fallen off the wall and down the stairs. But when she got up to look – our father, having heard it too, rushing to the bannister opposite – there was nothing to be seen, and the clock was ticking peacefully on the wall.

I'm not sure if I really remember it, but my mother has told the tale so often I feel as if I do. The memory is visceral: the sound assaulting the guts, the stomach-dropping shock of there being nothing to be seen.

There's something I do know I experienced for myself. It was early evening. Our father was home and the building beneath us was vacated and silent. I was alone on the L-shaped landing playing with our Woolworth's plastic figures, sending Maid Marion and Robin Hood across a plain with a wagon and a herd of assorted animals, when I heard footsteps in the corridor below the flat. They got louder, coming towards the door of the insurance office just below. They didn't stop at the insurance office; they came on. They came right to the other side of our door and then they did stop. And then, to my horror, they passed right through the door, muffled now on the threadbare carpet, approaching inexorably upwards, although there was nothing to be seen. I fled for the living room, my heart hammering.

After that, I didn't go out onto the landing alone if I could help it. If I ever had to fetch something from our bedroom I'd have to force myself across the dip in the stairs, breath held, mind squeezed.

Somehow I had the strong sense of having to keep it to myself. I didn't tell my mother. I was surprised, therefore, when, she told us years later that in that flat she'd experienced the very same thing.

'Did you tell me?' I asked, curious.

'No, no, I wouldn't have wanted to frighten you!'

She did mention it, she said, to a colleague of our father's who came to tea with his wife, and he told her straight away that the employee and his family who'd had the flat before us had left because they too had thought the flat was haunted!

I must have been hanging about listening, I supposed.

So there you go, I thought: my mother and I unintentionally putting the wind up each other, as we would go on spectacularly doing.

In those days, in Prestatyn, I was always hanging about listening, always watching for clues. Clues to what I didn't know. All the time I had the sense of something important, significant, just out of reach.

When we walked with our mother after school, I'd peer into the murky caves of the amusement arcades, and the lights winking inside seemed to be sending a secret message.

Across the road from the flat was a sweet shop with a bon-bon machine in the window, its metal arm churning the dead grey bon-bon mixture and seeming to be flailing a frightening, unfathomable signal.

There was something important and disturbing about the songs echoing from the dance hall at night, hollowing the air with longing and loss. It was there, too, in the couples on the prom. I couldn't take my eyes off the way, in those days of sexual prudery and decorum, they touched each other slyly and slid, as if helpless, together.

There was a secretary in the insurance office, a young woman called Pam with dark hair and big puffy dresses. One summer Saturday afternoon she offered to take me and Cathy to the prom. As we walked along, there happened to come towards us the colleague who'd been to the flat for tea with his wife, a man with a stark-black moustache and a tight little belly beneath a waistcoat. We were just passing a fruit stall, and Pam said quickly that we could each have a peach, and made us sit on a bench to eat them. The man hadn't walked on. He had stopped, a little way off, and she left us and went towards him.

I bit into the peach. As the flesh closed around my teeth and the juice dribbled down my chin, I watched Pam and the man, standing apart yet somehow swooning together. Although I couldn't have named these things then, my mouth was filled with the taste of squalor and desolation and loss, and I swallowed the flesh and felt sick.

Years later, it would occur to me: they would be meeting in the office after hours, and once perhaps they knocked something over that reverberated up our stairs, which in front of his wife he'd be quick to confirm as the sound of a ghost.

But it wasn't just ghosts or underhand adulterers who disturbed me. As I walked beside my mother, her silk dress billowing and wrapping round my legs, my eye snagged on a couple clasped together on the emptying teatime sand. The sun had gone in; the sand had gone black and the water coming in around the sandbanks looked icy. His arms were fast around her; their mouths were clamped. He bent over her as if in supplication, and she was bent backwards like a wilting leaf beneath him. Her dark hair floated in the breeze, his struggled upwards, their clothes nudged around them, but inside all the restless movement they were perfectly still, making them together a single stark figure, a mysterious sign that somehow filled me with an aching sense of loss.

Every so often on Friday evenings our father would bring us a secondhand volume of a children's encyclopaedia. ('Put that in your pipe and smoke it.') We would sit on the floor with it, the reflection of the coal fire licking along the lino towards us. One evening we turned a page and froze in horror. A line drawing of a man or boy, we couldn't tell, barrel-chested with huge electric hair and long cruel nails, standing on a plinth.

'What is it?' Cathy whispered.

'I don't know,' I said, and shut the book quickly.

Man or boy? Villain or victim? I couldn't tell.

I put the book right at the end of the shelf so I'd know where it was and not make the mistake of opening it again

What was frightening was the not knowing, the way the image seemed to shift between something threatening and something crippled and pathetic. And so I shut my mind to it altogether (and thus never read the tale of *Strewelpeter*).

As I peered and stared, my sight was going. I'd become short-sighted and my eyes were deteriorating fast. I was frightened I was going blind. I was frightened that my body was failing altogether. Since we'd come to Prestatyn, in spite of my ability to run pell-mell on the sands, I got aches and pains in my legs that could make me collapse on the pavement and kept me awake. Growing pains, the doctor called them, and said they couldn't be cured, but while he was examining me found I had flat feet, which could. So on Saturday mornings I had to attend a clinic with other similarly handicapped children, where we sat in our vests and pants on icy lino, and picked up pencils and little bean bags with our toes. Along with my National Health glasses, sticking-plaster pink, with arms like surgical wire, I now had to wear brown lace-up shoes to support my arches, while Cathy, lucky Cathy, got to wear red sandals punched with holes in flower shapes. And a glove in bed, suggested by the doctor: I sucked my thumb, the only way I could get to sleep, a matter of shame for a child my age, and which was starting to make my teeth stick out. I was dismayed at my own disintegration. I was normal no longer, no longer whole. I wasn't natural or independent: I had to be corrected, aided and propped with artificial devices, I couldn't get by without them like other people.

Our teeth were rotting – Cathy's too – and we had to climb more brown-lino stairs to a dentist's, and sit in a chair like the executioner's one I'd seen in the paper, and have a drill drag at our skulls. Now if I bit down on a piece of silver paper, a shock would go through my brain, reminding me I was no longer fully human.

I stared hard at a girl wearing callipers, a red-raw gash in her calf exposing a pinned bone. I stared at the people in wheelchairs. You could get polio, I knew; in fact, Daddy's only brother did. Mummy had told us: during the war he had joined the RAF in the footsteps of his elder brother, Daddy, but the very first time he went home on leave he fell ill with polio and never returned. Now, a grown man, he still lived with their parents, unable to work, dependent on the charity of the nuns, a permanent cripple. You heard of people ending up being unable to breathe, and having to spend the rest of their lives in something called an iron lung.

These things could happen to people, and then they became part of a different, lesser population. Already with my cramps and my artificial aids I was no longer one of the healthy, beautiful people, no longer the same as my handsome athletic father and my beautiful mother and my chocolate-box-pretty sister. I was odd, an aberration. And naughty, a child who fidgeted and stared. 'Don't stare!' Mummy would hiss, pulling me away from whatever I was staring at. You could get into trouble for staring, for trying to understand the mystery of it all. 'Smile!' she would tell me, as she dragged me away. 'A smile costs nothing! You've got a duty to be happy! You look pretty when you smile!' 'Take that bloody scowl off your face!' Daddy would growl, 'or I'll take it off for you!' The kind of child who deserved to get sent to a children's home. The kind of child a father could find hard to love.

I took refuge in books and stories. I would read to Cathy – Little Women, A Christmas Carol – sitting on the floor with the book laid flat so she could see the pictures, and at school I excelled in writing my own. In books and stories things always made sense, or if there was a mystery it was always solved in the end.

After two years in that flat in Prestatyn, we moved to another three streets away, up similar stairs and corridors with similar brown lining.

In later years, our mother would explain: our father just wasn't earning money in the insurance. He had come to Prestatyn to be an inspector, overseeing agents and sharing with them the commission on policies sold while he was in charge of them. The trouble was, in that seaside town in autumn, when everything closed down and people were no longer making money out of holidaymakers, they stopped paying their premiums, which meant that the commission would have to be paid back to the firm. When a client 'took up' their policy again the following summer – in reality they would be buying a new policy – the agent would get commission again, but our father who had moved on to oversee another agent, would lose out.

One Christmas in the first flat we were so poor that our mother had to make the Christmas crackers, and all she could afford for the dinner was a tiny piece of pork (it must have been before his ban), which, due to an unfortunate incident, was even tinier in the end. She was turning the meat when she dropped it on the cat's back. She would relate it afterwards crying tears of laughter: how the cat howled, and then, as the pork dropped from its back to the floor, leapt away through the door to the fire escape, left open for the steam, and jumped onto the railing, a raw bloody patch right down his back. He turned once to glare at her, his eyes flashing luminous green, and then leapt, out into space and the thirty-foot drop to the yard below. She thought he must be dead, but when she looked over he was staggering to his feet. He shot across the yard and under the wooden gate and didn't come back. And she picked up the pork, cut off the side that was covered in cat hairs and skin, and popped it back in the oven!

We'd laugh too. But I'd think of her legs that the cat had been roiling around, white and bare even in winter because she couldn't afford to wear out her stockings in the house, and my father lying flat on his back in the living room, all Christmas afternoon, and the fact that his moods were blackest on Christmas Day.

It was after we moved away from that ghost-haunted flat, that the cat came back to us. Cathy and I were playing in the different but similar alleyway beyond the different but similar fire escape, when the cat came creeping round the corner, covered in something white like flour, unrecognisable but for the scar all down his back. The fur grew over the scar in the end, but whenever you stroked him your hand came up on that troubling knot of skin and I'd think of the shadows and the aching feeling in the kitchen that Christmas day.

Our father, our mother always explained, had decided he just had to get out of the insurance. In the meantime, he gave up his position as inspector and went back to being an agent and collector. And we'd had to get out of the flat, because it had come with the inspector's job.

He'd come back one day, she always told us, and announced that he'd found another: it was all set and sealed, no need to worry any more, the contract was signed and we could move right away. And then he mentioned the little matter of the couple who were leaving having run a clandestine bed-and-breakfast business (against the rules of the lease), and that, this being March, there was a full summer's bookings which our mother, with a baby and two small children, would have to take over!

She protested: but the other couple had been childless – we wouldn't have the room! And she didn't have anything like enough crockery and linen!

He thought she'd be pleased, he said (I can imagine his face screwing in irritation): after all, there'd be extra money coming in . . .

So our mother had no option but to borrow more money from Nanny and Grampa to buy the equipment. And that summer we would have to sleep on mattresses in the attic (to which there happened to be a proper flight of wooden stairs, which no doubt our wily father had taken into consideration) while strangers occupied our bedrooms, the odd family but mainly groups of young people, girls in our parents' room and boys in mine and Cathy's. And then there it was again: that disturbing thing with men and women: the bedroom doors below creaking open at night, and the sudden sound of giggling, like a plug being pulled on a secret, and then stopping quickly again.

As soon as we moved, the first guests were imminent, and, busy with the baby and unpacking and preparations, our mother sent me and Cathy to collect the crockery she'd ordered from the shop across the railway bridge near the flat. We took a large canvas holdall, and the woman in the shop filled it with blue-and-white striped crockery. As we carried it back, listing on Cathy's side, I had the sense that everything, our whole life somehow, depended on our not dropping it. The wall was too high to see the railway beneath us, but I was filled with a panicky vision of the contents of the bag, cups and plates and jugs and bowls, smashing on the shiny rails below, and with a tight, tight feeling that I sensed was also my mother's, of determination knotted with wearying shame.

At the end of that summer, when the bed-and-breakfast guests had gone, I came upon my mother and father embracing. I was shocked. I had never, within my memory, seen them do it before. I ran from the room and threw myself on my bed. They followed, laughing, saying I was jealous. Eight years old, I lay on my bed afterwards, wondering: was I jealous? I tasted, tested the feeling. It didn't feel like jealousy. It felt like something else, something strange that I didn't understand at all. A kind of creeping dismay.

The following spring, I went out onto the landing and a terrifying figure was coming up the inner stairs, unimpeded by the flat door. A man entirely in black. It wasn't just his clothes, the black jacket and beret; his skin was the colour of deep night.

I screamed and ran for my mother. She came, wiping her hands on her pinny and laughing. 'That's Daddy!'

She explained: he was no longer working for the insurance but at a power-station site. My father hadn't spoken, and he still looked alien, the lips a red slit in the black, and the blue-and-white eyes bleakly glittering and sliding.

And so he began working away, which I remember as a time of relief, a summer when we didn't need to take in bed-and-breakfast guests but went walking with our mother for miles along the prom or jumping on buses, just to see where they'd take us.

And then we moved to England, to the Midlands, to join him.

A CONUNDRUM

'**D**OES HE REALLY love us?' Cathy would ask me, holding tight to my arm as we walked on a Saturday afternoon down a high-hedged lane in Easton in the Midlands, escaping the house after a beating.

The lane led off the road we lived on, a road of modern red-brick houses and bungalows, of which ours was one of the largest, new and detached. We had left the gloomy flats behind. Before we moved, there had been excitement. Daddy had written to us in Prestatyn describing the amenities: central heating, radiators in every room! A shower as well as a bath! Picture windows! And modern easy-clean tiles on the kitchen floor! And eventually we would be able to buy it: our father had been made a foreman, with a foreman's wage, and the couple who were letting it had moved to Canada and wanted to sell. Daddy had done a deal with them, which was that once they'd got themselves properly sorted out in Canada, they would sell it to our parents.

The day we arrived we tumbled stiffly from the car. The house was a raw-looking block in a sea of mud, built with rough sharp bricks that would graze your arms if you didn't take care running round the corners. The inside was stark, the picture windows exposing both sides of the downstairs through room, and glass doors making the rooms leak coldly into each other. And yes, it was cold: although Daddy was a foreman now, somehow it turned out we were poorer than ever, we still owed all the money to Nanny and Grampa, and the central heating couldn't be put on. And, although we'd come to be with our father, not long after we moved he started working away again, in the north west of England, back over the Pennines we'd crossed to join him.

He came home to Easton at weekends, but we dreaded him coming: his temper and moods were worse than ever. Now he hit us with a biting cane, kept ready in a gap between the unit and the cooker in the kitchen with its floor of dark-green tiles like black ice. I couldn't pass the place without inwardly flinching. On Friday nights, when we'd been naughty in the week - which we were, more than ever - and Mummy had threatened to tell him, we'd be in terror as we heard his van on the drive, as the headlights glared, searching, through the glass door and threw shadows swooning down the hall walls. We'd beg her not to, swirling, frantic to escape our own doomed skins. Mostly she wouldn't, but over the weekend something would erupt and he'd smack us anyway ('Line up!').

Some weekends the workmate he gave a lift to came in, and as their voices sounded outside, we'd breathe with relief. Now, instead of coming through the door looking grimly up through his brows, his cheek rippling, our father would be all bonhomie, ushering in Mick Daly. But we knew Mummy didn't like it. She'd play the generous hostess and get out the cake for which she'd had to scrape to buy the ingredients, but we'd recognised by now that sometimes the more irritated or upset our mother was by an acquaintance, the harder she worked to give the opposite impression. Our father knew that too, and even while Mick Daly was still there, his cheek would start going again, and once Mick Daly had gone and we were in bed we'd hear our parents rowing.

The week-times without him weren't so great now, either. At this time our mother started getting the crippling migraines she would have forever more. I would come upon her at the little Formica table in the kitchen with her head in her hands, and she would say she had flashing lights in front of her eyes. Sometimes she'd been weeping, and would quickly wipe her eyes on her pinny and rise. She would stagger and catch the table to steady herself. I didn't know what I'd do if she fainted, in this place where we'd been for only a few months and still knew no one, with our father away and little David only four years old.

I became afraid to leave her. We were meant to stay for school dinners, but at lunchtime I'd think up a ruse to get to run home with Cathy to check she was all right. I'd break the arm of my glasses, or take Cathy into the toilets and snap the elastic on her knickers, and under the pretence of rushing home to get them mended, we'd run pell-mell, Cathy holding up her knickers, and burst through the back door, to find with relief our mother sitting having lunch with David and looking up in surprise.

This was also the time that my mother, distressed and losing patience, began sometimes smacking me too (the eldest, the one who should know better), with her slipper rather than the cane. But she was always beside herself when she did it (and, unlike our father, she wasn't any good at it, she flailed and missed), and always loving afterwards, so it never dismayed me the way my father's stony, calculating punishment did.

'Does he love us?' Cathy repeated in the lane with its high enclosing hedges. She was still shuddering after the beating. Little curls of black hair, escaped from her plaits, trembled around her pale troubled face.

'I don't know.' I never knew. I couldn't puzzle it out. Before we moved there, Mummy had read out from his letter describing the shower: *The kids will have a high old time splashing about.* And he'd gone round the Easton schools and had had a long talk with the headmaster of the one he had chosen; he chose it, he said, because he thought we'd like it and would do best there. But he'd since shown no interest in the school, and we'd surely be for it if we dared to have any high old time splashing about.

We hated the school. Woodland Grove it was called, but there wasn't a tree in sight, just knee-grazing concrete and boys with green teeth and musty-smelling, ill-fitting clothes, who flicked custard and gravy into our hair and waited for us at home time on the demolition site and threw stones.

One Saturday teatime we told Mummy about the bullies. (We'd come to dread weekend meals, Daddy sitting silent and absent-seeming, though if he caught us eating with our mouths open or holding our knives wrong, he'd explode.)

Mummy turned pointedly to Daddy. 'Patrick, what should they do about those boys?'

He focussed, came back from his reverie with an effort.

He said, 'If you're bullied, run like hell,' and then went back to the place he'd been inside his head.

But running like hell was what we did already, and it didn't seem to make any difference; in fact, I was beginning to see it made it worse.

There was something about us that seemed to attract the bullies' attention. They never bullied the girl who sat next to me in class, Gillian Arkwright. The day I arrived she told me eagerly about herself, about her dog and her many dolls, and the fact – announced proudly – that her mother said she was 'highly strung'. She had invited me to tea, in a large brick semi in an older part of town, and the smell that hit me as I stepped through the door, a sweet, musty smell of deep carpets and plump cushions and permanence, told me straight away that this was a different kind of home from my own. There was a piano, and Gillian went to it immediately and started playing, demonstrating for me her oeuvre. It was clear right away that she had the run of this place. I was sure right away that her father didn't hit her.

She had a freedom, a confidence, of which I was dimly jealous, and which I began to realise created a forcefield around her that deterred the bullying boys.

We'd become scaredy-cats, Cathy and I, that was the trouble. We were scared of everyone and everything. On a couple of Saturday mornings in Prestatyn, Daddy had dropped us off at the cinema for the kids' matinee, and although we'd been excited to go, we cringed at the massed violence of the kids waiting for the film to start, the roar of the organised sing-song and the sweet-paper pellets arcing through the air. And now here there were rough boys, boys who I was sure got beaten like us at home, probably worse, but took it in their stride, who got the cane in school and came back swaggering and grinning, who sensed our fear and knew they could bully us.

But knowing this, working it out, didn't make me stop flinching, I couldn't.

We felt lacking, inadequate. We envied the confidence of other children, but we didn't like it, either, it felt threatening. The other girls shouted in their blunt flat accents, and slammed across the playground in their unfamiliar games, with a casual acceptance of how the world was. 'Are you stopping?'

they would call, turning and seeing me still standing (which was their way in this place of asking *Aren't you coming?*). Stopped, that was exactly how I felt in this place. Uncertain, unknowing, shivering and frozen to the spot.

There were girls who, as spring came around, we played with in the road. They all went to Sunday School. 'Why don't you go?' they asked us, looking at us curiously. We stood there, curiosities who didn't go to Sunday School, who didn't even have a religion, who hadn't been baptised, who could end up buried on a wild hillside, our graves grassed over so that no one would know we were there, or had ever lived. For whom religion was a knot of tension.

We had asked Daddy, in one of his better moods, about the fact that his grandfather was Jewish.

He'd become serious. He had given us all his attention for once. He said they'd come from Europe, Germany I thought he'd said, to Dublin; they'd had to leave because of a *pogrom*, people were persecuting Jews. Yes, his grandfather had taken him to the synagogue in Dublin. But weren't his family Catholic, we asked? He replied, a bit grimly so I thought perhaps he was getting irritated with us: The girls were brought up as Catholics and the boys as Jewish. This seemed very strange. I couldn't imagine it. So what was it like in his family? I asked, dared to go on asking. (There wasn't a single photo.) He answered: So poor that they'd had to eat nettles, and had no table, just a board to eat off, with holes dug in the earth floor for their legs. But by then he was grinning, and we didn't know whether to believe him or not.

We wanted not to be different and strange. 'Mummy, can we go to Sunday School?' we asked.

'They *can* go, can't they, Patrick?' she asked him at the

weekend. She was reminding him, I knew, of their agreement to let us decide our religion for ourselves. But there was tension in her voice, for this was Methodist Sunday School, and indeed it sounded like a challenge.

He levered up his eyes under his brows. He looked hostile. His lip curled.

'They can if they want to hob-knob with bloody hypocrites,' he growled, and went back to his plate, and it felt as though, rather than being given permission, we'd been dismissed and condemned. It felt as though we had made ourselves more alien than ever to our father.

We didn't much like Sunday School. We didn't fit there. We couldn't pray there. When the teacher told us to close our eyes, all I could think of was the sun showing up the blood in my eyelids, and of the sight before I closed them of the long shadows made by the splinters on the board floor, and the horrid big dirty crayons she made us use to draw scenes from the Bible while she sat on one of our low chairs with her knife-pleat skirt in a perfect circle all around her and picked pills from her pink angora jumper.

I didn't know what to think about any of it, and I didn't know what to think about me and Cathy. What were we? We were poor, but the rough boys jeered at us for being posh. Though we weren't as posh as Gillian ... Were we good girls, or bad ones? We were teachers' pets in school, the acknowledged *nice* girls, impeccably behaved and constantly praised, yet at home we seemed to need to be punished all the time. Were we girls whose Daddy loved them, or not?

Sometimes he seemed to hate us. 'Shut the hell up!' he would yell if we made a noise when he was doing his pools, hunched above the yammering radio, or tuning into foreign stations that only he could understand. 'Belt up or I'll belt you, you noisy bitch!' And the wireless emitted buzzes and screams and gobbets of the prickly-sounding Polish he'd learnt in a Polish squadron in the RAF, and the guttural German he must have got from his grandfather. He had rented a TV, specifically to see the pictures of the Sputnik in which the Russians had sent a little dog into space. They showed a picture of the dog and the tiny capsule in which it was imprisoned, and a chart of the huge black universe in which it was travelling. I was frightened for the dog. 'Will it be all right, Daddy?' I cried. He turned to me nastily. 'Be quiet, I didn't pay to get a TV so you could drown it out!'

But I couldn't shut up. The thought of the little dog trapped up there filled me with terror. 'But *will* it, Daddy?'

'Shut the hell up or you'll get what's coming!' and he scraped his ice-blue eyes at me in a look that seemed pure hatred, as if he wished to God I didn't exist.

'The breedin' beats the rearin',' he'd say with disgust, a phrase that puzzled me until I decided that it meant that nothing anyone could teach us, nothing we could do ourselves, however hard we might try, could erase our wayward natures.

Yet hadn't Mummy told us that he was the one who had named us, me and Cathy, that he'd absolutely insisted on the names he wanted? Didn't that mean he cared? Mummy had wanted to call me Georgina, she said, after our Grampa, George, but Daddy had insisted on Josephine. And wasn't that the female version of the name of his younger, crippled brother, Joseph, of whom, she told us, he'd seemed quite fond – pleased when he came to England and joined the RAF, planning a meet-up that was only foiled by Joe's falling ill? And Cathy, she had the same name as his youngest sister,

Cathleen, the nun, who wrote to him once a year, one of the two letters she was allowed to send each year, in gratitude for buying the habit and the ring. In fact, Mummy told us, our parents had agreed on *Catherine* for Cathy, but when Daddy, with his maverick tendencies, went off on his motorbike to register the birth, he put down *Cathleen*, which he'd wanted all along. Didn't that mean he was *involved*?

Yet now he seemed anything but involved.

There was a story connected with my birth concerning my father and a jackdaw. One June night after I'd been born, coming back from the hospital on his motorbike he saw a jackdaw's nest and took two of the nestlings home in his sidecar. One of them died, but the other thrived, and when my mother came home with me from hospital, it had already taken up residence in the living room of the cottage. There was bird shit all over the floor and chairs, and the bird glaring at my mother as if to say, Who are *you*? What are you doing here?

I would imagine my father stopped for a fag on one of those hump-backed bridges we would later race up in the Austin, the motorbike parked nearby. Tall trees all around, marching off along the stream, sun dropping in milky diagonals between their trunks. A sudden rustling in the air above him, and then a cacophony: a flock of jackdaws coming down into the trees above. *Jack*, *Jack*, they'd be calling, wheeling acrobatically, the name he had in the air force. One dropping into a hole in the tree directly above, the tell-tale sign. My father up on the wall and climbing, the bird flying out in fright at his approach. Inside, a nest of four baby birds ready to fly, cloudy brown feathers that would later be black, and the soft brown eye that would turn that eerie jackdaw blue. A fledgling lying in his palm like a throbbing heart, before he slips it in the sling he's made of his shirt.

He taught the jackdaw to fly, Mummy told us. While she was in hospital learning how to breastfeed and change a nappy, he was coaxing the jackdaw across the room with titbits.

Mummy banned it from the house, of course – they had a baby with weeping skin, open to infection – but it stayed on the roof and in the nearby trees, and every time our father went out of the door it swooped down in joy to sit on his shoulder. It would swoop on hers too, she said, when she went to hang out the washing, nearly knocking her over!

I would think of it sitting at night in the swaying trees beside the cottage from which it had been banned, where now lay its usurper, me.

He had to get rid of it in the end, she told us. One day when I was out in my pram, it flew down from the roof and tried to peck out my eye, and it was only the neighbour coming running at my screams and sending it flapping off that saved me. He took it out to the country, she said, but the damn thing came back. He took it further; it came back again. Three times he tried, and three times it came back. In the end, he had to wring its neck.

All because of me, I'd think now. 'She's like a skinned rabbit!' Mummy had said he'd cried when he first saw me, which had seemed funny when she told us. I thought now: he'd been repulsed by me, raw and unformed as I was. And then he'd looked in the nest and found those bundles of perfect, pulsing new life.

I thought of him miles off in the country, flinging the bird, his namesake, into the air. 'So long, pal,' I thought of him saying grimly, sadly. I thought of him having to wring its neck, all because of me, and felt desolate.

He didn't like us as much as other children, it seemed. The girls in the road would call for us sometimes, and if he was there he'd invite them in, and chat to them in a flattering way he never used with us. Cathy and I would hang back, embarrassed, strangers to the side of our father he was showing to them. I had the sense, as time went on, that the other girls had cottoned on to this. They were becoming superior, beginning to boss us around. We began to prefer being on our own, wandering down the lane or staying close to the house, the muddy space where our father was meant to have planted a lawn, but hadn't.

One darkening late afternoon as I ran in the gap between our house and the bungalow next door, I looked up and saw, framed in the lighted kitchen window of the bungalow, the young couple who lived there in a deep embrace. I looked away again quickly and deliberately kept running. Such images were everywhere, on the cinema hoardings, in my mother's magazines, but somehow, like the sight of my parents embracing, this real-life image filled with me with a dismay I didn't understand.

What if our father really did hate us? He had special powers. He could see fairies, he could lie on the floor and do what he now called astral projection, flying up out of his body, he said, and looking down on the world. He could put curses on people. Once in Llanfair, Mummy had told us, he put a curse on a woman he didn't like, and next time she came calling she fell on the path and broke her leg. What if he hated us enough to curse us too?

'Your Daddy loves you really,' she would insist as we left

the house after a beating, escaping our father and the oppressive shadow he cast over the place. 'Yes, go,' she would say, intent and distressed: the sooner we and our father were apart the better. I couldn't avoid the dismaying implication that the house would be better off without us.

'Roll on Nanny's,' I said between the high hedges, clasping Cathy's arm tighter. In Llanfair we were thought of as good girls; in Llanfair we knew we were loved.

Though a new, worrying thought was creeping in: what if Nanny and Grampa and Uncle Gwilym discovered we weren't good really, that we were naughty enough to be beaten so often, and even to be threatened with the children's home? They might not go on loving us then . . .

The high hedges fell away, and the lane opened out onto a vast ploughed field, with only the tops of a mining village on the horizon. There was a single dead tree with one branch remaining, that made me think of a gallows. Above, a grey steel sky with its unseen flying metal and the little dog lost in the blank silent universe.

One year, that was all that we lived in that Midlands mining town, Easton.

Our mother would relate how, one weekday, when our father of course wasn't there, there was a knock on the door. There stood the owners of the house, back from Canada: they had decided not to stay after all. They no longer wanted to sell the house to us; they wanted it back, and they wanted us out forthwith.

So much for the so-called matey deal our father had done.

Our mother tried to hold out, to argue, but – wouldn't you

know it? – there was nothing in writing. Next thing, a court order dropped onto the mat.

After all the plans, after Cathy and I had managed at last to adopt the local accent and had mastered italic script, the only one allowed in the school, we moved again, in a hurry, back across the Pennines, to the north west of England where, after all, our father was working.

Flitting, they called it in that place, as if we were birds, flying up any old how, as if, I always thought afterwards, we had something to fly from.

All that year in Easton there was a song on the wireless, a song about singing the blues. It drove me mad, clenched my stomach, but Cathy and I couldn't stop singing it, couldn't get it out of our heads: a song with a message at odds with its upbeat, skiffley sound.

DANGER

As soon as we arrived in the new place I sensed it: danger.

An old industrial town perched on the side of the vast watery spaces of the river Mersey. Two weeks before we moved, we travelled over to look at the house our father had rented. That time we'd had to drive a long way round: our father had had to visit a power station on the other side of the river beforehand, and afterwards we'd had to cross by a transporter bridge. It was January, getting dark already by the time we drew up above the water. Far out in the giddying spaces, the transporter platform crawled towards us, impossibly suspended from a great metal structure arcing above. A sleety squall came up and the platform carrying the cars and people started swinging, and once it reached our shore they stopped its operation until the storm was over. It was properly dark by the time we got to the house, a blackened end-terrace on a hill, and, as it turned out, the electricity had been turned off. We waited in the van on the cushions and blankets in the back where we kids sat for the journey, while our mother and father viewed the place by candlelight.

Even by candlelight, she would always tell us afterwards, she could see stalactites of grease hanging from the kitchen ceiling, and mouse shit in the kitchen sink. Driving back in the dark that evening our parents quarrelled. How could he have committed them to such a disgusting hovel? my mother cried. He'd had no option, he bawled, being in such a hurry, he'd had to take it sight unseen. But how could he have *done* that? my mother spluttered. And this time he *had* signed a contract – they were stuck with it! It was snowing by now and on the tops of the Pennines there were drifts each side of the road. On a bend on a hill we skidded; for endless, terrifying moments the car fell backwards and sideways across the road to whatever precipice lay behind us in the dark. We landed, thankfully, in a snowdrift. Stuck. Our father had to get out and trudge across a snowy field towards the lights of a farmhouse to ask to borrow a shovel.

On my lap was a plastic box I'd been holding to stop the cupcakes we'd brought for the journey from sliding and squashing, and which I'd clung to as we plummeted as if it could save us. 'Would you like a cake?' I asked, when our father had gone. 'Mummy?' She had said nothing. She still didn't answer, but shook her head, looking away, so I knew she was crying. I gave one each to Cathy and David, and took one myself. The cakes had green icing I'd helped my mother to colour. I sunk my teeth into the acid-coloured crust. Always afterwards the sight of green icing made me feel sick.

Now, two weeks later, we had moved. We arrived late afternoon. Our parents made us wait in the back garden while inside the house they cleared up the worst of the mess. There was new snow on the ground, and I occupied the others in making patterns with their footprints. While they jumped and exclaimed, I looked around. A long garden stretched in torn rags of snow and shadow to a small bare orchard at the bottom. On the left was the garden of the next-door terrace, and on the right a wooded wilderness which would turn out later to be the grounds of a gloomy abandoned house.

There was a smell in the air: something chemical, poisonous.

Our parents were taking a long time cleaning. Afterwards our mother would tell us that the place was so filthy there was shit on the bathroom walls. The dark came down altogether and the patches of light on the snow from the kitchen window turned sulphurous.

At last our mother called us in.

I stepped into the doorway. The kitchen was a dark, wet-looking cave, its walls painted in dark-blue gloss paint. And then I saw what was just inside the door, and stopped short. An old-fashioned, Victorian-looking gas cooker, dead blue-grey with cruel-looking antlers of pipes and knobs, standing on curved legs. It looked as if it could break free from the wall. A hoarse roaring came from its pipes: our mother was boiling a kettle on its hob, and a hot gassy smell filled the room. Here was danger of gassing or explosion.

I had to force myself past it, through to the downstairs back room and up the stairs, all painted that dark blue, like the dead yet glittering walls of an underground tunnel.

I had to force myself past it next morning to join my mother outside. She was in the garden, talking to the next-door neighbour. They stood with the fence between them, their arms folded against the February cold, their aprons flapping in the wind. The neighbour seemed to me an elderly woman, dumpy and grey. My mother was talking about the mess the house had been in, and as I approached, the neighbour was saying it had been occupied by soldiers from the nearby base. 'There was all sorts going on,' she said, and added, cryptically: 'Nowt s'queer as folks.'

The garden stretched away in blue shadows, and something

black flapped at the back of my mind.

Just then, a lanky boy of about fourteen came out of her house and, although she looked like his grandma, she introduced him as her son. He looked down without speaking, a hank of charcoal-coloured hair half-hiding his yellowish face. Colin. Still without speaking, he went off down the snowy garden, and his mother explained: his father, her husband, had died in the summer.

I watched his progress down the garden. He had a drifting walk that made him look as if he'd lost contact with the ground.

Here, in this place, there was death.

I had more than ever the sense of something hidden. I was watching out more than ever, and everything around seemed to signal spoilage and death.

The front doors of our terrace led directly onto the pavement. Colin had a married sister who would visit with her baby, leaving it in the pram outside the front door. One day I peered in at the baby. He wasn't asleep, but he didn't grin the way David as a baby would. He didn't even seem to see me. I pushed my head in further, which had always made David chuckle and kick. Still the baby didn't seem to notice; his grey eyes looked right through me. And then I knew: there was something wrong with him.

And there was still something wrong with David. Five years old, he still had those turns when his face went white and clammy and his eyes rolled away up; in the end he'd be violently sick. Mummy had taken him to the doctor, who'd diagnosed 'biliousness' and prescribed a special diet. He was quiet and withdrawn. When I buttoned his coat or lifted him onto the table to tie his shoelaces, or smoothed away his dark-brown fringe to check that his forehead wasn't damp, he was passive, acquiescent, and somehow removed. It was lucky, I would think, that Daddy didn't hit him. He was so quiet, in fact, that he hardly seemed to notice him.

That summer Cathy and I were banned from playing down the garden because Colin was always down there next door with an airgun. We would watch him from our bedroom window, a boy whose father had died, a boy who by all ac-counts was failing, who hardly ever went to school, shooting over and over at a piece of corrugated metal, obsessive yet somehow absent. Instead, we played on the pavement in front of the house. We had a game that seemed extremely wicked and daring, of sweetly saying hello to adults who passed and seeing how many would say hello back. There was one woman, posher than most, tall and erect with fuzzy black hair and a bright-green coat, with a handbag over her arm, who never seemed to twig the game we were playing, and greeted us every time with sincere delight. We hadn't seen her for a while when something odd appeared down the hill: a bright-green contraption, an alarm-coloured vehicle. A wheelchair, being pushed towards us by a man. Slouched inside it was the woman, horribly transformed: long skinny legs akimbo, her black fuzzy hair on end. She caught sight of us as they neared and shrieked with glee, flinging her arms and legs wide, gabbling unintelligibly, while her husband smiled at us, rueful and embarrassed.

We didn't know how to respond. I stood stock-still, taking it in, not wanting to take it in: the inexorable damage that could overtake you, out of the blue, at any time.

The papers had announced that smoking could cause

cancer. Smoking, that thing that characterised our father, a fag always in his hand, curtains of smoke in any room where he sat, his *smell*, a sharp yet musty mixture of smoke and tobacco, if you went too close. Though nowadays we dared not get too close. The high-biting cane had been lost in the move to be replaced with the stinging but less painful slipper, and now and then his snapping leather belt, but also now he'd strike out unexpectedly with his hand, clipping you on your arm or your ear without warning. Sometimes now I couldn't help flinching as I passed him, and he'd bellow, 'Don't you bloody flinch at me, you insolent bitch, or I'll give you something to flinch for!'

Yet it was hard to avoid him. He was around more now, no longer working away, taking up a huge space in the kitchen – he was a stout man by now – poring over his time sheets, elbows on the table, and calling for cups of tea ('Any chance of a cuppa, Missus? Where's that bloody tay, Woman!') and puffing away.

At the sound of his van pulling up on the cinder yard at the side of the house, our mother would warn, 'Now, don't make him angry.'

Increasingly now she meant especially me. Increasingly nowadays I seemed to rile him more than Cathy.

'You shouldn't answer him back,' our mother told me. 'You make it worse for yourself.'

It was true, I did. I was going on for eleven and developing a sense of injustice: when he threatened to beat me I'd protest and justify myself. 'You insolent bitch,' he'd bellow, grabbing the slipper. 'What are you?' And I'd have to answer, 'An insolent bitch', before the slipper came down. And it was true that I screamed louder than Cathy when he hit us, I was in such fury and despair, and the more I screamed the harder he hit me, and afterwards I went on crying for longer. Later I'd feel shame and guilt, thinking of Mrs McGowan next door hearing it all through the wall. *Nowt s' queer as folks*, she'd said about the previous occupants, and no doubt she said that about us now.

It was me, the eldest, who had to run down the hill to get his dangerous, cancer-causing cigarettes. 'Run and get us a packet of fags, will yeh, Jo.' All of a sudden he'd be almost matey, but we knew his need was so pressing that if I didn't jump to, drop what I was doing and belt down the hill, he would turn: his cheek would start pleating, his mouth would screw, and any moment he'd be taking it out on someone.

That first summer, because of the news in the paper, he tried to give up, and his temper became truly frightening. He didn't last, and we breathed with relief as well as dismay when, after not very long, he started smoking again.

'Run and get us a packet of fags, will yeh, Jo,' he'd say again, less matey than before, with a hint of warning that if I didn't do it sharpish I'd be for it.

Players Please it said on the creaking sign outside the shop. The shop doorbell cracked like a pistol. 'Ten Players, please,' I'd ask every time, and every time the newsagent would laugh, and I'd have to make myself smile. I'd rush back up the wearying slope, along the grey stone wall enclosing the wilderness, in the packet's slippery cellophane the feel of anxious anticipation.

'There you are, Daddy!'

He would turn and take it with a strange piercing look, somehow resentful yet at the same time conspiratorial, as if I was his private Angel of Death. He'd tear the packet open, jam a fag in, and visibly subside, and in the newly curling smoke we'd all breathe easy again, for the moment.

But in the mornings Cathy and I would wake in our shared bed to the sound of his coughing, a volcano of sound along the dark-blue-painted landing. The sound would cut; I'd stop breathing: had he choked? Had he finally had a heart attack, like Colin's father next door? And then with a monumental sound of tearing he'd start again, and we'd relax, before our stomachs knotted once more on his continued presence.

He had always smoked in bed, he kept falling asleep smoking and singeing the sheets, and we lived in constant fear of a fire.

'Don't make him angry,' my mother would constantly tell me, but she couldn't help making him angry herself. Why did he have to be the one buying the after-work drinks, she would ask him, when we could hardly afford the rent, when there was money still owing? 'You mean-minded Welsh witch!' he'd growl. At night we'd hear them having terrible rows, a churn of clashing voices coming from the kitchen through the back downstairs room and up the dark stairs. Sometimes we'd come in from outside and find our mother with her head in her hands at the kitchen table again, quickly lifting her pinny to wipe the tears away. We began again to be afraid for her while we were at school.

The school was perched in the high white light above the river, near the transporter bridge. It was a smaller, kindlier school than the one in Easton, yet we found it hard to settle. The bridge towered above the playground, a giant scaffold. All day long ships moaned as they approached, warning of possible collision. We had developed a fear that our mother would put her head in that hissing gas oven, and we reverted to our lunchtime ruses, running like mad down the long road beside the canal and up our hill, clutching our broken knickers.

But that autumn Cathy had to be at that school without me: I had a place at grammar school.

I was to start a few days later than her, so her first day back I went in the afternoon to meet her. I turned into the steep cobbled lane. Here, behind one wall, was a bakery, and the smell of yeast filled the lane, a brick-and-concrete bowl of sun. There was no one about. I was early. The concrete ticked in the heat. I stopped and stood still, looking around and listening, antennae out as usual. Always, alone in places like this, cut-off pockets of sun, in the alleyways in Prestatyn or the lanes at Llanfair, where everything small, bits of rubbish on the ground or ivy-leafed toadflax growing in the walls, was sharp with magnified shadows and outlines of light, I would get a particular feeling: that sense of something huge and swelling, but hidden.

I walked down the hill and stood outside the school gates. Just beyond, the hill became even steeper, and as I waited, someone walking very slowly came up from below, showing first as the top of a tangled head of hair. Progressively he was revealed as an unkempt-looking figure: floppy jacket, baggy trousers, shuffly gait. He came and stood at the gates. He was early, too. I looked at the watch Grampa had given me: another ten minutes to go.

The man spoke. 'Waiting for someone?'

'My sister.'

There was a silence. The concrete clicked. He moved closer and spoke. 'Not at school yourself?'

'I'm just about to start at grammar school.'

Something sparked and spilled in his eyes, and suddenly I wanted to run. But I felt uncertain. After all, he was probably just waiting for his child to come out of school.

'How old are you?'

I didn't want to answer, but politeness forced me. 'Eleven.'

He looked away then dragged his eyes back to me. And it wasn't so much what he then said – I didn't even know what he meant: 'Have you tossed any boys off yet?' – as the hollowness of his voice as he said it, and the helpless slide in the whites of his eyes.

Here was danger. I turned on my heel and slammed my legs up the hill, past the bakery and down the half-mile to home. My chest banging, I crashed through the back door, where my father happened to be home.

He jumped up and drove me straight back in the van. We turned into the lane and it was empty. School wasn't yet out. 'Stay there,' my father said grimly, locking me in for safety, and went to look for the man.

The man had gone.

He got back in the van and we waited for Cathy.

I thought: *My Daddy loves me really.*

But as we sat in silence, I stole a look at his grim profile, his jaw sinking into his bull neck now, and saw that he was miles away already, lost inside himself.

I sank back into my own thoughts. I thought about the man and his helpless sliding eyes. That was the horror, the real and absolute danger. The man's helplessness, his squalid guilt and lack of control.

Then there I was, dressed up in a green gymslip and blazer and a green felt hat, and carrying a stiff brand-new satchel, things that there had been a struggle to afford, waiting for the school bus at the bottom of the road beside the glittering canal and the blood-red brick tannery, with two other, strange, identically clad girls.

96

We'd been to Manchester to buy that uniform, the only place you could get it; my father had driven us all. We descended to a basement. My mother held the list that came from the school, and the woman counted out the regulation number of baggy green knickers for gym and laid them on top of the pile of all the other expensive garments, the green gabardine mac, the green-and-yellow striped tie, the cream shirts, the two pairs of knee-length socks, the PE blouses and culottes for outdoor games, and I was overcome with a feeling of not being able to breathe, and had to go up to the entrance in the square to get some air.

And now the school bus would whip me off several miles, to where I couldn't be with Cathy at lunchtime, or rush home to check on Mummy. Mummy would be more dangerously alone now, as David had started at nursery school – though so unwilling was he, so frightened, that she had to pretend to be sitting on a chair outside the door all morning.

And I wasn't too different. Primary school had always been a haven for me, the place where I could be a different, better person, someone who excelled and got praise, a place where I could sink into the predictability of numbers and the comfort of stories, where no one would guess the ragged, shameful scenes at home. But the grammar school terrified me, with its huge size and milling green-clad girls, the gowned teachers with looks that could freeze you, whose sarcasm shrivelled you with shame. And there was one especial thing, a danger. As soon as my class walked into the science lab for the first time, I smelled it: gas. I stopped, petrified. I couldn't help it, I cried, 'There's gas in here!'

There was no teacher present: in that school the teacher

would sweep in after the girls like some grand dame in her gown. The others looked at me curiously.

I felt more panicky. Didn't they understand the danger? 'It's dangerous!'

A wicked look came over one girl's face. She leaned across to the nearest tap and switched it on, and the lethal stuff hissed into the room.

I fled. Down the corridor, banging through the double doors, and slamming into the approaching science teacher, who stopped me short and fixed me with a Gorgon glare.

As she took the class to task for messing with the gas taps, issuing dire warnings of punishment, I could see the others eyeing me, the tell-tale-tit who would have to be punished by them. And so I was: every science lesson, before the teacher arrived, or whenever she left the room, someone would rush and switch on the nearest gas tap to me, and the rest would laugh at my terror.

Now, for the first time ever, I was failing at school. I couldn't keep myself neat and organised, as you were especially supposed to do in this school. There was always dried gravy or custard on my gymslip; I forgot things all the time: my PE kit, my ruler, my books for homework. The moment the bus pulled away I'd realise what I'd forgotten, and would spend evenings in terror of the consequences next day. Before this I had never, ever been in trouble at school, I'd been a model pupil, but now I was in trouble for such things all the time. It upset me dreadfully: I was reduced to tears by the teachers' sharp tongues, another thing for which I was despised. Permanently tense and often upset, I couldn't get my head around the lessons, and my work was going downhill.

I had become one of those hopeless kids, like Colin

next door, for whom school was a place where they were condemned.

My leg-aches, which had never gone away, now became severe. Most weekends I'd have splitting headaches when luminous dots would float at the edges of my vision, one time, for a few terrifying minutes, growing and blotting out my vision entirely. I began to be afraid once more of losing my sight altogether. I couldn't bear the dark: I had to have the landing light on and the bedroom door open, or else the bedroom walls would seem to move towards me and I'd feel I couldn't breathe.

Then, out of the blue, something happened to break the tension of our lives.

AUNTY CATHY

OUR FATHER'S YOUNGEST sister, the nun for whom our father had bought the habit and ring, was coming to stay.

Mummy explained:

Our aunt (we had an Irish aunt!), Aunty Cathy (she had the name that Cathy had inherited!) was leaving her convent on the south coast of England. (England?! We'd always thought she must be in Ireland . . . !) A couple of years ago, the convent, a teaching convent, had agreed to send her on a teacher-training course. Now, in the convent they had a terrible problem with headlice among the children, so bad that the children's scalps kept getting infected, and on the teacher-training course she discovered that there were chemical treatments of which the convent couldn't have been aware. So when she got back she went to the Mother Superior and told her. And the Mother Superior had been furious! How dare she imply criticism of how things were run in the convent! And Cathy – *Aunty Cathy* – was punished for insubordination, sent to a boys' boarding school to scrub the stairs, four storeys, from top to bottom day after day, whenever she reached the bottom starting straight away at the top again.

She wasn't cowed. When it was over and she'd returned to the convent, she went straight to the Mother Superior to plead the case again – and lo and behold, she was sent back to do the punishment all over again! And so, like our mother losing faith in the organised side of her religion before her, Aunty Cathy began to lose faith in the life of the convent, where unthinking rules and the Mother Superior's pride could come before the health of the children.

From the punishment house, Mummy said, she had written her yearly letter to our parents describing her plight, and now she had written to say that though the priest had counselled her long and hard, she was leaving the convent for good, and was throwing herself on the mercy of her elder brother and benefactor, Daddy.

This seemed to me monumental. Here was someone who'd been punished for speaking out, for protesting, as I so often was by my father. Here was someone who'd break her solemn vows to God over the very principle. Who would change her whole life, throw herself onto the world all alone, over the principle of the mistreatment of children.

Surely she would have influence over our father. Surely she would be our saviour.

One late-October afternoon our father went to meet her from the station in Manchester.

We waited in acute anticipation in the kitchen. The kitchen was cosier now; in the eight months or so we'd been here, our mother had painted over the dark-blue kitchen walls and sewn remnants from the market into cushions and curtains. She had polished up the black and red quarry floor tiles, and they flickered and glowed in the light from the fire behind the range. (There was nothing she could do about the cooker, of course, standing vicious sentinel near the back door.)

The van nosed into the yard. The van door opened with its usual squeak, but this time seemed to open a new angle in the air. We heard our father's low rumble and a woman's soft voice, and then their feet on the steps up to the back door.

She was like an apparition. Squat and matronly-looking (not at all like the beautiful sister who had once spurned our parents), dressed in a headscarf and a grey old-fashioned coat reaching down to ankles ringed by wrinkled lisle stockings, and flat lace-up shoes. Her face and hands were white (like those of the sister who had spurned our parents, and unlike our olive-skinned father's). She took off her headscarf, and her hair, black like the other sister's but shaved in the convent, stuck up in uneven tufts as if electrified on a descent through the clouds.

'At last I've come to you,' she said, putting her hand on my mother's arm. 'Praise be to God.'

Her voice was Irish, even more Irish, after spending her life with Irish nuns, than Daddy's. She gazed around at us all, her dark eyes flicking like touched water.

She was so different from our father in every way: deep-black and pure-white, while he was so all-over tawny; open and still while he was like a coiled spring.

She reached out and touched the heads of each of us three children in turn.

And already she was having an effect on Daddy: he put his hand on her back, solicitous, protective, and led her to the chair beside the range.

She stayed until her hair grew respectably long enough for job interviews.

It was a time of pure relief for me and Cathy.

Our father *was* miraculously changed: he was home more in the evenings, and he sat and talked to Aunty Cathy for hours, patiently explaining to her all the things in the modern world that life in the convent had shielded her from: she hadn't seen a TV until she saw ours; she'd never read a newspaper until, just before she left the convent, they brought her some in preparation for the outside world. And she drank it all in, trusting and calm, taking for granted this side of our father so strange to me and Cathy.

The first Sunday she was going to Mass. She asked our father if she could take us girls. Shocked, I looked up at him reading the paper at the table, for his reaction. He waved his hand with casual, friendly permission.

I stared at him, wondering. It came to me: he didn't want her to know that in our household there were strange tangles over religion.

On the way to church we held her hands tightly – we did that all the time; she took us for walks and we clung to her hands as we clung to Grampa's and Gwilym's in Llanfair; we sat close to her in the kitchen. But in the church we were uncomfortable, out of our depth, sitting rigid in the big cold space, amongst the brittle rattle of the censer and the chanting of the impenetrable Latin, acutely embarrassed to be the only ones not rising for sacrament.

And then, before Christmas, she was gone, gone to be a nanny to a vicar in Birmingham, and life in the house plunged into tension once more.

I thought about it, lying in bed and listening to our parents rowing again. Our father, I knew now, had simply been putting on a show for Aunty Cathy. Treating her in a special way reserved for her, but nevertheless acting differently as he always did with strangers, with his workmates, with the antique dealers, with those girls who came to the house in Easton.

And it struck me: my father and Aunty Cathy were indeed strangers. I worked it out: she was twenty-seven; my father by now was forty. Thirteen years' difference. He had been sixteen when he left Ireland and went to live with his aunts in Birkenhead. She would have been only three. And before that hadn't he been living with his grandfather? Hadn't he in fact gone there at the age of ten, three years before Aunty Cathy was even born . . . ? They had hardly ever known each other.

I realised: she'd been a clean slate on which he could draw a different self.

And the moment she had gone, his thunderous self had risen up once more.

She was not the saviour I had hoped. She couldn't change our lives. She came back at weekends, which made oases of calm, but it wasn't the same: always to the forefront now was the knowledge that we were all putting on a show for Aunty Cathy, and always, all weekend, there was the dread of Sunday night when she'd be gone.

Down the years our mother would recall that time when Aunty Cathy was visiting. There was a fuss, she would tell us, of which we weren't aware at the time, when for two weekends (two awful weekends for us) Aunty Cathy didn't come because she'd gone back to Ireland to visit her parents, taking the vicar's little girl with her. She didn't think to keep in touch with the vicar while she was gone (so unworldly!), and the vicar, worrying that she'd absconded with his daughter, had rung our parents in a panic.

We had a phone now, our first phone, though only our

father ever used it. (None of our Welsh relatives had phones, so our mother had no one to ring; we simply weren't allowed, not that we, either, had anyone to ring.) He'd had it installed in the back room which up to now had always been very cold, but now he'd get our mother to make up a fire there ('Light us a fire, will, yeh, Gwen!') and then settle with his fags, pick up the phone and dial. 'Now what's the story?' he'd begin and then he'd be there chatting to a workmate crony for hours. ('Yeah, yeah, yeah . . .')

Needless to say, our father's parents didn't have a phone, so he'd had to ring the shop in the village two miles off. Many years later, our mother would tell us how he happened to have the number. His parents had run up a debt in the shop, and since our father was the eldest son who'd gone off to seek his fortune, our parents were paying it off in instalments – another expense when money was so tight and their debt to Nanny and Grampa still unpaid.

Aunty Cathy returned, surprised about all the fuss (so unworldly!), bringing a brown-paper parcel for our father, sent by his mother.

We stared at the contents: a pair of brown child's boots and a blond plait complete with tiny dead nits, which greatly amused our mother. Our father's first pair of shoes, the shoes that the schoolmaster coming down the lane had told our father's mother to buy him, and one of the plaits into which she'd tied his hair in order to cut it as instructed.

We stared and stared, Cathy and I, taking in this concrete proof of something that by now had the quality of fairytale or legend.

And our father's mother had sent them. She must want to make contact with us all.

We got excited. The notion crystallised: we had a grand-mother in Ireland! Grandparents!

'Can we write to her?' I asked our father.

He was silent for a moment, then said: 'I can't stop you.'

I felt a little dashed, but my excitement overcame it.

We had to ask for the address. I stared at it, written in the copperplate hand he had learnt in the church school. 'Where is it in Ireland?' I asked.

He got out his big old atlas and laid it on the table. We sat each side of him to look, which felt strange – we usually kept a wide berth from him now – smelling his tweedy cigarette smell, watching as his yellowed finger came down in the centre of Ireland, in a great green empty space.

We wrote our letters to our grandmother, telling her briefly about our hobbies and our schools, and asking her to tell us all about Ireland. (We had asked Aunty Cathy, but we hadn't had a satisfactory reply. 'Oh, fields,' was all she said, and then turned in amazement to watch a bright-blue car with sharp modern angles drive by.)

We popped the letters in the post box, excitement fizzing like lemonade in our throats. We waited impatiently for a reply.

None came.

In the end we gave up rushing each morning to the cold front room where I didn't like being anyway, and which I'd rather shut my mind from: the door leading straight to the pavement and making the house seem vulnerable, unsafe, and the landlord's alien furniture piled wonkily to the ceiling, an unsteady barricade.

We'd forgotten all about it and summer had come round again when two letters arrived from Ireland, one addressed to me and one to Cathy.

They were identical.

Dear Josephine/Cathleen,

Thank you for your letter. You ask what it is like here. We have geese and hens and a small field in which we grow vegetables. We live a long way from the nearest town and we have a pony and cart to take us to market. It is a hard life and very different from the one you lead in England, and you would not like it here.

Your grandmother Jackson.

We were taken aback by the formality, by the lack of any of the expression of affection we were used to in our letters from Nanny and Grampa. Or interest, even. We studied the wording. *You would not like it here.* But we would love it! Geese and hens, and a pony and cart! *A very different life from the one you lead in England.* Did she think we were town girls – we who were so ill at ease in the poisonous industrial air of this town, who longed all the time for the countryside of south Wales?

You would not like it here. In the end we understood: it was a brush-off. She didn't want to know us after all. We felt hurt. I realised I should have known from the formal way she addressed our mother in her letters to our parents, *Dear Patrick and Mrs Jackson.* I wondered, with a dreary feeling, if perhaps the reason she had sent that parcel to our father was that she didn't treasure those things any more, she was washing her hands.

We put it out of our minds. We put her out of our minds, and no longer thought of ourselves as having a grandmother in Ireland.

There was another incident connected with that visit by Aunty Cathy to Ireland. The weekend before she went, our mother would tell us, Aunty Cathy was sitting at the table as my mother made scones. She picked up the cookbook our mother was using. She stared at it curiously. 'Why would you use a Jewish cookbook?'

'Patrick bought it for me,' our mother replied.

'Why on earth would he buy a Jewish cookbook?'

'Well, your grandfather was Jewish, wasn't he?'

Aunty Cathy cried, '*What?!!*' and went whiter than ever.

Maybe she never knew, our mother thought: their grandfather had died not long after Patrick came to England. Cathy must have been very young at the time.

Aunty Cathy had gone red now. She seemed uncharacteristically angry. She said, uncharacteristically remonstrative: 'Of course he wasn't Jewish! There are no Jews in Ireland!'

So when our father came home our mother asked him straight out in Aunty Cathy's presence: 'Patrick, you said your grandfather was Jewish, didn't you? Cathy doesn't think he could have been.'

Our father drew himself up, she said, straightened his shoulders in a way he hadn't done in a good while, and looked Aunty Cathy in the eye. 'When you go to Ireland next week,' he told her, 'you ask our mother and see what she says.'

When she came back he asked her: 'Well? Did you ask our mother about our grandfather? Did she say he was Jewish?'

'Yes,' said Aunty Cathy, looking at the floor. But she'd said it in a whisper, lowering her head, and dropped to the floor to help David with his game.

After our mother told us, I would wonder if it was the catalyst that made our father's mother wash her hands of the little boots and the plait: if, by resurrecting something so successfully buried, he had shown his true non-Catholic colours.

Aunty Cathy stopped coming so often. She built a life for herself in Birmingham. In no time at all she went from being an innocent nun to a woman of the world. She got a job as a teacher in a primary school; she bought a car and learnt to drive. Once, while walking to school with my mother, this ex-bride of Christ had stopped and clung to church railings in fascination at the sight of a woman marrying a human man; now she began going out with one she met in church.

A few times she brought him to stay, a small man with sandy hair and a raw complexion. Our father hated him, I assumed for the same reason that Cathy and I didn't much like him, his quiet yet half-cryptic and possibly even sneering manner, and the way his large glasses slewed and magnified his eyes that seemed to be slyly watching all the time. Even while they were there, my father couldn't keep up his social manner, becoming notably less expansive. And when they were gone he'd let loose: 'Bloody creepy little bastard.' They got engaged and, our mother would tell us later, he tried to persuade Aunty Cathy not to marry him, urgently pressuring her whenever she came alone. No wonder, I would think, she stopped coming in the end.

We would go to the wedding and Cathy and I would be bridesmaids – cold in our ice-green brocade-satin dresses and once more unsure and awkward in the Latin ceremony – and a few years later she and her husband would come to mine and Cathy's, but by the autumn of the year I was twelve she'd stopped visiting us. She never did so again, and though our mother would keep in touch with her via letters at Christmas, and in later years the occasional phone call, she didn't even come to our father's funeral.

A REALISATION

IN THE AUTUMN in that house there would be one
weekend when our father would get a ladder and with now
uncharacteristic husbandry pick the fruit in the orchard. He
would store the apples for keeping in the loft of the garage
across the cinder yard, wrapping them in newspaper and
laying them out with care. Or mother, happier than usual,
would be busy preparing to bottle pears and make pickles.
Autumn sun came through the trees and slanted into the back
rooms of the house, making the red quarry tiles glow in the
kitchen. The second year, the year I was twelve, our father,
with uncharacteristic amenability, let me climb up and pick a
few apples, holding the ladder steady.

But the apples were always greasy to the touch and covered
with black flecks from the tannery, impossible to wash off, so
they had to be peeled.

And the fruit was in, and the autumn grew cold. Aunty
Cathy had stopped coming, and our dark life closed around
us once more.

Now our father began to terrorise us in a calculated way. We
weren't supposed to read in bed, but we did: reading was our
great consolation, our escape. One night we were lying in our
bed on our bellies, our books propped on our pillows, when
I was slammed so hard on my backside that I shot up the bed
and hit my head on the board. He'd sneaked up on us unawares.

III

After that we read under the covers and kept the door wide so we'd hear if the door to the back room opened at the bottom of the stairs. But then I'd look up and there beyond the banisters on the stairs was his big head with its shock of hair. The look on his face was worse than the beating that followed: his gimlet eyes glinting with nasty triumph.

And all around bad things kept happening. Mushrooms of H-bombs filled the TV screen; out on the road the woman in the wheelchair shrieked and jerked every time she caught sight of me and Cathy, signalling from the dark mad trough of existence she'd slipped into. Mrs McGowan's daughter's baby died.

One Saturday morning, on my way to the library, I paused at a side street, looking out for traffic. On the pavement just down the side street, outside the Co-op which was oddly shut up, was a bright-red stain inadequately covered with sawdust.

Later that day Mrs McGowan would tell my mother that the manager of the Co-op had committed suicide, thrown himself from the window above the shop, because his wife had run off with another man. But in the brief second of catching sight of that stain, I already knew what I was seeing: seedy despair. And part of the horror was a thud of recognition.

David's turns got worse. He spent a lot of time off school.

I went one afternoon to check on him in his bedroom, sleeping off an episode. He sighed in his sleep, a deep shudder, his long dark lashes, greasy with sweat, flicking on his pale sallow cheeks. I tucked the covers around him. I turned to the window. The window, at the side of the house, looked out over rooftops to the deep cut of the ship canal in the distance, and from here you could see what our father had said was a famous illusion: ships going inland appeared to be going uphill. I could see one now, the funnel of a tanker crawling impossibly upwards. However I looked at it, tipped my head to adjust to the horizon, the effect was still the same.

What you saw was not always the reality.

I thought: what if this dark, unfathomable life we were leading at the moment was not the reality? What if it was a dream, my own, or someone else's? What if we were all characters in someone else's imagination?

I had just got home from school one November afternoon when a car pulled up on the cinders outside, a different engine from my father's. A short scuffle on the crunchy ground, and then a man brought in my father huddled over, his left hand ballooned in a bloodstained bandage.

Another accident. He had caught his little finger in a machine.

He sat in the kitchen, his face like wet putty. It was strange, seeing him like that. A victim of chance spinning up with metal blades. Not super-powerful after all, not superhuman. Humanly vulnerable.

I had a sense, for the first time ever, of having the power to alter my relationship with my father.

Some time ago he had replaced the broken-down fence between our garden and the wilderness next door, but hadn't got around to protecting it with creosote. One day in January, when the skin of his mangled little finger had healed, he announced that he was going to do it that weekend.

I told my mother I wanted to help him. She looked doubtful (he could say no; it could cause trouble), but said she would ask him. On Saturday morning she told me he'd agreed.

I was filled with growing confidence.

It was cold. I put my woolly hat and coat on and followed him down the garden. He went ahead without speaking, but I didn't let it put me off. It was his normal manner, and after all, and I was the one who was going to make things different between us. And of course, he was forced to show me how to use my brush, how to run it flat on the rim so as not to drip, and how to scrub the creosote into the wood. I began to feel elated. As we got to work I chatted, about the creosote, the wood, and the process – though not easily; I felt self-conscious.

He grunted monosyllables in answer.

I began to run out of thing to say. After half an hour or so, I fell silent. There was only the scratching of the brushes and a blackbird rattling in the trees above, and now and then the mournful hooting of a ship on the big canal. My courage failed me. Through the stink of the creosote, the smell of rot came up from the ground, and through the trees the gloomy frame of the bridge loomed over all.

Every so often I glanced at my father: his profile was stony.

It dawned on me slowly: he *knew* I was trying to make friends with him, and he didn't want me to. He wouldn't let me.

I had no power, after all, I realised, to change my relationship with my father. This was the situation, and it always would be, and I had no idea why.

&

The night-time rows between our parents got worse. One Saturday afternoon a row erupted in front of us kids. I quickly ushered the other two into the cold back room and tried to distract them as the sound of our parents' raised voices came in crashing waves through the door, our mother's cries of angst and our father's bellows of rage.

I wanted to listen, but I didn't want to, either: there was something particularly terrible about this row, something so ruinous that I didn't want to know.

At length there was a crash, followed by an abrupt silence.

I rushed through, telling the others to stay.

My mother was slumped backwards in the armchair beside the range, eyes closed and unmoving. My father stood at the table, gathering up his fags and keys. Upside down on the hearth beside my mother was the aluminium teapot, dented, the leaves spattered across the range and along the floor.

'Mummy!'

She didn't move.

I turned to my father. 'Daddy!'

He shot me a thunderous look and was out through the back door and had gone.

My mother twitched, and I was flooded with relief.

Tears squeezed out from beneath her shut eyelids. A bleached lump was swelling on her forehead.

'Mummy!'

She opened her eyes. They were blank behind the tears.

I didn't know what to do.

Helpless, useless, I picked up the teapot, finding with relief that it hadn't been hot.

I forced myself to be calm. I cleaned up the tea leaves.

'I've cleaned up,' I told my mother.

She nodded numbly, but her tears kept falling.

I had to do something to somehow make things better. 'Shall I go and buy another teapot?'

She came to a little, focussed. Then nodded numbly and pulled herself up slowly out of the chair and went and fetched her purse.

As I stepped from the house with Cathy, I thought: it's up to me now. As Cathy caught my arm and we made our way beside the blackly glittering canal, I thought: we're on our own now. The grey February afternoon seemed to simmer with loss. But as we stepped into the hardware shop, into its paraffin-smelling interior, announcing our entry with the snap of the bell, as the shopkeeper showed me the alternative aluminium teapots – one exactly like the one our father had ruined, plain and slightly angular, and another, short and rounded and covered in scrolled engravings – I had a sudden feeling of detachment and control.

'That one,' I said, pointing to the decorated one, tasting for the first time in my life the unusual sensation of making a decision for my parents. 'That one.' Different from the one they had had before. Different from the one my father had ruined.

Now that Aunty Cathy came no longer, beatings had once more become a feature of Saturday afternoons. Now, when we walked the streets arm-in-arm afterwards, sorrowful but also now angry, we'd think about escaping in the future. We'd have a ranch, we told ourselves, with horses that would take us anywhere we wanted and love us whatever, with a big white gate with a lock through which we'd let only the people we wanted, and definitely not Mummy and Daddy. No, not

Mummy either, we thought angrily and sadly. So often we felt on her side against Daddy, and so often she would plead with him on our behalf, but also all too often she seemed on his side against us: Don't make him angry; Run quickly and get the cigarettes; Don't answer him back, you bring it on yourself.

At the end of that summer, the summer I was thirteen, I stood on the back doorstep and watched my father scything the orchard. A stout man in early middle age, no longer the lithe hero of the RAF photos, rounded in the middle (all those cups of tea saturated with sugar), his trousers so wide that they had to be held up with braces, his hair, as always when he was at home, floating wide.

He had just driven us back from Llanfair. For the past two summers Cathy and I had been allowed to go on the train on our own, and towards the end our mother came with David to join us, and then our father drove down and brought us all home (Cathy and I distraught at having to leave, as usual).

My father scythed steadily, unaware that I was watching, working with husbandly patience in the way he could sometimes, swinging the blade with firm, sure sweeps, his trouser-legs swaying.

I felt a surge of guilt. I couldn't love him the way I could my Grampa in Llanfair. I couldn't love him the way a daughter was supposed to love her father, the way my mother obviously loved Grampa, the way the girls in books, *Little Women*, *What Katy Did*, loved theirs. But he made it so hard. He didn't let you love him. The way he held you off, remote and mentally absent.

The way that, even with others, he could switch off that engaging charm if he decided, as he had with Aunty Cathy's boyfriend.

And he was so prejudiced. I thought back to a time two years before, my first term at grammar school. We'd been told by the form teacher to get our parents to come to the school play. I had received the instruction with dismay. It would be impossible: apart from his aberrant show of interest before we went to the Midlands, Daddy had never been to any of our schools. In any case, if he came there'd be no one to look after Cathy and David. And if he didn't, how would Mummy and I get there and back, without him to drive us? All the way home on the school bus I worried about it. What if I didn't manage to persuade them to make it happen? I had taken it, in that rule-bound school, as a strict instruction (by which the other girls had seemed quite unfazed, perfectly accustomed it seemed to getting their parents to do things). Would it be yet another thing to draw down the teachers' disapproval? Another thing to make me a source of fun and contempt to the other girls?

As soon as I could, I broached the subject with my mother. She was dubious, but agreed to ask my father. She was making the tea and he was sitting with his paper at the table when she opened the subject. He dragged his eyes up and asked me: 'What's the play?'

My heart leapt: he wasn't dismissing the idea outright. I told him.

He went very still. Then looking back at his paper he said, 'I'm not bloody going to that.'

I cried in dismay: 'Oh, Daddy, why not?'

He raised his eyes, a scrape of blue. 'And neither are you.'

He stood up. 'In fact, I've got a bloody good mind to complain to the headmistress.'

'Oh no – Daddy, don't! Daddy, why?'

But he'd left the room.

I turned in confusion to my mother who had her back to me at the cooker, stirring the stew. 'What's wrong with the play?' I didn't know it: *The Importance of Being Earnest*.

She put down the wooden spoon and introduced me with some awkwardness to the phenomenon of which up until then I'd been in total ignorance, sexual attraction between men, for which she told me the author of the play had been imprisoned, and by which my father was so disgusted.

Eleven years old, I was astounded by the notion. In all my reading of classic novels, in all of the media culture of the time, the early sixties, I had picked up no hint of it.

'Oh well,' my mother said, rather coyly, in reaction to my astonishment, 'I didn't even hear the word *homosexual* until I was twenty-nine!'

I was too astonished by the notion itself to think at the time about my father's prejudice, and too exercised by the problem at school: because of my father's injunction, none of us went to the play, and I was the only one in my form class who didn't.

But I heard the discussions about the performance, and the play was clearly nothing to do with the homosexuality of its author: it was considered suitable for a girls' grammar school, for goodness' sake! It was a famous and loved play! No one, none of the teachers – no one beside my father – judged it by its author. Or judged its author, either: he was, I had discovered, a famous and loved playwright!

My father, I thought now, was ridiculous: ignorant and prejudiced.

I turned away from the sight of him in the orchard.

REBELLION

ALL OF A sudden the dark life was over.

Our father was promoted to the kind of white-collar job he'd promised himself from the beginning: an engineering inspector with a company car. By the following Easter we had moved back east, to Thwaite, the small Yorkshire market town where at last my parents settled, where everyone except me ended up (only I, and not Cathy, got away in the end).

To our utter relief, Cathy and I found ourselves dropped into an existence approaching the *normal*. We had a brand-new bland-fronted semi-detached house exactly like everyone else's on a housing estate bubbling like mushrooms at the edge of town, the first house our parents had owned. We had a mother who sang as she painted the new rooms, and a father who stuck around and dug and raked the new garden as a matter of course rather than grudging exception, and whistled and hummed as he did it. They had stopped rowing.

My aches and pains vanished.

I was at a school I could walk to along a river fringed by May-blossom hedges, a small school that had once been a Victorian Young Ladies' Academy and still retained some of that ethos, with kindly elderly spinster teachers in tweeds and stack heels and with a suffragette ambition for their girls. There were 'preparation' periods, like in the schoolgirl comics and annuals I loved, where homework could be done away from the historic tensions of home.

I began to do well in school again.

Not that our father stopped beating me and Cathy. (He didn't hit little David, which was one mercy.) Not that there wasn't still the feeling that we were a blight on his life – the one blight nowadays. His moods could be good now, he would join the conversation at mealtimes, sniggering at anything funny. He would even joke with us (sneeringly), and in those moments Cathy and I would feel relief. He'd play practical jokes (though we didn't find those so funny): jump out and stick up his little finger, the mangled last joint of which he'd finally had surgically removed, wiggling it in our faces, shiny and raw with two little ears where they'd sewn the skin over.

But often, too, he could be stonily hostile. In a bid to bring us and our father together, our mother now petitioned for us less often, making us go and ask him ourselves for money or permission. He would turn, raise his head slowly and slew his eyes towards us and tell us we didn't deserve it: *You can come asking for money when you start pulling your weight round here!* So unfair when now in this new house we had weekend tasks: dusting the rooms, wiping up the pall of his ash on all the objects he'd brought back from antique shops down the years and which now our mother had the chance to properly display; every so often cleaning the brass and silver and gagging on the ammonia; every Saturday morning walking the mile into town to get the vegetables from the market. Or he'd deliver an insult: *I don't slog my guts out working so you can buy clothes to go round looking like a tart!* Or give us an ultimatum: *You come back here and ask me when you've shown some good behaviour*; and we'd have to wait, sometimes days, and then go through the unnerving ritual again. Whenever I brought home my school reports, which invariably described me as polite and conscientious, he'd snort and say, with varying degrees of nastiness depending on how far I was in his bad books already: 'Street angel, house devil.'

And he could still lose his rag. He didn't beat us so often now, but when he did – for not dusting properly (our mother had absorbed only too well her lessons from Miss Protheroe when they were first married), for the heart-stopping times when, in spite of all our fearful care, we knocked something over while dusting or broke a dish while washing up, for coming in later than commanded, or me for arguing and answering back (which Cathy didn't) – well, then he beat us more viciously than ever.

Now, in fact, we led a more double life than ever. For in that genteel school of mine, who would imagine that the most polite and helpful and hard-working pupil, the one who excelled at everything, who was in the choir and acted in the school play, could be cowering on the floor in a corner of the tiny kitchen trying to ward off the blows of a slipper? Who in Thwaite would guess of her respectable father – he had joined the Conservative Club and would eventually join the Masons; he did occasionally come to school events now with my mother, in a smart dark suit, his hair swept in distinguished waves above his ears – that he stood above her in his braces, flailing the slipper over and over, bellowing in anger, hair wild? (Though he usually kept enough presence of mind to hit us where the bruises wouldn't show, on our buttocks and shoulders and backs.) What would the girls at school think if they knew, the doctor's and vet's daughters, the girls whose fathers owned the farms around? I had friends now at school, but I didn't meet them often outside school hours. There was too much to be ashamed of, and we couldn't fit in: money was still tight – there was a mortgage to pay now, as well as Nanny and Grampa's debt to pay off (at last!) – so we didn't have the clothes, but, ignominiously in this more middle-class setting, must wear our school gaberdines out of school.

But we no longer saw our father as part of the real world. We saw him now as the blight on our lives that we'd always been on his, the enemy to be avoided, of whom we must free ourselves as soon as possible. We stayed away from the house as much as we could, escaping, as soon as our housework and homework were done, along the river out to the countryside, or later, when we'd begged secondhand bikes and he'd finally grudgingly bought them, to the outlying villages.

By the age of fifteen my whole plan was to get away from that world of home. I lay in bed at night scheming and fuming. I was sick of all the hypocrisy, the vast gap between how things were in the house and the face we all presented to the world.

Such a hypocrite, my father, on so many levels (*Street angel, house devil!* I'd think in despairing fury). If we swore he would tell us off with a curse; if our talking or singing got on his nerves, he'd cry 'Shut the hell up, you noisy bitches!' at the top of his voice. One rule for him and another for us. 'Who laid the bloody table?' he'd bawl if a knife was placed the wrong way round, a rhetorical question since the job was mine and Cathy's. Once, out of my raging sense of injustice, I dared to cry, 'Well, obviously not *you*!' and got one of my worst beatings ever.

My mother, too: if anything, I was angrier with her than with my father. My father I had written off as ignorant and primitive, but my mother ought to know better. Once upon a time she had wanted a career, and the stories of her life had impressed upon us girls its importance, and the unfortunate unfairness of Nanny and Grampa's old-fashioned view of the role of women. Yet here she was now, immersed in a life of domesticity, cooking and sewing and scrubbing, creating a lovely home to cover up the truth at its heart, a home as elaborate but neat as the lie. Dedicating her life to saving our father's face in the world and for himself, enlisting me and Cathy in the stressful project, and woe betide us if we slacked.

Here she was, jumping up at our father's peremptory commands and running like a slave to make him cups of tea, or making us do it – after the way he had always treated her, dragging her through all those years of gloom and struggle, being so nasty and calling her names, spending all her money, embarrassing her for years over other people's (Nanny and Grampa's) money, spending on luxuries for himself when she was struggling to buy food and clothes . . .

'Your father needs a long rope,' she would say to me now. I'd think of him doing his astral travel: he'd said that a spiritual rope kept you connected to your body, and you used it to get back down again. 'And I've always given it to him,' she would add, 'but I've always pulled him back on it again!' And I'd feel dismay at her indulgence.

Whenever I complained about him, she'd quote, airily or intently, the assurance by Jesus that he'd keep a place in heaven, and in his heart, for all of his disciples: *In my Father's house are many mansions.* I resented her for coercing me into her forgiving philosophy.

'This house is like a museum!' I had cried in protest one day – another time she saw red and had a bodged go at hitting me with her slipper.

'You're just like your father!' she cried as she flailed, an accusation she would often fling at me now, guaranteed to make me boil.

The stories of her life, and her own attempts to stand up to our father, had impressed on us the importance of intellectual freedom for women, yet now, it seemed, she was bent on shutting me up.

'Do it for my sake!' she'd cry, begging me not to argue with him. She meant for *his* sake really, I thought, though it would stop me, for tension brought on her migraines and gave her bilious attacks, and I was beginning to resent the way she used it to silence me.

When I wept with despair and injustice she'd say I took things too seriously. (*Your Daddy loves you really.*)

'You cry too much,' she would tell me. And I have to say that Cathy didn't cry nearly so much; because she didn't argue, she didn't get hit so often.

I felt oppressed by my mother as well as my father now. I didn't understand her any more, any more than I understood my father. I was meant to be clever, I was well read, but I didn't understand anything of my family. And I no longer wanted to. I was sick of it.

The sound of the television came up through the ceiling. The news was reporting that someone had escaped to freedom and culture over the Berlin wall. Across the field beyond the house, the night sleeper rattled past on its way between Edinburgh and London. I thought of those cities – places, as books made clear, of solid fact and reality, where people were straightforward and words meant what they said.

I was thoroughly sick of being a bit-player in my parents' overwhelming Alice-in-Wonderland story, where things were never what they seemed and nothing made sense. I would make it an irrelevance to me. I had my own life to lead.

If you're bullied, run like hell.

At the first opportunity, I'd leave.

⁂

And I did, I did leave, I lived a life elsewhere, in conscious opposition to everything my father stood for.

Yet here I was, all these years later, compelled by the mystery of him again.

PART THREE

In which I ponder some further mysteries

PATRICK'S PAST

M Y MOTHER WAS pleased. I knew what it meant to her: after all those years of enmity, here I was wanting to understand my father, and not only that, immortalising him in a novel.

We spent hours on the phone as she reminisced for me all over again, with quite a few laughs – the cat glaring daggers at her before leaping from the fire escape; Miss Protheroe's earphone – and of course some more sober moments.

But the more we went over it all, the less I felt I understood.

'Your dad was very unhappy,' she said by way of explanation, becoming serious.

'Yeah . . .' I tailed off, thinking of the things I thought she must be thinking of: the shame of it all, after his vow to himself. The cultural cringe. All the stuff around religion, his getting cut off, excommunicated like that . . .

He went on for some time identifying with the Jewish religion.

In the brand-new house on the housing estate he worked for hours out in the garage making shelves and fashioning leather straps to hang the horse brasses on. He also worked in brass – which my mother now told me he'd done as a hobby in the RAF – making his own horse brass in the shape of a Star of David. He'd given up the ban on bacon, far too fond of a bacon sandwich, but he still had the *Jewish Chronicle* delivered. And he'd designed his own ring, black jet inset with a gold Star of David, and had the jeweller in town make it up, a big ring that could catch you a nasty blow when he lashed out.

The first summer in Thwaite an engineer came from Poland on a fortnight's exchange to my father's engineering firm, and my father jumped at the chance of taking him under his wing. He was buoyant, in a good mood, for which we were glad: he'd be out of the house, showing the visitor around and entertaining him; but we were also, as usual, half-wearied: we'd have it shoved up our noses as usual that our father preferred the company of strangers to that of his family, and when he brought the visitor home we'd be forced to collude with his great-guy pretence.

The man stood in the kitchen (out of habit, our father had brought him through the back door), a tall stiff man of about forty. Jan Malikowski. He clicked his heels and bowed to my mother and me in turn in a way that seemed possibly satirical, and I knew what my mother would be thinking: here's a man who's seen a sucker coming in Patrick Jackson. And lo and behold, it turned out, that very evening, that my father had told Jan to leave the digs the firm had provided and about which he had privately complained to my father, and stay in the grand hotel in a village outside town at my father's expense.

My father took Jan off into the best room, the front room, and got out the Polish cherry brandy he'd had the wine merchant order in specially.

'Nostrovia!' he cried, exercising with relish his smattering of Polish, and raising his glass. 'Here's to our shared ancestral homeland!'

The man looked at him cynically, almost with a smirk, and I thought: Polish? I was sure that when I'd asked him in Easton about his ancestors, he'd said they were German.

My father and Jan went off to be wined and dined at my father's expense at Jan's hotel, and I didn't see my father again that evening. Next morning, a Saturday, I asked him: 'Dad, didn't you say your ancestors came from Germany?'

He went still, serious and intent, as he'd been the other time I asked. This time, however, he was full of purpose. He said, 'Sit there,' pointing to the table that took up most of the space in the little dining/living room. He went through the front room and upstairs. I was shocked to have provoked such a reaction. I sat and waited, uneasy. He came back carrying an envelope, and the big old grey atlas from a shelf in the front room.

He sat down beside me – I felt awkward – and opened up the atlas at Eastern Europe. He pointed with his yellow finger to a town north of Krakow, in the area marked *Silesia* which he said was part of the German Empire at the time. *Rosenhein*, the town was marked, a German name. You wouldn't find it, he said, on any modern-day maps of Poland.

And then he opened up the envelope and took out a photo. A middle-aged to elderly couple in peasanty clothes, the man with a long moustache and beard. When they'd got to Dublin, he told me, they'd changed their Polish name to the English equivalent, *Jackson*, our name.

There was none of the irony, none of the amused sneering at my original question. He was handing the information to me in all seriousness. As if he was giving it to me in particular . . . I glanced up at him. I couldn't believe it. I was screwed with confusion, and embarrassed. And then, before I knew it, he had put the photo back in the envelope and was taking it through the door to the front room and stowing the atlas away.

Our father's 'Jewishness' was just another instance of his self-romanticising, Cathy and I decided in the end. We treated it as a joke. It was easier, psychologically, to cope with our father if we could see him and his doings as a grim joke.

Now on the phone my mother and I laughed at the time it got me and her into a pickle, while he, as usual, got off scot-free.

Coming from school one afternoon, I stepped off the river path near our house at the bottom of our road, only vaguely noticing a dumpy young woman at the top, coming my way and scanning the bland house fronts as if looking for an address. I was preoccupied with our driveway: my father's bright-blue Anglia wasn't there, which meant I wouldn't have to get straight upstairs out of the way, but could sit in the kitchen with my mother, chatting and reminiscing.

I was just settled at the little Formica table where my mother was making David's special cake without butter, when the front doorbell sounded through the rooms of the house. My mother went through to the little hall at the bottom of the stairs. Guessing it was the girl I had seen, I curiously followed.

She was standing at the door with an intent yet hopeful look on her face, trussed up in a stiff tweed skirt suit, her face framed by a chrysanthemum-shaped hairdo, a crocodile handbag clutched tight.

'Mrs Jackson?'

'Yes . . .'

The girl's shoulders collapsed in relief. 'Oh, thank goodness I've found you!' and then, in response to my mother's bewilderment: 'You *are* the Jacksons who take the *Jewish Chronicle?*'

'Oh – ! Yes . . .'

'It's *such* a relief! I've just started at the teacher-training college, and would you believe it, no one else there is Jewish! So my tutor suggested I come into town and ask at the news-agent's who takes the *Jewish Chronicle*. And you're the only ones in the whole town!'

'Ah . . .' My mother trailed off, clearly deciding how to handle this latest complication my father had got her into.

The girl said, as if having to state the obvious: 'I'm looking for someone to celebrate Shabbat with!'

My mother said kindly, 'You'd better come in.'

She brought her into the front room. Expectant, the girl sat on the sofa against the bank of embroidered and needlepoint cushions, her handbag propped on her knees.

My mother took a breath. 'Well . . . you'd be very welcome to spend time with us, but I'm afraid we don't celebrate the Sabbath in the way you do . . .'

'What do you mean?' She looked alarmed.

'Well, you see, it's my husband who takes the *Jewish Chronicle* . . .'

The girl looked dismayed. 'Oh! So it's only your husband who's Jewish?' She seemed to draw herself together. She was looking around now, I presumed at the lack of signs of Jewishness (the Star-of-David horse brass was hanging in the other room).

My mother, struggling as always to present my father in the best light possible, said, 'Well, he's what you might call a liberal Jew.'

'What?!' the girl stood, covering her chest with her handbag.

I was suddenly very glad she couldn't see the horse brass.

She made quickly for the little hallway. At the door she turned and said hotly but instructively: 'There are Orthodox Jews and there are Reform Jews. But I can assure you categorically that there is no such thing as a *Liberal* Jew!'

She was through the front door and was gone, and my mother was doubled up, laughing in silence in case the girl heard her, and I had my school skirt stuffed into my mouth.

It was thirteen years after my father showed me the photo that I thought seriously again about his identification with Jewishness.

I was a young mother with my first baby, newly moved for my husband's work to an unfamiliar city, my career as a teacher stalled, and stuck in an endless red-brick suburb where I didn't know a soul. Trapped for a time, after all my designs, in the biological imperative, and living a life not too different from my mother's, which I'd sworn to avoid. I fought it: I had begun to write, which I did now in the snatched hours when the baby was asleep, and I set about the task, not easy in that suburban place and long before the advent of the internet, of making like-minded contacts. I pushed the pram into the library and looked at the noticeboard. There was a notice for a class in Family History Research.

The picture my father had shown me flashed into my mind. I didn't remember it all that well, just a peasanty couple, the woman in a dress or skirt down to her ankles, the man with a beret, maybe? I wasn't sure. And who were they? His grandparents, or his great-grandparents . . . he'd told me, but I didn't know. From what I remembered of the clothes they could have been either, just the generic clothes that working people wore for a century or more.

And what had he said about them? I'd been too embarrassed by his unfamiliar attitude to take it all in. What had he said their name was before they changed it to *Jackson*? Janowski? Jacobski? But I remembered the seriousness with which he had told me, and his seriousness the time before in Easton, the care with which he'd impressed on us that they'd been escaping from a pogrom.

As I stood there in the library foyer, I remembered something else.

About a year after the visit of the Polish engineer, my father had made a return visit to Poland. One dreary winter late-afternoon not long after his return, our mother asked Cathy and me to sit down at the dining table. She went away and came back with two large hard-backed books that our father had brought back with him.

'He wants you to look at them,' she said, looking very much as though she *didn't* want us to, and, leaving us to it, went into the kitchen.

I felt rebellious about the coercion, and disinclined to sit and coo over evidence of our father's adventures. Besides, they were dull-looking books, monochrome and plain with impenetrable Polish text on the front. However, duly instructed, I opened the nearest one.

Full-page black-and-white photos.

We were growing cold. 'What is it?' we asked each other in whispers. A pile of leather boots. Another of clothes. A third made up entirely of metal-rimmed glasses. A mountain of naked emaciated bodies.

It was 1962. We had never seen such things, they had yet to become widely distributed. Only slowly did I understand what they were.

Our mother, back in the doorway and looking worried, saw the looks on our faces. 'I think you've seen enough now.'

I put my hand out to stop her.

She hovered, anxious, as I turned the next page, as we went on turning the pages and seeing the horror she'd rather protect us from, but which our father specifically wanted us to know and understand.

Standing in the library foyer twelve years later, I thought: It was as if he had been giving it into our safekeeping.

And I'd squandered it.

I went hot. My hand was sweating on the handle of the pram.

I was overcome with an urge to acknowledge what my father had so consciously given to me. I would join the class, I would research my father's persecuted Jewish ancestors.

I rang home, and my mother answered. I told her what I'd decided.

'Can you ask Dad if I can see the photo again? Can you ask him to tell me all about that couple again?'

She said she would.

She rang back next day. Instantly I could hear in her voice the old familiar panic whenever I wanted something from my father. 'Jo, your father doesn't want you to do family history research.'

I actually felt my jaw drop. 'Why *not*?!'

'Now, Jo, don't get like that . . . I'm sorry, but he really doesn't want you to do it.'

'*Why ever not?*'

'It's the Masons. Well, I don't really understand it all, you know I don't take an interest.'

Yet she sits and embroiders his Masonic paraphernalia, I thought, with the gold and silver thread she has to send off for specially . . .

'He doesn't want his Catholic background bringing up. There's no love lost between the Catholics and the Masons, he says.'

'But it's the *Jewish* ancestors I'm interested in . . .'

'Yes, but if you do family history research his Catholic background is bound to come up. He's getting high up now in the Masons, you know, and he's worried that could spoil things.'

'But why would they know in the Masons what I'd researched?'

'Well, I don't know. It's just, if you start writing things down . . . and other people, in the class, say, knowing . . . You never know who knows who. So he really doesn't want you to do it.'

I thought hotly, He's *forbidden* me to do it. And this is her code, her attempt to soften the blow. To soften me up towards him . . .

I said furiously, 'How does he think he can stop me? Anyone could research it! There are records in the public domain!'

'Oh, Jo!' She was pleading now, a wail in her voice. 'Please! I'm sorry.'

I put down the phone feeling whacked in the belly. How could I have forgotten my father's intransigence? The way he blocked me, refused to have anything to do with me, prevented me having anything to do with him? Of course, he hadn't even wanted to speak to me about it himself but had sent my mother as his messenger: whenever I rang, if he happened to answer, he'd hand me straight to my mother as if I were radioactive. How could I have thought that that incident with the photo had been anything but an aberration?

Well, fuck him, I thought. Fuck him and his family history. I wouldn't waste my energy on his ancestry or his past. It was probably all a pack of lies anyway. I had my own life to lead, my own future (as soon as I could get the trapped-young-motherhood phase out of the way).

I didn't do family history research, I went to a writing group instead. I made a point of putting it all out of my mind.

And yet I was haunted by the sound of my mother's voice as she told me. Somehow it conjured a strange image of lonely telegraph wires with the wind howling through them. And left me with a sense of a deep taboo I didn't understand.

A year later Cathy told me: 'He was in the IRA, you know.'

Since I'd had the baby and moved nearer, to Manchester, she'd started coming over sometimes for lunch, on her days off from the library.

'What? How do you know?'

'He told me when we were driving back from Nanny's.'

Nanny, who had survived by fifteen years our sorely grieved Grampa, had lately become infirm, and every so often our father drove our mother to see her and help out, dropping her off, and then, as in the old days, driving down to get her again. If Cathy could get a couple of days off she'd go along too, driving back with our father, to keep him awake, she said, by talking. I was amazed. I couldn't imagine sitting alone with my father and talking, let alone for all those hours. I was amazed to learn that that *he* would talk to *her*. When we were teenagers he'd drive us in silence, to the station, or the dentist's in the next town, turned away at the wheel in stiff silence as, post-extraction, I spat blood onto the verge.

'What did he say?'

She was leaning on the sink with her coffee mug, the sun glistening through her black curls, one arm folded beneath her ample bosom, one fantastic leg – delicate, like our mother's – crossed over the other. My eighteen-month-old, Luke, kept trundling on his plastic motorbike between us.

'Well, he said the IRA came recruiting round the villages, and all the lads joined up as a matter of course.'

'And did you believe it?'

She shrugged.

'Well, why has he never mentioned it before?'

'He's wanted to keep it quiet. He said the trouble is they won't ever let you forget it. Once you're in, you're always in. And once you've carried an IRA coffin, which he says he did . . . They're always ready to touch you for money.'

'My god. And now he's in the money . . .'

Six years or so before, he had left the engineering firm and started one of his own. It had been an instant success. At long last there was enough money for him to spend without our mother panicking and fretting, and money for our mother to spend too: she was a director of the firm, with a director's salary. For the first time ever in their marriage she could buy herself clothes, high-heeled shoes and ballgowns which she wore to the Con Club and golf club dinners and ladies' nights at the Masons, making the age gap between herself and my middle-aged penguin-suited father look in the photos even larger than it was. She was a woman with a career at last – though still in service, of course, to our father: a director with more than a director's burden of work, since our father, needless to say, spent a lot of time entertaining and travelling away to Masonic meetings. And of course she still ran around like a slave at home.

I said, musing, 'Perhaps that's why he didn't want me digging up his past with family history research . . .'

Cathy shrugged, non-committal, a little dismissive even.

There had been a certain reversal of things between Cathy and me. After spending her childhood in my shadow, always turning to me for explanations, she now had the air of being the one with the low-down on the family, and of considering me, who had lived away, uninitiated, even naïve.

I thought of the day I first knew she was pulling away from me. It was the first winter in Thwaite. She had started at a different school from mine, a larger, technical grammar in the next town. All that first summer I'd walked home from school along the river, but now, remembering my own experience of starting at a large distant grammar, I waited where her school bus dropped her off and walked with her up the road. Besides, that autumn our beloved Grampa had died: for a while I felt as though my world had fallen apart, and needed her company.

One afternoon she got off the bus, swerved past me without speaking and set off walking. I ran after her. 'Cathy, what's wrong?'

'Nothing.' It was a sullen grunt, and she'd had to force herself to answer. She kept her head down, walking very fast.

I had no dignity. I didn't fall back and let her go, I scrabbled after her. 'Did you have a good day? . . . Did something happen? . . . Did something go wrong? . . . Are you OK?' All the time getting irritable grunts for answers and sometimes no answer at all. In the end we walked in silence, and I did fall back behind her. She walked ahead, skirt rolled up around her waist and flapping at the backs of her thighs, as was the fashion amongst the girls at her co-ed, streetwise school, clearly trying to lose me, her nerdy, posh-girls'-school sister.

It was my first realisation – at fourteen years old, two years older than Cathy – that she wasn't simply my shadow, that she didn't necessarily see the world the way I did, and that – in that moment, at least – she didn't actually want to. I was shocked and upset. And the way I felt brought me a revelation: that though I'd always considered her dependent on me, it was I who needed the comfort of solidarity between us.

Well, I had to forgo it. Of course, she grew away from me. She had friends I didn't know, more friends at school than I had, and of course she hardly ever brought them to the house. She was popular, in a way I couldn't imagine being. She developed a social manner quite at odds with her childhood shyness and fear. She was a flirt. In the end, when we went downtown to get the groceries on Saturday, she had boys tripping over each other to talk to her. And no wonder: as she grew she became beautiful: that mass of black curls, those grey eyes that in certain lights would turn green. Those legs.

Though of course, we still had our father to negotiate and battle together. We kept our solidarity on that, a battle that didn't stop after we left home.

THE GREAT
ATTRACTIVENESS
OF OTHERS

H E WAS SO unhappy, my mother had said to me now
on the phone.

As I put down the receiver I thought: But didn't he overcome in the end all the things that had been making him
unhappy? Didn't he get what he wanted? The prestige and
respect of a small-town businessman? The material success?
The big house they bought once the business was established,
a small early-Victorian mansion in an acre of grounds?

And a religion. 'He was always looking for something to
believe in,' my mother had said to me on the phone, 'and
he found it in the Masons.' And yes, he did: his obsession
with Jewishness became subsumed in an obsession with the
Knights Templars and the Rosicrucians, the Star of David
caught within a Masonic sunburst in the gold pendant he
designed himself and had the jeweller make up.

But hadn't he found many of those things before Cathy
and I left home? Hadn't he already joined the Con Club and
the golf club and the Masons?

So why did he go on being so unhappy with *us*?

And depriving us. We didn't like to think it (or I didn't;
I could no longer speak for Cathy), but it was as if he were
flaunting his new-found wealth in our faces while depriving

us. He lavished gifts on others, paying the golf caddies outrageous tips that were the talk of the club while refusing us
money or giving in only grudgingly; buying brand-new bikes
for the ten- and eleven-year-old brother and sister who had
become our parents' regular caddies, while Cathy and I had
to have secondhand ones, and dud ones at that: mine had a
left-hand veer for which I had to compensate while steering,
and Cathy's brakes were dodgy, sending her more than once
over the handlebars.

'Now don't make a fuss!' our mother warned, wretched and
apologetic, when we found out about the bikes for the caddies,
glancing at the door in case he came in from the garage. 'You
know how your father always likes to impress other people.'

I cried: 'But why does he want to impress *them?*' An ur-
chin-like pair from the council estate, whom we might have
expected him to despise, with none of the manners he insisted
on in us, from the kind of family he might have been expected
to call *rough as assholes.*

'Oh, Jo, *please!* For my sake!'

His shock and displeasure at the financial implications
when I said I wanted to go to university. 'Bloody good job
when you get out to work and start contributing to this
household,' he'd been in the habit of saying to me. His silent
hostility when I asked for the clothes I needed for leaving;
the way he'd had to be persuaded by my mother to buy them.
The ominous air as he drove us to the city to buy them, the
stony implacability with which he handed over the money in
the department store, so that the girl at the till looked from
one to the other of us nervously.

Meanwhile, he went on buying expensive gifts for the
two caddies. His own particular caddy was Sandra, Sandra

Suggate, whom I'd glimpsed only once early on, a skinny underfed-looking girl with straight dull hair and a grubby pale complexion. After he started his business, when she was coming up to leaving school at sixteen, he offered her a job as his personal secretary, on, our mother told us with deep frustration, a salary more suited to a London graduate PA. So Sandra Suggate worked in the office alongside my frustrated and resentful mother who, true to her own tradition, kept up towards Sandra a pretence of acceptance and even compensating flattery. By then I was leading my own life elsewhere, but it still stung me to hear of it.

I was teaching in Scotland, twenty-five years old and four years married to the husband who'd been my headlong escape, when he and I visited those offices for the first time.

We were due early, in mid-afternoon, so, following my mother's instructions, we drove to the premises in town. We almost missed the entrance, an alleyway between the haberdasher's and the baker's, a narrow squeeze for any good-sized vehicle. We came out into a courtyard winking with lined-up cars and vans, including my father's latest, the Rover, the nearest he would get to the Rolls he'd once promised himself. On each side, low eighteenth-century buildings slumbered in the May sunshine. Ahead, from a barn-like workshop, came the secretly distant sound and splashy flash of welding. The little windows on the left, which my mother had said were those of the offices, shone blindly.

My mother appeared at the top of the enclosed flight of stairs, and it crossed my mind, not for the first time, that she looked panicky at my reappearance. The look, if I hadn't imagined it, quickly faded, and she ushered us up in welcome.

My parents, I discovered, were ensconced in separate offices behind big Victorian desks, my mother sharing hers with her own assistant Janet, and David, who, nineteen years old now, was working his way up the business from the bottom. My mother was surrounded by stacks of invoices and orders that had to be processed by the end of the day, but my father in his office was sitting at a clean desk doing nothing much more, it seemed, than smoking.

'Come in, come in!' he said genially to my husband, Terry. 'Sit down, sit down. How's the Fellowship going?'

He hadn't liked Terry in the beginning: too working-class, his Derbyshire accent too strong, his table manners too un-refined (objections he didn't of course apply to his caddies). But then I'd met Terry at Methodist Youth Club, where, aged sixteen and lonely since Cathy had got her own social life, I'd gone to try and make friends, running the gauntlet of my father's alienated disgust. I knew, miserably, once I'd brought Terry home, that my father would be nastily sneering about him behind my back, just as he'd sneered at Aunty Cathy's boyfriend. And Terry sensed it, and would fumble and drop things at the table, his dark eyes trembling with the anxiety my father could induce if you weren't in his good books, and I'd be furious.

Terry was then already at university, he'd been home for the vacation when I'd met him, and as time went on and Terry seemed bent on academic career, I guess it dawned on my father that he could end up with a university lecturer for a son-in-law. He'd started buttering him up. He bought him the expensive textbooks for his science course, which his own father didn't see why he couldn't buy out of his grant as I did mine. I didn't feel discriminated against at the time. After all, my own textbooks weren't nearly so expensive, and I was relieved by the evidence that my father had taken to Terry at last.

'How's it going?' he asked Terry now, waving him into the chair opposite the desk.

I sat on the only other chair available, a little way off.

Terry told him about the Fellowship, and my father listened, emitting his traditional social, comfortable mutters of agreement. 'Yeah, yeah, yeah . . .'

He hadn't asked me about myself.

In a lull in the conversation I told him my own news: that I'd decided to start writing, and was teaching myself to touch-type. It sounded, from my place across the lino, like an intrusion, an announcement, a cry for attention, which I guess it was.

There was a silence. My father lowered his head, as if embarrassed by my childishness. I was embarrassed by it myself.

'Oh aye?' he said finally, then looked up and continued his conversation with Terry.

The door opened and in walked Sandra Suggate – she was such an important PA that she had her own office. She was nineteen now, no longer the waif she had been, her thighs bulging in her miniskirt, but her chest was still flat and she still had that dull grey look, her hair now hanging in flat tapes on her shoulders. She'd brought papers for my father to sign, and she laid them on his desk.

As she did so, my father said to me brightly: 'So you've been learning to type, eh?' glancing at Sandra Suggate as he said it. And then, without looking at me, but with a smirk at Sandra Suggate: 'Well, if you ever learned to type as fast as Sandra, I *might* consider offering you a job.'

He paused, still smirking. 'Of course, I could only offer

you a minimum wage.'

Sandra Suggate was smirking, too, looking straight at me with a kind of sly triumph.

I could hardly believe it had happened. I had to believe it had happened.

She had moved behind his desk to put down the papers, and she stood there now beside him, beyond the sunbeam that came in through the little low window, in the place I couldn't go, my father's favour.

When we visited again that Christmas, however, my mother told me that my father would like to see something I'd written. I was shocked by that in turn. I handed her a couple of pieces to give to him.

He gave them back to me himself. He sniggered briefly at the one about the sexist schoolboy taunting the teacher, in a way that made me uncomfortable: it was the teacher I felt he was sniggering at. That was his only reaction. He didn't mention the other story, a more complex, fragmentary and overtly feminist piece about the exploitation of a younger woman by an older man. Altogether his reaction was odd, somehow stiff and contained. Well, I thought, he wouldn't have made head or tail of my writing, would he, with his old-fashioned, primitive views? And I wondered, more sympathetically, if it had made him feel somehow inferior, with his life-long consciousness of his lack of formal education.

A couple of years later I understood a bit better.

On one of those summer days when Cathy came to visit me and my toddler, she got off the train looking grim.

'What's wrong?'

'Dad's been having it off with Sandra Suggate.'

'*What?!!* How do you know?'

'Mum rang me on Friday evening. They were running away together.'

'*What?!!*'

'Yes, apparently Dad walked into Mum's office and threw his keys on her desk and said, "It's all yours, the business, everything, I'm finished with it all." And he got in his car and drove away. When Mum got home he'd cleared out his wardrobe and left.'

'My god! So where was Sandra Suggate?'

'She was still at work when he left the office. She told Mum she'd no idea where he'd gone, but obviously he was planning to leave with her. Turns out they've been carrying on for a while, and Mum's known.'

'My god!'

I tried to digest it. 'But he didn't go?'

'No.'

'So what happened?'

'Well, I went straight round to Mum's and sat with her. I told her: Don't you worry. They'll be in some transport caff now and he'll be trying to persuade her, but when that gold-digging bitch realises that running off with him would mean a future tied to an old feller without a business any more, she'll get cold feet. And she must have done: he came back at two in the morning with his tail between his legs.'

She paused. 'Stupid bastard.'

I had a moment of feeling sorry for my father, hoist on the petard of his long-standing habit of buying the affections of others.

Then: 'Oh god, poor Mum . . .'

'Yeah, it's been going on for ages, apparently.'

Right under her nose in that office . . .

Something occurred to me. 'But I thought Sandra got married a couple of years ago . . .'

'Yeah, she did, but she left her husband. It only lasted a few months.' Cathy paused. 'I did wonder, when Dad bought her those golf clubs, and all that golfing equipment, while she was still married . . .'

I remembered that my mother had complained about that on the phone at the time, but I'd hardly taken any notice, too used to her lifelong complaints about him lavishing money and gifts on others.

I was staggered. *I'm finished with it all* . . . Everything he'd always worked towards, the business, the settled life, the flamboyant respectability, the goals he had put before any of us . . .

And now he'd put Sandra Suggate before it all. That greasy plain girl. When our mother was so beautiful, looking half her own age, and had bent over backwards all her life to please him.

When Cathy had gone on her train, it dawned on me:

She had said that Sandra's marriage had lasted only a few months, she'd implied that the affair with my father had been going on while she was married . . .

It must have been going on eighteen months ago.

⁂

Eighteen months ago I had ended up back in the house on the housing estate, thrown on my parents' mercy with my new baby.

After the way my father had treated me in his office, I

149

had vowed, bitterly and proudly, never to ask my parents for anything again, but less than a year later I had no option.

Things had gone badly wrong. I was eight months pregnant when Terry applied for and got a job at Manchester University which was due to start in four weeks' time. We had the prospect of a move coinciding with the birth, or my being left in Scotland alone with the baby. Worse: Terry now had to work out his notice, and wouldn't be able to take time off to be at home for my return from hospital as we'd planned.

We put our house on the market, and while I was in hospital it sold, far more quickly than we could have expected, which meant, according to Scottish law, that we'd have to vacate in four weeks. Yet we hadn't even begun looking for a house in Manchester. I arrived from hospital with the baby to a house being measured up for curtains by the purchaser, Terry due to leave for Manchester in a week, and only three weeks before we had to get out altogether.

Worst of all, I felt ill, which I had never expected. It had been a problematic birth, and, it would turn out later, I was suffering an unsuspected complication. Alone in the house with the baby next day, I almost fainted as I was carrying him up the stairs. I decided I had no option but to ring my mother for help.

She rushed north. She looked around at the mess in the downstairs room of our tiny modern terrace, baby things all over the floor, the milk-soaked baby - slightly premature, hungry all the time yet unable efficiently to feed - me in my dressing gown dizzy and faint, and said in distress: 'There's nothing for it, Jo. I've discussed it with your father. I don't see any other solution: you'll have to come to us until you find a house in Manchester.'

I clamped my mind against the implications: that it depended on my father; that he'd had to be persuaded; that the only reason he had been was that there was no other solution.

A week later Terry drove me and my mother and the baby south through a frozen country, back to the house on the housing estate, and I couldn't avoid the feeling that he'd abandoned me, back to the past he was meant to have helped me escape.

That first evening, as I sat in the cramped dining room feeding the baby, I was tense, dreading the arrival of my father, the man who had been so irritated by the presence of his own children. My mother had been helping me bath the baby by the electric fire, and the plastic bath seemed to fill half the room. Dirty nappies, filled one after the other in quick succession, were piled on the floor. My mother was still hurriedly tidying up when my father walked in through the door.

He wasn't scowling. He came and bent over the baby, Luke, on my knee, poking his eagle face towards Luke's and grinned. 'Well, well, well,' he said, mildly amused.

In the days that followed, he went on being benign. I knew that my mother was in the habit of rushing home from the office earlier than my father and David to have the evening meal ready for when they arrived. Often now, however, although she had taken some time off work to help me, with a particularly fretful baby causing such disruption, she hadn't even begun the preparation before they turned up. Yet my father didn't complain. Never once did he make his traditional demand: 'Hows abouta cuppa tay, Missus?'

He wasn't around much – keeping out of it, I supposed

– but never once did he betray bad temper or even irritation. One weekend he even drove us, me, my mother and Luke, to Manchester to look at houses Terry had lined up for viewing. He even came inside with us and now and then contributed, if somewhat distantly, to the discussions.

I didn't have the space to be more than just grateful. I was too preoccupied, too besotted with Luke, his elfin face, his velvety torso, too overwhelmed by the physicality, the tug on my breasts and womb when he cried, the seep of milk and blood. The lack of sleep and increasing exhaustion: like me as a baby, Luke never slept for more than an hour, and cried all the time. I was in a dazed bubble. The day we went looking for houses I trailed behind the others, desperately frustrated by my lack of control of the situation, but utterly incapable of exerting it, giddy and removed. The houses blended one into the other, one variegated carpet or one glass front door into the next, so that afterwards I couldn't picture the one we had chosen.

And I was trying to suppress the notion that Terry had put his job before me and Luke. I was afraid he had emotionally abandoned me. I needed him to prove that he hadn't, but when he came at weekends he couldn't easily engage with the new world of the baby. He found it hard to wake with me for Luke in the night, and I felt that when he left on Sunday evening for Manchester and his digs, he was relieved.

I had the sinking feeling of history being repeated.

And I was worried that this was Luke's problem, that I'd failed him already in the way I had vowed never to do: transmitted to him my own angst.

So I had no room to wonder why my father had become so strangely benign, leave alone to suspect he was caught in the euphoria of an affair.

I realised now that with that second story I'd shown my father, I'd unwittingly pressed a button.

I thought of that awful visit to my father's office. I remembered the intimacy with which Sandra Suggate had moved and stood behind the desk beside my father, the knowing smirk that had passed between them. The way she flaunted herself, flapping her tabs of hair, as she left the room. And – I remembered, with a lurch of the stomach – the sly, almost triumphant look she had given me, a flaunting of the secret she was in on with my father.

Sandra Suggate wasn't then yet married, but the brewing affair with my father had been a subtext even then.

But why, I wondered, did he need to put me down the way he did on that occasion?

OK, I understood now why he paid that ridiculous salary to that minimally-educated girl, but why did he need to make that nasty quip about paying me, his graduate daughter, a minimum wage – in front of her, indeed specifically for her benefit, it seemed?

I wondered again: was it resentment at my education? I thought of how he'd been when I said I wanted to go to university . . .

So pointed, though. And so very nasty.

And it wasn't just Sandra our father favoured over me and Cathy.

Cathy had warned me, about the Sandra Suggate revelation: 'Mum doesn't want David to know.'

'He doesn't know?! Even though he works down the office?'

'Well, you know what Mum's like – she'll have been pulling out all the stops to hide it and put up a good front.'

'Huh. Protect him from having his son know what he's like!'

No, it wasn't just Sandra who saw a different side of our father. There was David.

DAVID

A LTHOUGH I'D ALWAYS been glad that our father hadn't hit David, we did, at a certain point, begin to wonder about the discrimination.

Not long after he bought the caddies new brand-new bikes, he bought one for David too.

Our mother told us, intently: it was his compensation for failing the eleven-plus.

Unlike us, he had failed. He had lost too much schooling. While my aches and pains stopped once we moved to Thwaite, David went on having his turns. For a year after we moved there I took him to school in the mornings and he'd clutch my hand all the way, and watch through the school railings, his white face panicky, as I left for my own school. But all too often I didn't need to take him, he was too unwell to go. He struggled as he sat with our mother over the eleven-plus practice papers, his hand going up to his forehead and pushing up his flap of dark-brown hair, his face growing sweaty.

Our father hovered, silently concerned, in a way that surprised me, since he'd shown so little interest when Cathy and I were practising ours, and since for most of our childhood he had hardly seemed to notice David.

Was it, I wondered as I watched, because David was a boy? Did it matter to our father, even though up to now he'd shown so little interest in him, that David did well, simply because he was a *boy*?

I even began to wonder if *that* was why he didn't hit him: because he was a boy.

I didn't mind, though, that as David became a teenager, he had luxuries we hadn't had – the clothes, the watches, the bikes (he ended up with several) – after all, our parents were so much better off by then, and I wouldn't have wished our experience on him. And though I noted the patriarchal paradigm when our father took him into his business, I was glad for David, since he'd ended up leaving school with few qualifications, which, although I was leading a distant, different life by then, had been a continuing source of worry to me.

We were exercised, though, when our father bought him a car to drive the mile from home to the office, while Cathy, four years older, struggling on a student grant and living in a flat in town, had to get the bus every day to college five miles off.

Outdated patriarchy, we decided, and felt better about it. Infuriating as it was, despicable as it was, it was after all just an entrenched social attitude in which our father was steeped. It made it all seem less personal.

Until, that is, we heard about our father's will.

ॐ

It was a sunny evening in the eighties when my mother rang and told me that our father had willed his share of the house to David.

Thwaite House, the big house they had finally bought, once dower house to the nearby hall. David, aged twenty-three, was still living at home when they moved in, and thirteen years on he still lived there with them, notwithstanding his long-term relationship with our mother's secretary Janet who, presumably fed up of waiting, had bought a house of her own.

'The thing is,' my mother said, desperately anxious about my reaction, 'what your dad thinks is, you've got Greg' – by then I was divorced from Terry and living with a different partner – 'and Cathy's got Nick' (her second husband) 'but David's got no one.'

I knew what she meant: David was a man, so had no one to keep him, as, she was implying, we did.

'And if David and Janet are going to get married . . . And you and Cathy have houses, and David doesn't.'

I could hear her flopping with dismay at the unreasonableness of what she was saying, so forbore to say the things with which I was seething: hadn't Cathy and I paid our own way through working; hadn't we bought our houses *together* with our partners? The fact that marriage for a woman was in any case no guarantee of financial security: we were both of us divorced, and at one time I'd ended up a cash-strapped single parent. That anyway Greg and I weren't even married, so, according to the laws of the time, I didn't have the protections of a wife. That Cathy, in her marriage, was the chief breadwinner. And anyway, didn't *Janet* have a house, the doing up of which, for some convoluted reason, my mother had felt forced to contribute towards?

Besides, I didn't believe her. I didn't think my father had bothered to use that reasoning. She'd concocted it herself, to soften the blow.

My mother was going on: 'And of course, David was meant to take over the business, and now that's gone.'

The miners' strike had done for the business, the electricity board unable to pay my parents. But also, after the debacle with Sandra Suggate, my father had never regained the same

interest. He was more and more absent, off at Masonic meetings, and my mother struggled on alone. For David had never
settled into it: made ill by the figures when he worked in
the office, as he'd been by the eleven-plus papers, and on the
power-station sites by the chemicals and fumes.

'So your dad feels he has to make up for that.'

I couldn't speak anyway. I stared at the sun pouring down
the stairs of the house I lived in and pooling in the hall. I felt
punched in the gut. This *did* feel personal, after all. He could
do this to us: he could care so little about our feelings.

He never did love us after all.

My mother knew what I was thinking. 'Jo, it's not just
you. I had a battle to get him to leave half the house to me!'

I found my voice. 'What? But the house is half yours!'

And then she told me: although the house had been bought
with her money (our father of course being in the habit of
spending all his), he had gone behind her back to his solicitor,
a Masonic crony, and signed the contract without her. The
house was owned in his name alone.

She said, 'And I found out that he'd left it solely to David
in his will! I had such a battle to make him change his mind.
He wouldn't back down for ages. And Jo, I really couldn't
make him change his mind about you and Cathy.'

On her next day off, Cathy came over. We sat in the Italian
restaurant we liked to go to for lunch. Tears dropped like
rods from her greeny eyes onto the red-checked tablecloth.
(Cathy, who didn't cry!) 'It's not the money,' she said, her voice
strangled. 'It's the fact that it proves he never really loved us.'

She'd known for longer than me, yet still she was shocked
and deeply upset. I thought of the hours she'd said she'd spent

with him chatting in the car on the way to Llanfair; I thought of the times I'd watched her in recent years joking with him over the kitchen table in the big house, something I could never imagine doing. She must have hoped she was finally winning him round. I thought of her in our childhood urging me not to answer him back; the times she would warn me on the phone before I visited to watch what I said.

This is what comes of appeasing a bully, I thought grimly: it makes no difference, we'd both come out of it the same.

'David's always been mollycoddled,' she said bitterly.

And yes, he had. Right from being a baby, when he began to be ill. There was always the sense that he needed to be protected, from infection, from certain foodstuffs, from difficult situations like school. And increasingly from us girls.

It was when he was practising for the eleven-plus that I first had the feeling of being thought a specific threat to him.

I couldn't bear the sight of him struggling, and I wanted to help.

'No, you won't,' my mother said firmly, and went to help him herself, shutting the door. Of course, she would think that at sixteen years old I didn't have the skills. But I found it hard to erase the sense I had in that moment, of my physical presence, my *self*, considered a danger to David.

My first Christmas home from university, an old set of Dickens had appeared in my absence, placed on a new high shelf. I put up my hand to look at them, and my mother cried sharply, 'Don't touch them, they're David's!'

I dropped my hand as if stung.

Some golf crony had given them to him, apparently. And, my mother told me intently, they had said they were specifically for David and no one else must touch them. Which told me that I was considered some kind of danger to David. In danger, I thought, of damaging him by rubbing in my greater education . . .

And then there was the time I went to stay with the baby.

It was David, not my father, who came home from the office one day the first week and hung in the dining-room doorway looking put out as my mother and I scrabbled to put away the baby things.

Twenty years old then, he was the negative image of our younger father: the same sharp jawline, the handsome beaky nose. In spite of his illnesses and allergies, he'd become a trophy-winning cyclist, and he had our father's once slim yet stocky athlete's build. He hung there frowning just as my father, arrived back from over the Pennines or an evening at the Con Club to the hassle of his family, would once have done.

'Isn't tea ready?' he asked in a wronged tone.

It occurred to me, out of my dazed postnatal condition, that like my father he'd been keeping away out of the baby-occupied house, that in fact I'd hardly seen him since we arrived. He went on looking irritated, and I thought with an unhappy twinge: the favoured, pampered child, upset by the intruders in his nest.

In that moment, a tale that our mother would tell came back me. Those two summers when Cathy and I went to Llanfair on our own, our mother would take us to Chester and put us on the train. Down the years she would laugh at what David would say as our train pulled away, the little boy overshadowed by his elder sisters, relieved at having his mother to himself for once, with no one at last to covet his special cake, on one or two occasions even to raid the tin: 'That's got rid of them!'

'Well, any chance of a cuppa?' he directed now at my mother who was hurriedly picking up the nappies.

I was astonished. I wanted to ask him what physical or mental incapacity prevented him, in the age of feminism, from lifting the kettle himself. I didn't: something stopped me: some taboo that felt almost tangible in the room. My mother jumped up, anxious and hassled, dropped what she was doing and rushed into the kitchen, in just the way she'd always done for our father.

Weeks went by and I remained stuck at Thwaite waiting for our house purchase in Manchester to go through. And growing more and more exhausted: through moving so soon after the birth I'd missed the routine postnatal exam, and was too dazed to link it with the fact that, eight weeks after the birth, I was still bleeding profusely. And Luke went on failing to sleep for very long. In the end my mother took more time off work to help me.

In the evenings there was a panic to clear up before the men came home from their evenings out, to get Luke in his cot upstairs and tidy away the baby things. One evening we failed. David arrived home and Luke was only just falling asleep on my shoulder and the room was still in chaos. Shattered, hardly conscious or sane, I crept gingerly from the room and upstairs with Luke, and put him down in his cot.

I was coming back through the dining-room door when he set up squalling again.

'Oh god!' I cried in despair.

David snapped: 'For god's sake, pull yourself together!'

I was astounded. I looked to my mother, silenced by the taboo that now seemed to hang around David, expecting her to stand up for me and dress him down.

She looked at the floor, avoiding my eye.

How could she let him get away with it?

I did speak. I forced myself to be calm. 'Dave, it's not a question *pulling myself together*.' Yet I could hear how stiff the anger and hurt made my voice; I heard how it would sound: the voice of the educationally privileged elder sister talking down to the brother deprived of educational chances.

My mother shot me an alarmed look, and he was obviously stung. He flared: 'Don't be so bloody daft!'

'Dave, I'm not daft, I'm just exhausted!'

He had turned away, dismissive, but now he whirled back at me. 'Do you think you're the only one? Look at Mum: *she's* exhausted too, looking after the baby, looking after you, running the household and trying to keep up with all her work at the office – when she can get to it!'

My mind went cold. I thought: how dare he, he of the lordly demand for a cuppa? I thought coolly: he's jealous, pathetically jealous of his mother's attention being directed elsewhere.

I turned to my mother again, and was met with her look of alarmed warning: *Don't cause trouble*.

I let out a strangled cry of hurt and rage and ran upstairs to Luke, whose cries were now spiralling through the house.

As I got to the bedroom I realised David was following me. I turned. He demanded in disgust, 'Why don't you get your act together and stop behaving like a helpless brat?'

I wondered if I were hearing correctly. I wanted to cry, *Stop behaving like Dad!* but I couldn't, my mouth felt stopped.

I had dared as a teenager to answer my father back, but somehow now, as an adult, I was unable to answer back my younger brother. Somehow, with David, there was an even greater sanction. All that came from my mouth was an inarticulate cry of injustice.

He slapped me across the face, so hard I fell back on the bed.

He went away.

I lay still on the bed where once I would lie swamped by the image my father had beaten into me, madwoman in the attic, and which now threated to swamp me again.

Luke, as if in shock, had stopped crying in his cot.

Slowly, cold contempt overcame me. Down below I heard my father come in, his voice rumbling up through the ceiling. I thought: my father who had shown such unexpected forbearance would surely not accept this, David hitting a woman still weak and unwell from childbirth.

Well, I *wouldn't* be silenced. David should account for what he'd done.

Luke had begun to splutter again, so I picked him up and wrapped him in a shawl and took him downstairs.

As I went through the front room, I could hear the three of them talking in low voices in the dining room beyond the glass door. I opened the door and they stopped talking at once. My father was in his usual place at the table, his back to me. David was in the chair beside the door where I stood, facing away. My mother was in the chair opposite, and she looked up quickly and said with the false brightness that always made of her voice a squawk: 'Isn't he asleep yet?'

Protecting David, I thought. Pretending nothing had happened. Well, I wouldn't let him get away with it. Over David's head, I said to my father's turned back: 'Dad, David hit me.'

They all seemed to freeze. My father didn't turn, and my mother and David looked at the floor. No one said anything.

And then my father did turn slightly, just enough for me see that he was faintly smirking.

The silence went on. I could think of nothing to do but turn around with Luke and go back upstairs, which it seemed they were waiting for me to do.

I sat on the bed with Luke in my arms. All I wanted was to leave. I couldn't; I was trapped here in Thwaite. Trapped in the old narrative I was supposed to have escaped, in the old persona I had in this family. I had seen it, that persona, in their postures as they waited for me to go away back upstairs. It had been there in David's accusations; it was there in his face as he stood over me in the bedroom doorway. It was the notion, I realised now, he'd grown up with. That I was the one who caused all the trouble, the one from whom everyone else needed to be protected.

Luke was silent in my arms, his eyes wide open, wrapped in the shawl someone had given me, an old one, like a refugee shawl. He was staring at me, disturbed, I realised, by the pounding of my heart.

I had to calm myself, for his sake.

When I got up next morning, nothing was mentioned.

The incident was never mentioned again. I began to wonder if it had really happened. After all, I would think when we'd finally got into the Manchester house, I'd been insane with exhaustion, delirious maybe with loss of blood, maybe I'd even been unhinged.

The memory was so painfully vivid, but I felt unable to trust it.

For one thing, relations with my parents seemed immediately to improve. Once I moved to Manchester, the feelings I'd had when I left them, the despair, the determination never to go there again, faded through distance and a life of my own. And, stuck in a suburb with a new baby and lonely, cut off from my career, still ill since it would be another three months before the complication was diagnosed, and, as it happened, hassled by interfering in-laws who didn't like me, I needed to turn to my mother. And she wanted to see Luke; having a grandchild to take to see her did in the end ease relations.

Now, being nearer, we visited more often, but from this time on I saw little of David. He'd be out, whether by accident as my mother always airily made out, or by design, I never knew. I would wonder: was he still disgusted with me, still harbouring that old family profile of me? And in that moment, in the midst of the more cordial atmosphere, I'd be reminded, and feel a chill. Or was he keeping away out of shame for what he'd done, which, out of the saner world in which I was living, seemed only proper and therefore more likely?

But in the end his absence erased him from my preoccupations. I had other, more urgent concerns: working on making good any damage done already to Luke and creating a happy home for him, which meant repressing my dismay over Terry and making him my saviour all over again.

When I realised that during the time I'd spent at Thwaite my father had been conducting his affair with Sandra Suggate, it occurred to me that David had been in a state about that. In spite of our mother's plan to keep it from him, and her belief that she had succeeded, he would surely have known: after all, the two PAs in the office, his girlfriend Janet and Sandra Suggate, worked closely together. *What about Mum?* he had cried. *Trying to keep up with her work in the office – when she can get to it!* Inexplicably and perhaps seemingly unreasonably helpless with the baby, I was keeping my mother away from the office and giving Sandra Suggate and my father free rein . . .

Looking back in the light of the will at that smirk on my father's face when I told him David had hit me, I thought: besotted with Sandra, off in his own little world of adultery, he had abdicated. Passed on the job of keeping me in line. Passed on his mantle to David.

'We ought to have known,' I said to Cathy, as she wept in the Italian restaurant. 'Remember the year they moved into Thwaite house, and Dave stopped exchanging presents?'

It was the Christmas when Luke was coming up to three. After years of encouraging me to keep away for the actual days of Christmas, my father's most volatile time, my mother invited us for Christmas in the big Victorian house into which they'd just moved.

My father showed us round with pride, an attention I found gratifying (I always forgot!). A gothicky hall with arched alcoves, a sweeping circular staircase with a lush red carpet, long lounge and dining room with tall elegant windows, a crimson lake of a landing and several gracious bedrooms, all beautifully furnished with tasteful antiques and my mother's years of needlework. A separate servants' stairs leading down to a back kitchen converted from a scullery and banked with white goods; the big living kitchen, all gleaming wood and brass, in which my mother had put up a glittering Christmas tree, an object not seen in the Jackson household for very many years.

My father showed off his own handiwork, the stripped and varnished kitchen doors. David, he had said, had tiled the bathrooms.

'Where *is* David?' I asked, wondering why he, too, wasn't here to show off his work (I always forgot!).

My mother said, 'He's down at Janet's!' Brightly. Over-brightly. 'But he says he'll be here tomorrow!' She spoke with such emphasis and tension that I knew in that moment that he'd had to be persuaded.

Next morning, Christmas morning, Cathy and her first husband came over for the present-giving.

David hadn't arrived as promised.

We waited, all six of us: me, Terry and Luke, and my mother and Cathy and her husband. My father, of course, was out in the old stables he'd had converted to garages, uninterested as ever in family present-giving.

David didn't come.

In the end Cathy said, 'Well, shall we do it without him? We'll have to do it with him later.'

Our mother tensed. 'Well . . . He *did* say that if he didn't come I could give his presents out for him.'

We knew then that he'd never intended to be there. We knew then that though my mother had hoped against hope that he would be, she had known in her heart that really he wouldn't.

She took a deep breath. 'And he asked me to tell you: this is the last time. He doesn't want to exchange presents any more.'

'What?!' Cathy exploded.

'Now, Cathy, don't cause a fuss!' cried our mother, wretched yet sending her that look of warning.

Afterwards Cathy and I walked in the grounds with Luke. Cathy fumed. 'I bet he didn't even choose those presents! I bet she chose them for him – I bet she always has! I bet she even went out and *bought* them for him while he sat on his arse! I bet she paid! She probably wrapped them too! She probably had to put the pen in his hand and make him write the labels!'

'The worst thing, though,' I said as Luke came running towards us, 'is sending a message through Mum like that!'

The high-handedness, the dismissiveness.

Using our mother like that as his messenger. And our mother incapable, it seemed, of challenging that, and, though she clearly hated it, going along with it.

The sense that he felt entitled to do it.

Yes, his sense of entitlement.

The big white house loomed in the darkening post-midday, its pitched roofs lowering, black pruned holly bushes standing like guards on the lawns. A house built in early Victorian times for a widow ousted by the son and heir, in which an order not so very different was now taking shape, in which David had become our father's sidekick and double, our mother in thrall to them both, and Cathy and I discounted altogether.

'Yeah, we should have guessed then,' said Cathy bitterly, swallowing her tears.

Another incident came back to me, taking place only months before this lunch.

I was visiting Thwaite House with my two children and my partner Greg. David had gone on making himself scarce for my visits, but on this particular occasion he was there, and joined us, if a little absent and reserved, for tea.

During these last few years our father did seem to have changed in a way that must have put Cathy off the scent. To my two children, entering their teens now, he must have seemed a harmless old man. He would sit at the table with his fag, mostly silent but listening, sniggering now and then at the things they said. On this particular occasion, to my surprise and gratification, he became involved in a discussion we were having about dialect. He had always been so snobbish about the local dialect, but when I'd mentioned its elements of Anglo-Saxon and Norse, in spite of himself he'd become interested. And there we sat, around the big table in the big glittering kitchen, me and my partner and kids and the grand-parents (my mother bobbing up and down in her pinny) and the uncle: for all the world, it seemed, a cohesive family having a straightforward conversation with none of the old tensions. I was put off the scent myself.

David, silent up until that moment, spoke. He said, peddling our father's traditional line: 'People should speak properly.'

Not yet grasping the shift in atmosphere, I cried: 'But dialects are so interesting, Dave!'

He snapped, with a tone of finality: 'Nothing interesting about them!'

I realised: nothing had changed. He was the boy, the man whose word over mine in this household was law.

I had no authority here. I called on a higher one: I said, 'Well, it's interesting enough to be studied in universities. It was one of the things I studied.'

He stood. He flung back his chair and stormed from the room.

My stomach dropped. I had put my foot in it, in spite of

all Cathy's warnings. I had done it again, flaunted my superior education.

A silence had fallen. My kids and Greg were looking in wonder from me to my parents. My father was looking down at the table and my mother had a look of distressed horror – both of them, I thought, quite rightly acutely embarrassed by David's behaviour.

My mother spoke, her voice hollow with reproach. 'Oh, Jo, go and apologise to David!'

I stopped breathing. *Say sorry to Daddy. Say sorry to David.* I felt rage.

My children were watching intently, teenage boys watching their mother being told to apologise, to grovel, to a man, for, as far as they would see, simply disagreeing with him.

I couldn't have them taught that sexist lesson. I had to let them see me stand firm.

'No,' I said, though my heart was knocking with not only rage but fear, that old, old fear, and I could hear my voice shaking.

'No,' I repeated. 'I will *not* apologise to David simply for speaking my mind!'

My mother seemed to deflate. Her shoulders dropped, she closed her lips as if shutting up for once and all, and turned away as if accepting a fate she had tried to avoid.

And on the face of my father, who was still looking at the table, was that private half-smirk once again, as if something had been proved to his satisfaction.

'Well, David's got rid of us good and proper now,' said Cathy, as the waiter, discomfited by her tears, cleared away her uneaten lasagne. 'He's got all the cake to himself now, for sure.'

'Yes, *all* the cake! Well, that's what Dad tried to give him! It's worse for Mum! Why would he do that, try to leave the house to David, over her head?' The house that was bought with her money, that she'd worked so hard on, getting down on her hands and knees to polish its floors and weed its vast garden (as my father squandered his money and the business started to struggle, domestic help was no longer an expense our mother would brook – though in any case the cleaner and gardener they'd started off with had been unable to work to her standards).

I answered myself: 'It's precisely because she's always pandered to them both. She's taught them to treat her like a doormat. After all she used to say about Nanny and Grampa and Gwilym!'

And that was how I explained it to myself before, preferring not to dwell on it, I put it out of my mind altogether.

⁂

Twelve years later, stalled on my novel, I pondered it again.

I asked my mother on the phone: 'Why *did* Dad do that, try to leave the whole house to David when it was of course half yours?'

There was a pause. I could sense reluctance battling with her desire to help me.

She said: 'He was punishing me, Jo.'

'*Punishing* you?'

I thought she must mean the fortune in Australia she'd prevented him from claiming before it disappeared.

And then she told me something she'd never told me before.

PART FOUR

In which I get a revelation

A SECRET REVEALED

S HE BEGAN: 'WELL, you know he was always so jealous.'

'Yes, *unreasonably* jealous.'

'Well, that's it. So that time I went to Shropshire to tell him I couldn't marry him, I didn't tell him why.'

She paused.

'Do you remember that when I was engaged to your father, the minister at the chapel, Peter Baron, was in love with me? It was ridiculous, he knew very well I was engaged – he was even calling the banns! – but each Sunday he kept asking to walk me home after chapel. I always said no, but then he'd say he was walking to the beach anyway, and he'd walk down with me. I did actually really like him, as a person. We used to have these discussions while we were walking – arguments, really, about religion, but good-natured. Really deep discussions. Of course, I could never talk about religion to your father. He would just get nasty and end up being insulting: *You bloody tight-arsed Methodists*, and so on.

'Well of course I didn't mention Peter Baron to your father. He was already still so jealous of Arnold Hitchins, though that was all in the past. He had no reason to be jealous now – I wasn't in the least sexually attracted to Peter Baron – but I knew he would be jealous, and there didn't seem to be any point in making him.

'Well, one Sunday night a fortnight before the wedding,

Peter Baron had walked me home and we'd had a really good discussion. And it occurred to me that if only I *had* been attracted to Peter Baron, I could have a life of intellectual stimulation, I could have had an intellectual marriage. And it made me realise I would never have that with your father.

'And that was when I thought I just couldn't marry your father after all.'

'So why did you?'

'He was so upset when I told him. I've told you, I'd never seen a man cry like that before. And it upset me so much seeing him like that, that I knew I did really love him.

'And of course I didn't say anything of *why* I'd had doubts because I knew that he'd have been even more upset, I didn't mention Peter Baron.'

'But he knew in the end that Peter Baron was in love with you? We knew . . . you've always mentioned it . . .'

And then she told me how he found out.

She was proved right not to have told him. One week after their wedding, they went to the dance at the airbase in Shropshire where she danced with a pilot officer. She told me now: as she and our father walked home in the dark afterwards, he was strangely silent and walked apart from her. She asked him what was wrong. He stopped and spat at her out of the dark: 'You bloody tart!'

She was staggered.

He went on: 'Dancing with that bloody supercilious toff!' (The kind who had run him down on the road.) 'Showing off your bloody fanny like that!' She'd been wearing the blue woollen dress, she said, the one she would always describe to us girls, that she bought to get married in before she was lent the wedding dress, demure with a Peter-Pan collar, although the flared skirt, she said now, swung out when she twirled in the dance.

'Smearing yourself over that bastard like that!'

She protested: 'It was only dancing! You know I love dancing!'

'Yes I do! All those men you smeared yourself over! Your parents knew it, didn't they, what you were up to! That's why they wouldn't let you stay on at school: they knew next thing you'd be getting yourself knocked up!'

And then his hand came out of the dark, knocking her off her feet, and the knuckles of the hedge stabbed her in the back. And he was gone.

It was such a shock to her, she said. He could be nasty in arguments, but it had never been so personal. And he'd never shown signs of being like this . . .

I thought of all the times we'd listened to her expurgated version of this story and laughed at our father's jealousy – simply proof of his deep love for her, we'd thought. I thought of how she'd always stressed the demureness of the dress he'd seen as the dress of a tart . . .

He wouldn't speak to her for days, she said (and all the time there Miss Protheroe would be, watching and taking note and seeing the possibility of driving a wedge).

After that, as we knew, every man she ever had anything to do with was under suspicion – or, rather, *she* was under suspicion.

So of course, as time went on, although it ought to have sunk into harmless history, she knew it was best not to tell him about the minister Peter Baron.

There was an aunt who lived in the centre of Llanfair

beside the Rectory, a sister of her father's, of Grampa's. I remembered her: Aunty Ellen. I remembered squinting at her through the curtains of sun coming down through the elms around the yard of her cottage, a big woman, or so she seemed to me then, with floppy cheeks and pendulous bosom. She was particularly fond of Cathy, my mother said, as she'd helped at Cathy's home birth, so while Cathy was still a baby she would take her on Tuesday afternoons when my mother went on the bus into town and I was left down at Nanny and Grampa's. Later, at the end of his round, our father would collect Cathy from Ellen's before joining us all down at Nanny and Grampa's for tea.

Now, Aunty Ellen was also especially fond of our father: another old lady charmed and besotted. On those Tuesdays he'd often finish early, and the two of them would sit talking for an hour or so in her big cave-like kitchen or out in the yard under the elms. One afternoon when Cathy was just one year old, Aunty Ellen started talking about the long-departed Methodist minister Peter Baron. She said she'd never forget him: he'd come and chat to her, she said, sit for hours in the chair where our father was sitting, and go on and on about how *he missed every hair on Gwen's head*. How much he had loved our mother, and how terrible it had been for him having to marry her to our father.

For two whole years after that our father wouldn't even sleep with our mother, she said, but slept in his den downstairs.

He simply wouldn't believe that she hadn't been unfaithful to him with Peter Baron, taking the fact that she hadn't told him herself as proof of her guilt.

At this point in her telling, something flashed into my mind, something I'd forgotten, maybe repressed: running, more than once, with the pushchair beside my mother from the house on the council estate, running to Nanny and Grampa's, through a short cut, a gap in the fence up an embankment; one time my mother slipping in mud, the pushchair sliding backwards, wheels spinning, and my mother fallen in the mud and weeping . . .

So things had been going wrong before we even left south Wales . . .

My mother said, 'He was punishing me. But also he was disgusted: he really did think I was a tart.'

'But that's just ridiculous!' My prim and proper, conformist mother!

My mother paused. Then: 'Well, it was because when we started courting I had sex with him.'

I almost fell off the kitchen stool where I was sitting with the phone. My prim and proper mother, my religious Sunday-School-teacher mother, having sex, at the age of fifteen – in 1939! I had always assumed that mine was the generation of sexual freedom! Not that I'd had much sexual freedom myself; indeed, the sexual attitudes we'd had drummed into us made me pretty much repressed, had in fact for a while made me scared of sex. Had put me entirely off the scent about *this*.

My mother said, 'So he thought I was loose. He thought I'd have sex with anyone. And he couldn't have been more wrong.'

Once our father moved on with his unit, she said, she quickly began to feel ashamed. Because, of course, according to conventional attitudes, sex outside marriage was wrong. It was against her religion, after all. She felt so bad she confided in Nanny. (She felt able to confide in Nanny – in 1939?!) Nanny told her there was no point in feeling guilty (she told her *that*!), what good did it do?

But she went on feeling guilty, and this was the reason, the real reason, she said, that when our father was moved on with his unit, she decided not to keep in touch. She wanted to put it all behind her. She would never do it again, she vowed. And with Arnold Hitchins she was safe from it: the religious Arnold Hitchins believed fervently in the sanctity of marriage.

But because she'd had sex with our father, our father would never afterwards believe that she hadn't then gone on to have sex with Arnold Hitchins. And once he found out about Peter Baron, he wouldn't believe that as he stood at the altar, his bride and the very minister who was marrying them were secretly sharing a physically sexual past, conducted even during the engagement.

And of course he would remember how at the last minute she'd balked at getting married, and would see it in that light . . .

'So you see,' she said, 'he never forgave me.'

I thought about that.

'Put your bloody tits away, woman,' he'd say as she dished the dinner, if her nipples were showing through her jumper. And my guts would shrivel at the nastiness, and at the sense that it was her very femaleness that disgusted him.

And ours. 'Cover your bloody arse,' he would growl, if Cathy or I were wearing a skirt he thought too short, and it was his words, his disgust, rather than any sense of being provocatively dressed, that would make you feel indecently exposed.

I thought of the thing he used to say to us, *The breedin' beats the rearin'*. And understood it at last: the degeneracy he saw in our mother he saw repeated in us.

It was only now, with this revelation of my mother's, that I understood what was behind one of my worst-ever beatings, the night before I was due to start the new school in Thwaite.

'My god,' my mother had said to me only recently, in one of our long phone talks. 'I'll never forget the day you went off to the new school covered in bruises.'

He'd been too beside himself that time to beat me where it wouldn't show.

The previous evening a girl who lived two doors off, a year or so older than me, had invited me, the newcomer, to go for a bike ride, lending me a bike.

'Be back before dark,' my mother had warned as we rode off into the April early-evening: I had the new school next day, and there were no lights on the bike.

The girl set off ahead of me, turning many corners and speeding down winding lanes so that, in this new place, I soon lost my bearings.

We ended up at a sports field.

She threw down her bike and went into a hut where it turned out a boy was waiting for her, and I understood: I'd been used as cover for a liaison.

With no other option – I didn't know the way home, I was on a bike belonging to someone else, and I could hardly break her cover – I hung about outside, embarrassed and fed up, while inside they snogged.

The time went on. The light began to fade. The girl knew I had to be back before dark, but she was showing no sign of coming.

I opened the hut door. 'I need to go.'

'Coming in a minute!' she said, peeling herself from the boy and immediately clamping back to him.

She didn't come.

It was dark by the time we pedalled furiously home, me without lights and in a flat panic.

But I couldn't have guessed the extent of my father's anger. My explanation of what had happened did nothing to save me; in fact it seemed to spur him on to greater rage, and I really couldn't understand why coming back without lights was so great a sin that it couldn't be excused, even when I'd had no option.

I understood now, for the first time. I was not yet then fourteen years old, I had never had anything to do with boys. But my father believed that that night I too had been snogging on the sportsfield, and probably worse. He thought that I too was a tart, and, like my mother, a liar.

Now, for the first time, I understood the real reason behind the dusk curfew when Cathy and I rode our bikes around the villages. One night we didn't make it; it was already dusk as we raced against time into the estate, chests banging, thighs aching, forced however to pull up before we got to the house so as not to alert him with our screechy brakes. Sneaked our bikes as carefully and quietly as we could along the narrow space between his car and the rose bed (scratching his car would bring the worst kind of beating), saw with relief that the adjacent kitchen window was dark, which meant that, with luck, he'd be deep in a phone conversation in the dining room, not noticing the time; stowed our bikes in the garage and quietly opened the back door. Only to be pounced at out of the darkness with a slipper and beaten to within an inch of our senses.

When we went to town on foot he'd follow us, sneaking in the car to see if we were hanging around street corners with boys, and if we were, Cathy later being so popular, woe betide us.

Sometimes, by this time, he would take one look at Cathy and see red. She came back one night, all innocence, from the cinema where she'd been with her gang of friends, perfectly on time, and yet our father, for no apparent reason, went wild. 'What the bloody hell have you been up to?' And he grabbed her and threw her over his knee – her yellowing nylon knickers, her tired greying suspenders, all her burgeoning femininity on show – and beat her so hard that our mother came running and crying for him to stop before he did her permanent damage. We were confounded: we had no idea what it was all about. When our mother told us it was because of the marks on her blazer, the blazer she'd saved up for weeks to buy off the market, we still didn't understand. Up in our bedroom we stared at it, streaked white from the limewash on the wall outside the cinema where everyone leaned while waiting in the cinema queue. It was a while before we worked it out: she had been beaten for a scenario up against a wall that, streetwise though she may have been when it came to lingo and fashion, she was too innocent even to imagine.

I once cried, between blows, with angry irony: 'How come you know so much about immorality?' and he beat me for that, so hard that I thought he might destroy the only weapon I had to fight him, my brains.

But in the end I gave him proof of my sexual immorality: I had an affair.

BANNED

I WAS THIRTY, married to Terry with two small children. It was more than an affair. It was brief, but enough to give the lie to my precipitous and ultimately unhappy marriage to Terry. I ended the affair to save us, but once it was over I knew that our marriage was dead.

I was grieving and alone with my children. I'd cut off my lover, a writer who lived at a distance, but Terry, coming to the same conclusion, that there was no future for our marriage, had gone to Newcastle, to a job he'd applied for without telling me.

I was panicking about the children: they were picking up our unhappiness. Five-year-old Luke, previously confident and gregarious, had become quiet and withdrawn, and eighteen-month-old Timmy wouldn't let me out of his sight and would grab my leg if I started to move away. In spite of all my vows never to do so, I had visited upon my children the uncertainty and fear I'd once known as a child.

I had no one in Manchester to confide in.

I drove across the Pennines with the children to Thwaite House and my mother.

My father and David were mercifully absent.

'But it's over?' my mother asked, meaning the affair, distressed and wanting reassurance. I nodded, but could hardly keep my lips from trembling.

'Well, better not tell your father!' she said with all her old alarm.

I was taken aback. Surely, after his affair with Sandra Suggate, my father couldn't, wouldn't take his old, censorious attitude? My mother was being unrealistically alarmist, I thought, her old ingrained habit.

Nevertheless, when my father came in we both immediately stopped talking. He stood in the doorway sensing it, bulky in his jacket and wide trousers, looking from one to the other of us, like a great bear sniffing the air.

Next day, because we were there, my mother wasn't going to the office. When I came downstairs with the children there was no sign of my father, and I assumed he had already gone. At mid-day my mother was at the sink peeling potatoes for lunch, I was sitting by the Rayburn helping Timmy with his jumbo Lego, and Luke was away in the deep antique-filled spaces of the house plonking on the piano, lost in the world of his own to which he had retreated, when the door to the hall burst open, and my father, freshly dressed for the office, came in.

'Oh hello!' I said. 'I thought you were at work!'

He didn't answer or look at me. He picked up his keys and cigarettes from the table and my mother turned to him in a kind of panic: 'Do you want breakfast, Patrick?'

'Nope!' It was a bark; his face was grim. He brushed past her and was into the scullery, making for the back door.

My mother snapped down the knife and scuttled after him.

I didn't even tumble to it then. (I forgot!) I could see he was angry about something and wondered uneasily if, according to the old ingrained order, he was annoyed at my disrupting the peace of the household by descending with my kids.

Although it was January, such was her panic she had left the outside door open and I could hear the clashing waves of their voices, that old familiar sound, hers high-pitched and pleading, her Welsh sentences rising at the end, his low Irish boom monosyllabic and adamant. I couldn't have seen them even if I'd stood: outhouses separated the yard where they were standing from the section of garden overlooked by the kitchen window. Out there, the light was turning yellow and a single flake of snow unpicked itself from the sky and drifted down. Their voices went on. The notes of Luke's playing sounded through the house as if from very far away. My father's voice rose on an ultimatum, and then the yard door slammed and I heard him get in his car on the drive outside the kitchen window, and he roared off.

My mother came back in, wiping her chapping hands on her pinny. She looked stricken. 'Jo, you'd better go.'

It was only in that moment that I knew.

'You *told* him!'

'Jo, he guessed! He *saw* how upset you were. He's not *that* insensitive, your father!'

For one moment I was foolishly touched. And then I saw sense. I heard my voice come out as a snarl: 'Oh yeah, so sensitive he wants me out of the house with my kids!'

'I'm sorry, Jo!' She was wringing her hands. 'But he's adamant. I've been arguing with him about it all night – that's why he was up so late this morning!'

I snarled: 'Oh right! One rule for him and another for women!'

My mother looked as if she might faint. The affair with Sandra Suggate was something that was never mentioned. She was crumpled against the sink. She looked as if I'd hit her.

I surveyed her, collapsed there in her pinny, her home-made pinny, she had always made her own pinnies, the pinnies with which she'd so often wiped her eyes, as she made everything: the cushions, the bedspreads, the huge heavy velvet curtains, the cutwork tablecloths, the embroidered pictures that adorned the walls, constructing with her needle the sumptuous back-cloth and stage set for my father's big act as an English gentleman and lord of the manor. She looked so young, twenty years younger than her fifty-three, still slim, her perfectly-featured face unlined, no grey in her hair. She looked like my sister, as my teachers thought she was when we first came to Thwaite. It was as though she had become arrested in time, arrested in spite of all her early ambitions in the man-pleasing codes of another age. (And what good had it done her, when her husband had betrayed her with a Plain Jane thirty years her junior?) She wouldn't, couldn't stand up to him for her daughter.

'Right,' I said bitterly. 'I'll go first thing in the morning.'

She panicked. 'Oh – no, Jo! I think you'd better go *now* . . .'

And then I understood: his ultimatum had been for me not to be there when he returned.

I forced one word through my teeth: 'Right!' and scooped up Timmy and took him upstairs to pack.

We ate a miserable lunch, hardly speaking, my already disturbed children gazing wondering and troubled from one to the other of us, wide-eyed as I bundled them in to the car. My mother hovered, pathetic, the wind lifting her pinny, odd flakes of snow swirling around her. I drove out of the gate without waving as had been mine and Terry's habit, and though I could see her in the rear-view mirror standing on the pavement in the darkening afternoon, I didn't, as we were in the habit of doing, put my hand up out of the window to wave before we rounded the bend.

I put my foot down. I didn't think, I just drove, to get over the mountains before the snow settled on the moor, sped with my children through the fracturing sky, my throat as frozen as the road.

We got over it, my mother and I.

In the end, pleading with my father on my behalf, and with me on his (I had vowed, once again, never to go back there again), she brought us both round, and one day in mid-June I took the children for tea.

I was alone with both my parents and my children. My father sat with us for tea, which I thought my mother had probably had to persuade him to do. He was quiet during the meal, but I felt that by acceding he was making amends.

We finished eating and Luke went off to play the piano. My mother got up to go to the pantry in the scullery, and I expected my father, who had always so hated being alone with me, to rise too and go off out to the garage.

He stayed put. My mother didn't come back, but he went on sitting, intently rolling a cigarette. I realised he was preparing to speak to me.

He looked up and fixed me with cold blue eyes. 'I knew what you were up to.' He punched the words at me like posts in a fence. 'You came here one time with Terry, and I saw the hurt in his eyes.'

My stomach twisted for Terry, and for one moment I was stunned by my father's empathy.

And then I thought: he could recognise Terry's hurt, a man's hurt, but he can't recognise or care about mine, his own daughter's. Indeed, he had been giving me a reprimand.

He stood, collecting up his cigarette papers and lighter

with a familiar flipping motion of his hand. He said, censorious: 'And don't you hang around. You don't want to be getting stranded on the tops with those kids in that car.' (My very old car.)

And he left, the man who, six months before, had forced me over those very same tops in that very same car with those children six months younger, on a winter afternoon with the dark coming down and a snowstorm beginning.

I was hurt, and also angry with myself for being hurt.

But my larger emotion was contempt.

I watched in contempt as, three years later, he shook hands with my new partner Greg.

Terry and I had tried to make it work, but I left him in the end. For two years I lived alone with our children in a small Victorian terrace in a different, more urban Manchester suburb, teaching part-time and writing. And then I met Greg, the sociologist consulted by the women's theatre group I was working with, and in the end he moved in with us.

He had been living with us for two months when I picked up the phone to make a request to my mother. Through the window, he was playing with the children in the little back garden. I watched them as I dialled, Greg tall and languid with his soft charcoal beard, orbited by the two boys. As soon as he'd moved in they had relaxed. Their bodies softened, they slept more deeply. We all relaxed: now in the mornings I woke in my sun-filled bedroom, Greg's long limbs beside me, in a hammock of sensual peace. Outside in the garden now, he put his hand on Luke's head as Luke spoke to him earnestly. Four-year-old Tim, coming up to listen in, grabbed hold of Greg's leg and leaned against it with casual luxury.

I wanted my mother to know my new happiness. 'Can I bring Greg to meet you?'

There was a silence. Then, sounding doubtful and unhappy: 'Well, I'll have to ask your father.'

I was taken aback, stung. Surely, after all I'd gone through, the terrible year as things disintegrated between me and Terry, and my time after that struggling as a single parent, my father now understood that in leaving Terry I hadn't acted out of *choice*? That in the end Terry and I just hadn't been happy together. That it hadn't all been my fault?

Surely, I thought (once again), my mother was underestimating my father?

'Mum, why?'

'Well, it's the fact that Greg is still married.'

'Mum, I told you, he and his wife have split up! They're getting a divorce.'

My mother struggled, wretched. 'But they're still technically married. Your father doesn't think it's right that you're living with him.'

I had forgotten: here in this late-twentieth-century city, insulated once more from my father's hypocrisy, happy at last, I had forgotten yet again.

I said in anger and pain: 'Oh yeah, and *he's* such a saint! Not to mention the exception he made for Sandra Suggate with his rules for women and married men!'

I could hear how the reminder hurt my mother. I could hear her pulling herself together. 'Well, I'll try and persuade him, Jo.'

She rang back next day. Yes, Greg could come.

I felt triumph and joy. She had been wrong about my father, I thought, stuck in her old reflex.

Then I noticed her tension. She said: 'I won't lie to you, Jo. Your father took a lot of persuading.'

The following weekend Greg and I and the children turned in through the big wooden gates of Thwaite House, and pulled up on the gravel drive. It was a hot afternoon. The garden basked between its walls. The clipped holly trees stood sentinel on the luxurious lawns. A silence enclosed it all, scratched by small birds.

A trick silence. Something was wrong.

The drive was empty. My father's car wasn't there.

It turned out: Greg could come to Thwaite, my father had decreed, but while he was still technically married, while I was living with a man who was technically married, he refused to meet him (and so, apparently, did David).

The week Greg's divorce came through my father's attitude completed an acrobatic reversal. I watched in deep contempt as, emerging from the garage the next time we visited, he held out his hand to Greg in his old genial manner. A man to whom nothing mattered, it seemed – not the emotional reality, not the way you behaved in private – but the outward appearance and social forms.

David took longer to accept Greg and deign to appear when we came, which gave me a bitter laugh a year or two later, when David fell in love with a married woman at his cycling club and, briefly cheating on Janet, had an affair.

Not that it seemed even bitterly funny in the end. 'One rule for us and another for David,' I said to my mother, and she nodded, looking miserable.

AN EXPLANATION

THE WHOLE THING now took my breath away.

For my mother's imagined, indeed highly unlikely, sexual betrayal with a Methodist minister, it seemed that my father had harboured a lifetime's resentment, saved it up to mete out to her a spectacular final punishment, a punishment which Cathy and I, females in her imagined corrupt image, had also come in for.

I voiced my astonishment to my mother.

'Well, it wasn't just Peter Baron. I told you, he thought I'd have sex with anyone. The thing is . . .'

She stopped, and I waited.

'I told you, after Aunty Ellen told him about Peter Baron, he wouldn't sleep with me for two whole years. Except for one night. And that one night I got pregnant with David. And he couldn't believe it could happen. He said, "No bitch gets pregnant that easily." So he thought that while he hadn't been sleeping with me I'd been sleeping around, and that David couldn't be his child. For years he wouldn't believe David was his own.

'Jo?'

I had been silent with revelation. So *that* was why, when David was little, he seemed hardly to acknowledge his existence . . .

'But of course,' my mother said, 'when David got to be about eleven he started to look so like him there was no denying he was his own.'

Which was when he began to show an interest, to shower him with goods and attention . . .

It explained so much. There was more than just a child's bilious constitution fuelling our mother's especial anxiety and indulgence towards David when he was little. David was the child our father wouldn't even own, the focal point of the pain at the heart of her marriage. It explained our parents' joint focus on him later on, the emotional competition when our father claimed him, the boy who up until then had been solely, symbiotically attached to her.

I thought of the conflicts my mother must have experienced over David. Her relief at the change in our father's attitude; her desperation not to spoil the new relationship, the extra reason it gave her for indulging them both. Her consequent bitter helplessness whenever they teamed up against her . . .

Another thought came to me. 'But surely, Mum, it proved your innocence . . . !'

She gave an ironic laugh. 'Oh no. He believed David was his, he came to believe that that could have happened. But he still thought I'd been sleeping around. He never forgave me.'

And, I guessed, he never forgave us girls for being in her image.

※

I understood it all, now, I thought. I had the means to write the novel. I went back to my desk and the abandoned pages and removed the dried apple core sitting on top. I picked up my pen and wrote the crucial scene that seemed to explain it all:

Patrick can hardly hold himself together as he rises from his chair in Aunt Ellen's yard. The breeze moves the beams of sun and blinds him. He picks up the tottering Cathy. He puts her in the car. She looks back at him with her doll-like features. He turns away from her.

He noses the car down the short lane, through strips of sunlight and shadow. He comes out from under the trees and the village lies ahead of him, lime-washed cottages glowing in the sun, like a drawing in a fairytale book that promises a happy ending as flimsy as the paper it's printed on.

He stops the car and gets out, shuts the door on Cathy's round watching face, and leans on the bonnet.

When he raises his head he's no longer in the village but in a forest of fir trees spindling towards each other high above. The afterlife forest. And the car he's leaning on is the god-forsaken ghost of the broken-down Escort, its spectral but all-too-humanly-ugly owner leaning towards him on the other side.

All his life Patrick practised astral travel, and here he is in the afterlife dependent on mechanical transport and stranded. He looks up at the ugly bastard he's conked out with. 'You'd think that up here there'd be better ways than this of moving on.'

The guy comes round the bonnet. 'Oh, there are,' he says, and slaps Patrick hard on his back, and, unprepared, Patrick loses his balance, and he's falling, falling once more, down to the glittering kitchen where the body he's left behind lies on his deathbed, where his daughter Jo is dropping off beside it on the floor, on a crash-collision course towards her blond downturned head.

Which is where I ended my novel's first section.

PART FIVE

In which the book is judged by others

REACTION

EVERYONE I SHOWED the finished novel loved that first section. My mother loved it; it seemed that Cathy liked it.

They weren't so keen, however, on what I followed it with: Patrick, crashed from the afterlife into his daughter's consciousness and viewpoint, forced to face the reality for others as his suspiciousness and revenge played out through their lives.

Put bluntly, they liked my colourful roguish father and his viewpoint better than me and mine.

They especially liked the bedraggled man he met in heaven.

'Who is he meant to be, though?' my mother asked. 'What does he stand for?'

'His conscience,' I told her, although I was feeling a little uncertain that it was clear – a famous novelist who'd looked at the manuscript had taken him as a spirit guide and suggested that I'd have to ditch him unless I gave all the other characters spirit guides to match.

I told my mother: 'He's there to trip him up and force him to look at what he did in life to others.'

'Oh . . .' she said, sounding wondering and dubious.

Cathy said to me, 'You should make it all funny.' She lent me *Angela's Ashes* to show me how, the chirpy autobiographical account of resilience in the face of a poverty-stricken Irish childhood, featuring a feckless father and in which, in spite of all the deprivations and the father's absence, the protagonist is never in any doubt that his father loves him.

It was true that in much of the following sections of my novel, I the character, as I in real life, hadn't always been too chirpy or resilient. I'd recounted, for instance, how, sixteen years old, I lay beaten by my father in the house on the housing estate, my rebellious self, the clever sensible self I was in school, vaporised. How I tossed on the coverlet, unable to still my hopeless, worthless mind and body; I stood at the window feeling mocked by the neat patchwork gardens, then threw myself from the sight. How I'd pace, and then, too weak with despair to pace, throw myself on the bed again. I recounted how, long after I'd left, that lack of belief in myself would every so often grip me: long into adulthood I'd walk into a crowded room and suffer the acute anxiety of a child. How I battled with depression. For all my sense of relief in the university town I escaped to, despair could pounce, unexpected, from its stone walls; for all the moments of euphoria as I plunged on the bus between the tenements, escaped to Scotland with Terry, there were times when we walked in the hills and Glasgow lay below us, an alien city, and I was breathless with the effort of believing I was happy. From the big bay window of our little town house in Glasgow you could see the tumbled stones of Offa's wall, silhouetted in the evening against the sky. They made me think of nothing so much as fists, and the bare branches of the trees above them arms thrown up in despair. I related how I pushed Luke through the endless no-man's land of the Manchester suburb, where fallen cherry blossom gathered like scum and the poplars made a sound like the rattling of bones.

And quite frankly, as I wrote it, I felt it all over again.

There were days when I could hardly face it. I would pick up my pen and a sleepiness would overcome me, a desire for oblivion. And what reader wants to be dragged through all that? Who wants to have to share the psyche of a depressed rather than a chirpy and resilient protagonist, without the happy ending of at least a chirpy, narrative voice? As Cathy seemed to be implying: gross.

THE STANFORDS

I SAID TO Cathy, 'There's comic relief, though, isn't there, in the Stanfords?'

The Stanfords, Terry's family. My comic relief even at the time.

Although, actually, it was the Stanfords who found *me* funny, at least in the beginning.

I first met them when Terry and I called back at his house to pick up some records for Methodist Youth Club. The whole of the rest of the family was in the kitchen, gathered around the table where Terry's fifteen-year-old sister Brenda was icing cup cakes. The moment I stepped into the room a grubby little terrier made a sortie at me, then stopped short and howled as if at an apparition from the jaws of hell. My specs had steamed up, but when I'd wiped them I could see they were all grinning with hilarity, fuzzy-haired Brenda and Terry's barrel-shaped mother showing their little teeth and his eleven-year-old brother Paul and his uniform-clad fire-officer father grinning wide melon-mouthed grins.

There were no introductions. This was a house, unlike my own, where men and boys took an interest in baking, and where they didn't bother with formal introductions. Mrs Stanford's first words to me were, 'D'you want a go, m'duck?' and without waiting for my answer told Brenda to hand me the icing gun.

I didn't want to, but I didn't like to say no. Looking around for the sink I said, 'I'd better wash my hands,' and they all grinned wider, exchanging glances about the prim and proper new girlfriend of Terry's off the posh new estate, daughter of the well-known Patrick Jackson, Mason and Country Club member, known for splashing his money about.

'Ee, you've got to eat a peck of dirt afore you die!' Mrs Stanford laughed. 'Gerron in there! Pass her the gun, Paul!'

Paul, who seemed unable to take his eyes off me, reached for the icing gun, still staring, and knocked a spoon on the floor. 'Y'soft bogger!' Mrs Stanford laughed at him, and they all looked wickedly for my response, the girl they imagined to be too posh for swearing.

They liked to goad me.

'Does *your* mam use this kinda salad cream?' Mrs Stanford would ask when I went for tea, holding up a new brand, and Brenda and Paul watched with delighted faces as I had to say no, she didn't. 'Ee, eat your snap up, lass!' Mr Stanford would command me with his military air, as Brenda and Paul grinned at my hardly touched plate. I found it hard to eat there, with the dog rooting under the table for dropped bits and farting, and Mr Stanford snorting up his nose, bent slightly sideways from a fall from a fire service ladder. All of them, apart from Terry, chewed with their mouths open, Mr Stanford's false teeth leaving his palette and clonking around his mouth. He had a habit, shocking to me, of unconsciously scratching his crotch. And nothing in the Stanford household was very clean. Really, I had to admit to myself, rebellious as I was about my mother's obsessive housework and my father's snobbish insistence on manners, they had inculcated me well.

And the fact was, I was afraid of Mr Stanford. During the war he'd been in the navy, and he still had that commanding air. 'Get them pots done,' he would tell me and Brenda and Terry in a barking voice as soon as we'd finished eating, and I'd feel somehow reprimanded, and miserable. ('Does your mam use this kinda washing-up liquid?' Mrs Stanford would ask, tauntingly.) And the nervousness he induced in me was a further source of amusement for the family.

Still, I liked the antidote of the Stanfords. I liked their down-to-earth, no-nonsense approach, their simplicity: what you saw with the Stanfords was what you got. And bossy and interfering as they were – they would never let me and Terry alone; I was customarily hauled off to put Brenda's hair in curlers while Terry would be commandeered to help his dad with something – at least they were interested in their kids. They'd led ordinary lives with ordinary expectations, as part of a huge extended Derbyshire family, and there was clearly nothing troubling or mysterious in their pasts to distract them from making their kids their focus.

Though there was something all too familiar in the way they laughed at me. *You take things too seriously*, my mother would say if I failed to join in the laughter at one of her stories – the pork landing on the cat in north Wales, say, or Mrs McGowan in the terrace next door saying *Nowt s' queer as folks* – because for me it conjured the misery of those times. And here I was again at the Stanfords', the po-faced Aunt Sally.

Still, at the start, I didn't mind too much. Terry, after all, was my saviour – the handsome student with the crown of soft brown curls I'd first set eyes on in chapel, striding down the aisle of the gallery in his fashionable mustard waistcoat – and I could suffer a few discomforts from his family for that.

'Well, yes,' said Cathy now. She'd always seen them as comic characters; Fireman Fred was her satirical name for Mr Stanford. 'But they're not relevant. You could leave them out.'

'Yes,' my mother agreed, 'the book's not about the Stanfords, it's about you and you father.'

Well, my family had always preferred not to see the Stanfords as relevant to that.

There was no love lost between my family and the Stanfords.

As I soon became dimly aware, it was as a representative of my family that the Stanfords were amused by me. What was really going on was Class War. Proudly working-class Methodists, their hackles were instantly raised by my father's reputation as a middle-class big spender and, when they met my parents, the middle-class graciousness of my mother's social manner. Their initial weapon of necessity was amused contempt, though it quickly mutated into something colder. They sat in our front room on the housing estate, among the tasteful antiques and my mother's jewel-coloured embroidered cushions, while my mother fussed around them with cups of tea and cake, and they were stiff with discomfort and resentment and stony inverted snobbery, giving monosyllabic answers to my mother's questions. Mrs Stanford, my mother's best china balanced on her big knees, practically had her snub nose in the air.

And as for my father: he didn't even bother with his usual social manner; he hardly spoke. He detested them on sight.

When the Stanfords discovered some of the truth about my father, it all became more bitterly personal. It was very soon clear to them that, in spite of my father's reputation as a spender, I was not exactly a well-off student. Nothing was said; the Stanfords, I soon discovered, never discussed things: the more emotionally pressing a matter, the more it drove them into silence. But they would pointedly present me with gifts of cheap vests off the market or seconds from retail clothes outlets. Only slowly did I realise what was going on. I'd feel a vague discomfort, an inkling that they were making some kind of statement, and a growing sense of building up some kind of debt I didn't want.

And then they discovered that my father hit me.

I had told Terry that my father had hit me, but I didn't know what it meant to him. I didn't know what it meant to *me*, since the moment I'd started bringing a boyfriend to the house, he'd stopped. It seemed he'd stopped altogether. Terry and I were lying on the grass in the first weeks when we started going out together, our bikes flung down beside us. Terry replied that his parents had hit him too (though he hadn't been hit once he reached his teens), and all of a sudden it seemed nothing special, just the way that kids were brought up in those days. Terry told me that, like me, he'd sucked his thumb until he was twelve, and his mother had painted it with mustard, and I thought that really Victorian and cruel, far worse than the glove remedy my mother had employed. My parents, my childhood, didn't seem so bad after all. So the Stanfords were good in two ways: in some ways they were better than my parents, and in others they showed my parents as better than them.

Then one day in Terry's presence my father gave me one of his all-time priceless beatings.

I was in my first year at university, nearly nineteen years old. It was the Easter vacation. Terry's parents had now moved away from the town for his father's job, so Terry was staying in the spare room my father had created by converting the attic for us girls to sleep in. Afterwards I would have no idea what caused the row between me and my father, some trivial disagreement to begin with, but all of a sudden that deep something I could never fathom had flared up between us, my father bawling, puffed with fury, and I arguing back, angrier than ever that he should yell at me like that, *now*, when I considered myself adult and had a life elsewhere – and in front of Terry!

My father lost control. He grabbed up his slipper. I never expected it – I thought he'd stopped hitting me – I was off my guard, so he got me straight down in the corner of the tiny dining room with no time to cover my head.

At last he stopped.

He threw down the slipper and went off out to the garage.

Silence fell. Cathy had disappeared upstairs to avoid the flak. I've no idea where David was: outside playing, or watching, learning his lesson in how to control his lippy big sister. My mother stood wringing her pinny in the kitchen doorway, her face warped with dismay and panic. And Terry: Terry was frozen where he'd been standing seeing it all, his brown eyes burning with shock and horror.

I saw it through his horrified eyes: the violence, the sheer rage, the raw emotion.

Damage flooded with the silence into the room

Terry moved to the table and in silence, and all without asking, which was unheard of, picked up the phone.

My mother's eyes swivelled in panic. He was ringing his parents.

Shortly, his voice trembling, he told his mother that my father had beaten me, and asked if he could take me there straight away.

My mother looked as if she might collapse.

We came down with our packed bags and she was slumped at the sink (another time I had her slumped at the sink).

'Don't go,' she begged.

I said, 'We're going.' Terry said nothing, looking away at the floor.

'Jo, please – for my sake!'

I hardened. *For her sake.* I wouldn't do it any longer, demean myself *for her sake.* For the sake of her insistence on fake harmony, her inability to face up to the reality.

'We're going,' I repeated, and stepped away out of the back door.

The garage door was closed, a blank square.

As the bus made its way to the Stanfords' through the Yorkshire villages, Terry kept his arm around me. Cradled in his arm, and in his horrified, scandalised viewpoint, my ear throbbing where the slipper had caught it, I began to acknowledge how deeply upset I was, how deeply, existentially upset I had always been at these times, but for the sake of sanity and survival had suppressed. And it was such a luxury to acknowledge it, such a luxury to be rescued.

Terry, my rescuer, Terry my saviour.

The trouble was, the Stanfords saw themselves as my saviours too.

As the bus drew up to the stop in their village, Mrs Stanford was waiting there, a dumpy one-woman rescue party in sheepskin coat, self-important piety stamped in her posture. She swept my arm up in her sheepskin one and marched me off, leaving Terry trailing behind with the bags, her upturned nose pushed up even further in disgust at my parents.

It seemed a luxury to be made to sit by the fire and

wrapped in a blanket – while Brenda and Paul stared, for once not grinning – to be given milky coffee with a dash of brandy (a tip from *Woman's Realm*), and to fall asleep, washed out and exhausted. Such a relief to be made to feel, for the first time ever after a beating, entirely blameless and wronged.

But when I woke up to find the whole Stanford family tiptoeing around me, I was filled with the sense that I had woken up into a trap.

At the end of that week, when Terry went back to his university, I went back to my parents' for the two days left of my own vacation. My father kept out of my way, and my mother asked me anxiously: 'What did the Stanfords say?'

I could answer truthfully: 'Nothing.' They'd tiptoed around me, they'd coddled me, but nothing was said about what had happened.

But, having rescued me from my parents, the Stanfords, it had turned out, expected in return a loyalty I couldn't pay: they expected me to transfer wholesale my daughterly loyalties to them. During that week, whenever I mentioned my parents in the normal way (after all, I was pretty accustomed to getting over beatings), they were scandalised, silently offended. When Terry had gone, they expected me to stay, and were silently huffy when I didn't.

It felt like bullying. Mr Stanford, it was clear now, was a bully, just a different kind of bully from my father who at least ignored you if possible.

I no longer wanted to stay at the Stanfords'; I dreaded the thought of staying there in the long summer vacation.

And once I was back at university that term, back in my freer, more confident persona, the row with my father at Easter faded in significance – which, when I *did* think about it, made the significance the Stanfords gave it even more oppressive. We'd get summer holiday jobs in Thwaite, I decided, and stay the whole time with my parents.

I was unprepared therefore for what my mother said to me the day I got home.

'Jo, I think it's best if Terry doesn't stay here this holiday.'

'What? Why?!' She *knew* that Terry and I, at separate universities all term, were desperate to be together in the holidays! And she *knew* that I didn't much like being at the Stanfords'. She knew very well Mr Stanford was a bully – the way he'd bossed Cathy and David the few times they'd visited, forcing them to play cards when they clearly didn't want to. She disliked the Stanfords herself! And Terry and I had both got summer jobs lined up at the paper mill in town . . .

'I can't have Terry witnessing scenes like the one at Easter. And if you and your father are together for any length of time, it's going to happen.'

'Mum, I won't let it happen! I won't argue with Dad!'

'No, Jo, I can't risk it.' She was adamant.

And that was that.

I suspected it was an instruction of my father's, and my mother was covering for him.

And so I had to go to the Stanfords' for the summer, to be treated like their own child, to sleep with Brenda in her girly pink bedroom, to have to accept Mr Stanford taking me to the city for a summer job interview and, to my shock, coming into the interview and sitting beside me in his uniform bristling with sharp buttons, and speaking for me. (I was amazed I got the job, since I hardly got a word in edgeways.) To hardly see Terry in the evenings or at weekends, commandeered as we were into separate male and female domestic worlds. To be dragged around some weekends to visit the Derbyshire relatives, aunties in wrinkled stockings and Crimplene dresses who would stare at me curiously and with horribly knowing grins. And to have the Stanfords stiff with offence the week-ends we went, to my relief, to my parents': my mother had relented on the occasional weekend – less time for a row to brew between me and my father, and a lot of the weekend we'd be out with Terry's old youth club friends. As we came down with our bags on those Friday evenings, Mrs Stanford would be standing at the window with her back turned like an offended cat.

I just kept thinking: one day it would all be over, we'd have finished our studies and would no longer be reliant on our parents, we'd get away to a life of our own.

The following year, we got summer jobs far away from Yorkshire and just about managed to pay for digs.

In the autumn term of my final year we decided to get married. Really all we wanted was to be together, but if we didn't get married there was bound to be trouble with both my moralistic father and the Stanfords who policed our sleeping arrangements with tacit determination.

I came home at Christmas and told my parents. We were sitting in the little dining room, my mother opposite, sewing beside the electric fire, my father at the table with his back to me.

My father didn't react. He didn't speak; he stayed turned away inside his curling miasma of smoke. Then, his back still towards me, he said coldly: 'Well, you can get married in a bloody registry office, then.'

My mother said quickly, in panicky amelioration: 'Well,

your dad's got a lot of expense at the moment, with this business he's starting . . .'

I was stung, of course. But I felt triumphant to be able to answer: 'Well, that's exactly what we want! We don't want any fuss, we just want to be married!'

His big round shoulders went into lines of surprise. Silence filled the room again, and I thought the subject was being dropped, and though I was hurt I was busy telling myself I didn't care, it was nothing to do with them anyway, it was private business between me and Terry.

My father turned to me, and said in a mild, even friendly tone: 'Well, I'll buy you a second-hand car.'

I thought: My daddy loves me really! My daddy even understands me!

It would be years before it would occur to me that really it was Terry he was offering the car, since he saw cars as men's domain, to ingratiate himself with the future university-lecturer son-in-law who'd witnessed him beating me.

Two days later I joined Terry at the Stanfords'. To my surprise he hadn't told them. I assumed he'd been waiting so we could tell them together, which after tea that first evening we did.

Terry waited while Mr Stanford battled with his newspaper, flipping it repeatedly like an animal that needed beating into line.

Terry swallowed, and blurted it out: 'We've decided to get married.'

The Stanfords, as I'd expected, reacted with irritating smugness: in their Methodist world it was of course the only right and proper thing for us to do.

I added with pride, 'And my dad's buying us a car, because

we're getting married in a register office!' See, I was implying, my dad does love me, in spite of what you've been thinking!

There was a long silence. Mrs Stanford blew out her cheeks, leaned on her big spread knees and got up and stood at the window with her back to us.

At last Mr Stanford, in the chair with his newspaper, gave a rattling sniff up his occluded nostril. He opened his mouth, his upper false teeth disengaged from his palette and clacked back, and he said: 'I shoulda thought that anyone who wanted to do right by their daughter would gi'e her a proper wedding.'

'Oh no!' I said hotly at this slight to my father (who, it turned out, loved me really): 'Terry and I *want* to get married in a register office! Don't we?' I turned to him.

He didn't answer. I could see that he couldn't. His face was a picture of torture. And I knew then why he hadn't told them. He knew how they'd react about a register office, and he hadn't dared.

Mrs Stanford turned round in disgust and moved off across the room, barrel-stiff, and went to the kitchen to do the dishes, with the implication that things had come to such a pretty pass that there was nothing to do but carry on. I followed, to help as expected, and she handed me the teacloth with wordless disapproval. For the next ten minutes she passed me the washed dishes in silence.

We went back into the lounge where Terry and his dad were sitting, equally wordless, Mr Stanford reading the paper again and scratching his crotch. I thought the whole thing had been swept under the carpet in disgust.

Mr Stanford lifted his head as I entered. 'And it's not just a daughter. I wouldn't like to think of my son not having a proper wedding.'

I prompted Terry with my eyes to say he didn't want one.

He looked at the floor, stricken.

Mr Stanford went on: 'Yer weddin's the most important day of yer life. I wouldn't like to think of a son of mine not having that to look back on, like I have.'

A look of smug nostalgia crossed Mrs Stanford's face before she resumed her offended expression.

They were being so hostile. Hostile to *me*. I felt confused, and then I tumbled to it: they couldn't believe that Terry didn't want a traditional wedding, and they thought I was bullying him.

But Terry wouldn't, couldn't stand up against them for what we wanted. It would be years, we'd be well and truly married, before I began to wonder if maybe he *had* wanted what his parents wanted, a traditional wedding. That he didn't really *want* to stand up to their interference in the years that followed, and that the fact that I tried to make him made me the bully, the selfish bully his parents thought me, true daughter of my father.

Mr Stanford straightened his paper, shook his leg to rearrange his discomposed crotch, snorted up his knocked-sideways nose, and said decisively: 'Well, if yer dad's not going to pay for a proper wedding, I will.'

I stared. They would buck one of their preciously preserved Methodist traditions – the parents of the bride footing the bill – and pay for the wedding! But then again, I thought, because they had rescued me, they thought they owned me . . .

And that of course, was the last thing I wanted: to owe them anything more, let alone a thing they found so significant. As soon as Terry and I were alone together (we had to go out; it wasn't considered proper for us to be in each other's bedrooms), I said urgently, 'But we don't *want* a church wedding!'

He said, 'Well, if they're prepared to pay for it . . . And we did say it doesn't really matter to us either way . . . And it matters so much to them . . .'

That of course was the moment I should have asked myself: do I want to spend the rest of my life with a man incapable of standing up to his parents, even when it came to choosing their desires over mine? But I was blind, I was desperate; Terry was my designated saviour after all. So I decided he was right, everything beside our getting away together was irrelevant. The Stanfords, as my mother and Cathy would say as they discussed my novel all those years later, were irrelevant.

The last thing I wanted was having the Stanfords boss me around about the actual wedding, so when I made it clear I'd be getting married from my parents' house and they didn't demur, all I felt was relief. Terry and I booked a church wedding for late August, and I went off to concentrate on my final exams. It wasn't until I'd finished them and could apply my mind to the wedding that I began to wonder about the strange inconsistency: the Stanfords paying for it, yet uncharacteristically wanting no hand in it.

When I got home in June my mother told me that in all that time she hadn't heard from the Stanfords about the wedding.

She said, 'We need to book a reception. We need to know how much they want to spend, how many people they want to invite.'

We were both too embarrassed to ring *them* (the unspoken matter of the Stanfords' disapproval of my parents hung in the air). I rang Terry instead, still at his university in Scotland, and asked him to ask his mother. He sent a long list of the Derbyshire relatives. So it looked as if they were prepared to spend a fair bit . . .

My mother said, 'But I wonder what kind of reception they expect?' I pushed down my resentment – it was *my* wedding, after all . . .

I bit the bullet and rang Mrs Stanford and asked her. There was silence, and then she said, very stiffly: 'I think that's your mam and dad's job to decide,' implying, I thought with a twist of the stomach, that it was the least my parents could do when she and Mr Stanford were paying. I thought I understood at last their reason for standing back: they were forcing my parents to play their traditional role. I put down the phone, miserably wishing I hadn't given the Stanfords this stick with which to beat them.

In the end, my mother booked a room in my father's country club (special rates), and went ahead and ordered the cheapest reception menu. We engaged the cheapest possible photographer.

It came to a time in July when the deposit needed to be paid for the reception, and we still hadn't heard from the Stanfords. My mother said worriedly, 'You know, your father says he can't lay out the deposit, all his spare money's tied up in the business he's starting . . .'

My father ended up paying out the deposit. I was cringing. My daddy loved me really, but this could put him off me altogether.

By the time Terry arrived in July directly from Scotland, both my mother and I had come to realise with horror that maybe the Stanfords weren't paying after all.

As soon as he got there, I took him urgently out of the house for a walk. 'Do you think they're *not* paying?'

Horrified realisation melted his face.

Yet Mr Stanford had said with such self-righteous firmness that he would . . .

'Terry, you'd better clear it up with him!'

The pool of horror that was his face shimmered with sheer fright.

We were passing a phone box. 'Do it now, Terry. Ask him! Remind him he said he would!' I opened the phone-box door.

He stood with his arms hanging, his specs flashing and molten in the evening sun, his hair lifting like felt in the breeze. I had to push him in (another notch in the record of my bullying him). He looked at me as if asking to be let out again.

I picked up the receiver and insisted he press the keys.

The whole thing crucified him (and me). No, his father wasn't paying. Terry listened, his brow corrugated in agony, as Mr Stanford expressed his surprise and disgust, and finally his derision that we'd taken his statement that he'd pay for the wedding if my dad didn't as anything but a sarcastic comment on the outrageousness of my big-spender father even considering not doing so.

I broke the news to my parents. It nearly crucified me.

They sat in shocked but all-too-believing silence.

I said, 'Well, we can cancel it!' and had a surge of relief.

My father glared. 'We'll do no such bloody thing. I'm not having a fool made of me in this town.' (By now he'd invited a couple of Con-Club friends.)

He stood up. 'Well, you'll be doing without your bloody

car, then,' and went off out to the garage.

The morning of the wedding my father and I stood alone together in the house on the housing estate, waiting for one of his workmen to come in his car to take us to the church.

My father paced between the kitchen and the little dining room, his crinkled hair combed in distinguished sweeps above his ears. He was suddenly achingly familiar to me in his thickened frame and tawny skin. I wanted to say I was sorry to have caused him the expense, I wanted to assure him that I didn't want this ridiculous farce either, and more importantly that I hadn't meant to make him prey to the Stanfords' bullying and censure. I wanted to speak about the gift of the car, to say that I'd have given anything not to have thrown it back in his face, that I understood what it meant: that, in spite of everything, he loved me.

I wanted to tell him that I loved him, too.

My chest was hammering under the frilled and tucked wedding dress my mother had made me. He had stopped in his pacing and I took a step towards him.

He sidestepped. 'Where's that bugger O'Riley?' And went off to the front room to look out for him.

And then there we were riding to the church, with my father and O'Riley in his Fair Isle pullover discussing the bloody big bugger of a fan down at Ferrybridge. And then there were my father and I making our way down the aisle, and uppermost in my mind was the unfamiliarity of putting my arm through his, and the sight of the huge clan of Stanfords peering round and leering at the man who beat his daughter and had to be pushed into paying for her wedding.

As soon as the vicar pronounced me and Terry man and

wife I burst into tears, great gobbing, sobbing tears, and couldn't stop, and Terry started crying too, and the vicar bustled us in panic into the vestry and the register, skipping the bit about kissing the bride.

Thus I began my marriage, meant to be my escape, a marriage not so much to Terry, it turned out, as to the Stanfords.

They came with us on our 'honeymoon'.

Terry hadn't dared tell me until the wedding was over, by which time it was all arranged: they were driving us up. 'They'll help us look for a flat,' he said: just days before the wedding, the flat he'd taken in Dundee had fallen through. Which meant they would be staying . . . ! He said, in response to my despairing reaction, 'Well, looking for a flat is easier with a car, they can drive us around . . .'

I thought I might explode. They'd stopped my father buying us a car, and now they were using our lack of a car to impose themselves on us in our newly-married situation, and interfere in our lives – exactly what getting married was suppose to let us escape! And Terry hadn't been able to stop them . . .

They drove us up to Scotland (and I was meant to be grateful), and stayed with us in our temporary university flat for the whole first fortnight of our marriage.

'You can call us Mam and Dad now,' Mr Stanford announced to me the first morning at breakfast, introducing the new order, in which he, the head of our family of four, dictated the itinerary for each day: family outings where he and Terry walked together ahead and Mrs Stanford linked arms with me behind; in the evenings family meals, all of us cooking together, the menu dictated by them, followed by card

219

games. ('Get them pots done,' he would tell me and Terry, peremptory, as he got the cards out ready.)

For the whole fortnight they never left us alone.

I couldn't bring myself to call them *Mam* and *Dad*. They were obviously offended, and over the next days became increasingly frosty towards me.

And nothing was done about driving us round to look for a flat.

'Ask him!' I said to Terry as we sat up in bed, the only place we could be alone together. 'Time's getting on and we have to be out of here soon! If they hadn't been here we'd have been looking by now. Wasn't that why they came, to help us, after all?'

Terry looked wretched.

Still nothing happened.

In the end I asked Mrs Stanford myself as she and I were washing up. 'After all, it's why you're here. And time's getting on.'

She stopped with the teacloth in the air, a frozen look of sheer offence on her face.

She said, cold and censorious: 'Yes, Terry did ask his Dad. But he can't be using a fire service car to run you about looking for a flat. He's only got a certain mileage allowance.'

And I understood. They *weren't* here for that: they were here just because they wanted to be, putting their stamp on our marriage, incorporating us and our marriage into themselves. And we were supposed to be glad of it.

She put down the teacloth.

She walked away, and her stiff offended bottom told me what she was thinking: I was a girl in my father's image. I was ungrateful and grasping. And a bully, pressuring Terry to ask his dad for what I wanted.

Terry must have misunderstood about his parents helping us look for a flat, I thought. It would be a long time before it would come to me that, entirely incapable of standing up to them, he had suggested to me that they could help in order simply to appease me, and then hoped that they would.

At the end of the fortnight, when to my utter relief they had gone, I asked Terry: 'Did they give you money for the flat?' Our university grants weren't yet due (I was about to start a teacher training course), and, after the embarrassing expense of the wedding, it had practically killed me to have to ask my father for help with rent in the meantime. When it was announced that the Stanfords were coming with us we'd been forced to book an apartment with a second bedroom, so I took it for granted they'd pay the extra it cost.

Terry looked miserable. 'No, I asked them, but they said they thought your dad should pay.'

Things never changed with the Stanfords. For the whole of our marriage, they would come to stay for a week or a fortnight and take over: rearranging the cupboards, dictating the meal-times and menus, censoriously correcting our usual household habits. And yes, the censoriousness was directed at me.

I was ungrateful after all they had done for me, and I was a bully – not of course that any of it was ever voiced. Increasingly their attitude was one of keeping me in line.

'You've got to go where the work is!' Mrs Stanford told me sternly when I expressed my anxiety about Terry's applying for a job elsewhere, the start of which would coincide with the birth of Luke. They were staying with us in Scotland again, a three-week takeover of our household, and I was dreading them announcing they were coming again for the birth. To my great surprise they didn't. Forcing my mother into her traditional role, I would afterwards think. Later still it would strike me that they saw it as a matter of the Jacksons versus their son's career, and were actively encouraging Terry to apply for the job regardless. 'Why can't you ask your mother to come?' Terry asked me when they had gone. He said it tetchily, which surprised and upset me – he knew why! – but years would go by before I realised he was likely echoing his parents.

I tried to put my foot down whenever it was announced – or, rather, Terry sheepishly admitted – that they were coming to take over our house removals or our decorating, but rarely succeeded. Each time, Terry wouldn't dare tell me beforehand until it was too late for me to protest: Mr Stanford had already got time off work, the self-hire van was already booked, or the tins of paint bought.

'But I love that tree!' I cried out in protest, looking out to see Mr Stanford cutting down the willow at the bottom of our Manchester garden, a plan I'd been kept in ignorance of. 'Dad knows best!' Mrs Stanford told me firmly, as if I were a recalcitrant child.

To my surprise and relief they didn't interfere much with our children. They didn't even seem interested in them. Mrs Stanford took one look at the three-month-old Luke – her first sight of him – at his tan skin and blond hair, and stepped backwards, declaring: 'He's a Jackson baby, isn't he?' and turned away. They had little to do with them and when they did they could be stern, and now and then harsh. Meanwhile, averse as they were to their son's wife and infants, it turned out – I was belatedly informed – that they planned to build a bungalow to retire to at the bottom of our garden where the willow tree had stood.

They would taunt me, too, about my parents. 'As yer mam and dad been to see yer?' they constantly, pointedly asked, and when I had to say no would nod and exchange knowing looks.

The only thing to do was to decide, as Cathy and my mother were now saying, that the Stanfords were irrelevant, to grit my teeth and suffer them while they were there, and when they weren't to quash them from my mind.

Irrelevant, if you don't consider that at the heart of the fourteen painful years of my involvement with them was the spectre of my father: that he was what drove me into the arms of Terry and the Stanfords, that he was the prism that distorted my initial view of them and through which they consistently saw me. That it wasn't, in effect, a relationship between me and them so much as a feud they were waging on my father.

Not that any of that was clear to me at the time. I was too busy trying not to be depressed, and not to let my depression seep to my children – doing, in fact, what my mother had done before me – to think very clearly at all.

A distraction, you could say the Stanfords were, but a significant one. For a long time I tried not to believe the underlying truth of it all. For a long time I tried to see them as I'd seen them in the beginning, as simple down-to-earth folk more well-meaning than their manners conveyed. And when I no longer could, I told myself that their interference was the only and simple, if onerous, problem in my life. I couldn't let myself dwell on the bigger issues. That I'd married a man who couldn't stick up for me in the way I needed him to; and that the despair I felt so often was sweeping out of an unresolved past.

Irrelevant, if you thought, as a fair few people seemed to,

that the novel should be focussed on my father, and not so much on me.

⚜

When I heard that the Stanfords would be coming with us on our so-called honeymoon, I turned in despair to my parents. (Married only hours, and I turned in despair to my parents.) My mother murmured helpless commiseration. My father didn't respond. He stood. He picked up his fags. And on his face as he went to the garage, was a bitter, contemptuous smirk. As if he thought it served me right, I'd got what I deserved.

⚜

One time during my marriage to Terry my mother told me on the phone: 'Mr Stanford's been to the office to see your father.'

'What?' This was unheard of. Ever since we'd got married, the Stanfords and my parents had given each other a wide berth. 'Why?'

'He wanted money. He wanted him to donate to some fire service charity.'

I was taken aback. Pushy as Mr Stanford was, I was amazed that, under the circumstances, he should do this. The insensitivity, the blundering naivety . . . Or was it bravado? Or simple nerve? Even a downright taunting challenge?

The Stanfords had made no mention of such intention to me and Terry. They were of course famously lacking in communication, yet somehow it had the feeling of an underhand plot.

My mother, I realised, was sounding grave.

She said, 'Your father refused.'

This shocked me. Even taking into account the festering sore of the payment of the wedding, this was strange. My father, refusing to donate to a public cause and further his reputation, indeed risking damaging his reputation by refusing . . . ?

My mother said, 'God, your father was angry. He was shaking with anger when Mr Stanford had gone.'

Needless to say, the Stanfords never mentioned the incident. I felt it was another source of unspoken resentment and contempt, that it fuelled their growing coldness towards me.

THE FUNERAL

MY MOTHER HAD to admit, she said, that she didn't really like the depiction of my father's death and funeral.

I knew she meant she found it upsetting.

My father died of prostate cancer. Not that there was any open admission that he was actually dying beforehand, the man who'd always defied death, surviving all those crashes and falls and fifty-odd years of forty fags a day. He hadn't admitted to himself before it was too late that anything was even wrong.

'Watch what you say!' Cathy warned me intently on the phone. She had rung to ask me to come with her and David and our mother to visit him in hospital where he was having radiotherapy. 'For Mum's sake,' she said pointedly.

Greg went with me. We arrived at Thwaite House before Cathy. It was a warm July afternoon. The back door was open and propped in the gap was the knee-high board meant to keep out a rat they'd seen running in the yard and which I'd heard from Cathy David stalked with a gun.

With the business folded, it had become David's paid job to maintain the house he was due to inherit. He patrolled it with the shotgun, I'd heard, taking potshots at the squirrels who nevertheless defied him and bounced through a hole in the roof that had developed in the fourteen years they'd lived there, and which he kept not getting around to mending. If you stayed there now, which Greg and I and the kids had done a few times, you were woken at night by squirrels bounding and sliding in the attic above, like children at play.

We stepped over the rat trap into the scullery.

David was hunched in the doorway between the scullery and the kitchen, my mother in the kitchen beyond scuttling around getting ready.

He was barely able to grunt us a greeting.

'Whose car shall we go in?' I asked him.

'We'll go in our own,' he said shortly, and my mother, coming through, shot me a look: *Don't argue.*

She squawked, making us jump: 'The dining-room windows!'

The dining room was another point of potential invasion, with its long windows facing out over lawns towards bushes, good cover and a look-out point for burglars, and the park beyond. Once in the past few years it had indeed been the entry point for burglars. They had a dog now, meant originally to guard the place while they were all at the office and works, a fat black Labrador that had wandered as a stray puppy into the garden, pampered with sandwiches and daily treats of chocolate. It failed miserably, trembling in the hall as the burglars bagged the silver, and raced in relief towards my mother happening home through the back door just as the burglars were making off across the lawn and over the wall.

David snapped at our mother: 'The dining-room windows are locked! For god's sake, they're never opened, woman!'

I bit my tongue, automatically.

What I said was, 'I'll check the windows.'

My mother interrupted quickly, 'David will check them!' and he went, proprietorially, to do so.

My mother tried to catch the dog in order to tie him up outside – since the burglary, she had told me, he'd been too frightened to stay in the house on his own. 'Bruno!' she called, and he responded eagerly, but ran off the wrong way into the dead end of the scullery, skidded splay-legged on the high-ly-polished floor, bumped his nose, yelped, adjusted, and then shot through the outside door, leaping the rat trap, and once my mother caught him, wound the lead around her legs several times – an entertaining sight, I couldn't help thinking, for watching rats.

She came back into the kitchen and executed her customary manoeuvre for shutting the high light over the sink: pulling out the drawers beneath in a staggered ladder formation and stepping up on their edges to the draining board.

'Mum, that's dangerous!' I told her, not for the first time.

David, back in the room, shot at me: 'Leave her alone. Don't come here cramping her style and telling people what to do.'

My mother skipped back down the drawers and into her high heels and went to check her hair in the mirror, pushing out her Olivia-de-Havilland chin in her still very pretty face.

'Where the hell is Cathy?' growled David, pacing, just as our father would pace if kept waiting. Then, suddenly decisive: 'We'll have to go without her.'

'Oh no, Dave, please wait for her!' my mother pleaded.

At that moment Cathy's car pulled up on the gravel drive with a skid. Dave exploded: 'What the hell is she doing to the drive?'

She came rushing through the yard and tripped over the rat trap and fell headlong.

'Right, we're off!' said David, stepping around her as she picked herself up.

Cathy was instantly alarmed. 'Oh – aren't I coming with you?'

'Oh yes!' said my mother quickly, clearly having forgotten to ask him. 'She can, can't she Dave?'

He was already in the yard. 'Why can't she go in her own car?' he called.

'Because I don't like driving in the city!' Cathy called back.

'Of course you can drive in the city!' Contemptuous, he turned on his heel and was off to his car.

Cathy opened her mouth, but our mother stopped her: 'Don't cause a fuss, Cathy, please!'

'Come with us,' I said to Cathy, who was now spilling tears of anger and hurt. (Cathy who didn't cry.)

We sped through the countryside where once Cathy and I had gone cycling down lanes, now scoured by ring roads and patched with industrial estates, trying to keep up with David and our mother in his car. We lost them, and only caught up with them in the hospital corridor outside our father's ward.

Our father was sitting on his bed in his dressing gown, his feet hardly touching the floor. He looked small. A small man after all.

He scooped his yellow hand in hospitality, inviting us to be seated, though in fact there was only one chair. And a wheelchair: he was not allowed to walk. 'Does this thing have gears?' Cathy asked him, and he sniggered.

He seemed to have been subdued by the treatment. I felt none of the tension that my presence had always aroused in him.

He wanted a smoke, and I found myself standing and taking hold of the wheelchair handles, stepping out of the side-line role I'd now had in this family for so many years. I pushed him down the corridor, the rest of them following on behind, and when he'd had his smoke I pushed him back again.

I helped him back onto his bed. 'Thank you,' he said, looking up at me, abject and wondering, as if really seeing me for the first time ever.

I thought: the illness has changed him, made him see things differently. He appreciates me after all.

Some days later, when my father was home again, my mother, worrying about his continued deterioration, told me that he had no recollection of my being at the hospital that day.

Cathy called me late one December day. 'You'd better come tomorrow.'

For weeks, as he deteriorated, as he called up his cronies from his wheelchair and told them he'd be back at meetings any day now, as he took to his bed and the doctor began the morphine injections, yet the fact of his dying was unacknowledged, they had warned me not to come.

Now I had to come quickly, and next day I jumped on the train.

Dusk was falling as I turned in through the big wooden gates. The house ghosted across the lawns. The yard light wasn't on, and I made my way in the gloom between the converted stables and the old dairy that my father had made into a Masonic meeting place in which women were not allowed to set foot. The scullery was in darkness. I crossed towards the outline of light around the kitchen door.

I opened it, and my mother and David started in alarm.

Here I was, my father's Angel of Death.

He lay like a boulder on the bed near the Rayburn,

unmoving, eyes closed, a sheet tucked tight around his chest and under his arms. The skin of his face had a cindery tinge. His hair was thinner, plastered to his skull, the old scar in the hairline more obvious. His head looked enormous above his sheeted body, and he looked what he'd always been, but had never seemed: a short man.

'Patrick,' my mother said to his closed immobile face, 'Jo's here.'

There was no sign that he had heard.

'Speak to him!' she urged me.

I stared at my father's face, no more immobile than when he'd lain on the floor doing his 'yoga', no more impassive than when we'd begged him for money as kids.

'Hi, Dad,' I said at last, feeling inappropriate and foolish.

No movement. No sign. I began to turn away. As I did, his hand twitched on the sheet.

I stared at it. It was still now. His big yellowed hand. Could he really have been responding? Had he moved that hand, the sting of which I knew so well, in order to reach out to me?

I couldn't believe it. A twitch, that's all it must have been. I turned away.

We sat out the evening in the capsule of light that was the kitchen. David and my mother had gone back to the two chairs at the bed and I, unsure where to put myself, had sat at the table. The air was hot and stuffy, the Rayburn banked up because in the last days my father had been feeling cold, and unusually smoke-free and silent. The dog creaked in the basket under the table. The wall clock ticked above the bed, the same clock that we'd thought we heard tumbling down the ghost-haunted stairs in Prestatyn, an incident which, since

David wasn't even born at the time, must seem to him a mythical tale.

Cathy called round and left to get some sleep as she had work next day, asking to be phoned as soon as there was any change. As soon as she'd gone, our mother and David jumped up in unison. My father, it seemed, needed to pee; my father, it seemed, was conscious after all and had given some subtle signal I'd missed but to which they were attuned. They busied about him with a plastic bottle and I turned away, embarrassed to be there, embarrassed to be intruding on the intimate scene, the bond that the three of them shared.

At midnight my father's breathing became louder and more laboured. I noticed that his finger-ends were turning blue. I should say something, I thought, suggest we call Cathy. I said nothing, stopped by that sense that it wasn't up to me to make observations or suggestions.

My mother left the room with some linen and as soon as the door closed behind her David raised his head, looked briefly in my direction, waited a moment, and then, seeming to make a decision, stood and planted his chair with its back more directly towards me. It took me a moment to understand that he'd been waiting for me to leave the room too; he'd been waiting, the golden child and son and heir, to be alone with his dying father.

I was caught in a knot of emotions: embarrassment that I hadn't taken the hint; the desire to be gone, away from the embarrassment of the situation; and pain. And sheer fury at the expectation that I should jump to and accede, the old expectation of this household that the women should jump to and accede to the demands of the men, demands they didn't even feel the need to voice.

But also curiosity.

I stayed where I was.

David's shoulders slumped. He resigned himself to my presence.

He spoke to our father. 'Dad,' he said in a low private voice. 'I want you to know you've been a wonderful father.'

My mother came back and looked at my father.

'Why don't you go to bed, Jo?' she said.

I thought in pain: they want to be alone with him when he dies.

There wasn't a bed made up for me. 'Dave, can she sleep in yours?'

I'd hardly ever set foot in David's bedroom. 'He doesn't like people going in there!' my mother had told me once, finding me peering in. To my amazement – but of course he wanted rid of me – he nodded agreement.

I took my bag and went upstairs.

I opened David's door. Dark-green geometric wallpaper, dark-brown art deco furniture. Shelves with cycling trophies, stones and shells and bits of driftwood, books on cycling and the wildlife guides he started collecting at seven years old when we first came to Thwaite. And on a top shelf in the chimney alcove, frozen in the neatness of non-use, the set of Dickens my mother had once stopped me from touching, looking as if David was keeping them out of his own reach now.

I lifted the wad of blankets and was ambushed by an old familiar smell: the musty-sweet scent that rose up when I made his bed on the housing estate, or tucked the blankets round him after one of his turns.

233

He remembered nothing of that, I supposed. He remembered little, my mother had told me: one freezing night not long after they moved to Thwaite House, he'd had an accident on his bike, went over a pothole on the ring road and lay unconscious on the verge in dropping frost, until the lights of a passing car caught him. When he came round in hospital great chunks of his memory had gone. He now remembered nothing much, she said, of anything before the move to this house.

I got into bed, into the cat's cradle of blankets, and my brother's scent, the same after all these years, after all his transformation from nervous little boy to adamant thirty-seven-year-old man, wrapped itself around me.

I woke in darkness with the sensation of someone having knocked me hard in passing.

The landing light was on, showing under the door. My mother opened it and said in a small voice, 'Jo, your dad has died.'

The tortured sound of his breathing was gone from the room. I stood surveying the scene. My father looked little different. My mother was bent again now with David beside the bed, both of them weeping.

I went to the phone. 'Cathy, Dad has died.'

There was a long silence.

'Cathy?'

She gave a sob and I realised she couldn't speak for crying. (Cathy, who didn't cry.)

And I, the one who always wept too much, held the receiver as it dropped her great gobs of sobs, unable to cry, dry-eyed.

She was no longer weeping by the time she arrived.

'Well, what do we do now?' she asked in her customary dry manner.

Neither David nor our mother, still bent in grief, answered.

I said, 'We need to call the doctor to register the death. And then I guess in the morning we ring the undertakers.'

David's head snapped up. 'I'm not having my father taken out of this house.'

My father. Cathy's mouth tightened.

I quashed my own surge of anger. 'It's what has to happen, Dave.'

'I don't care what's supposed to happen! I'm not having those death merchants mucking my father about!'

A rush of fury that I didn't want to feel pushed at my tongue. Automatically I clamped down on it.

Cathy's bosom heaved. She said pointedly, turning protectively towards our mother, 'Well, what does *Mum* want?'

Our mother opened her mouth, but David cried: 'I know what she *doesn't* want! She doesn't want him carted off by those creepy bastards!'

'How do you know what Mum wants?!' Cathy's voice was trembling with anger.

'I *live* here! I know better than either of you what my mother wants!'

Cathy, Cathy who had always warned me to watch my tongue, exploded. '*What?!!* How dare you think you can speak for Mum!'

They faced each other over my father's dead body, both of them furious, and I suddenly felt a ripple of potential mad laughter.

Our mother spoke at last. 'Oh, Cathy, don't row! Please, not now!'

Cathy looked as though our mother had slapped her. Tears welled in her grey-green eyes.

Our mother went on weakly, 'Well, yes, I do want your dad here in his home.'

I said, 'I think you're missing the point,' and pushed down on my surging need to laugh. 'It's nearly the weekend, the funeral won't be for days. He'll need to be refrigerated.'

David groaned with horror.

'Yes,' said Cathy, with a sudden note of hilarity. 'We ought to shift that bed. He's already been near the Rayburn far too long.'

In the morning, David paced. We had reached a compromise: David would allow our father to be taken away – Cathy had given me a furious meaningful look – but we'd have him brought back two days before the funeral, to lie in the house.

David glowered and prowled, watching the gates through the kitchen window for the undertaking raiders. The big black car nosed in and he swirled on the spot in distress. I went to the front door, since neither he nor our mother had moved to do so, and when I came back with the two funeral directors, David was standing beside our father's body, shoulders squared.

He was still standing there when they brought back a cardboard coffin. The men looked at each other, hesitant, and finally he moved aside.

As they lifted our father, he cried in distress, 'Mind his head!' and the two men professionally desisted catching each other's eyes. He gave a groan as they placed him in the coffin.

After they'd gone he collapsed on the table, head in his arms.

In the midst of David's drama, our mother had become more or less forgotten. I said to her now, eyeing David crumpled on the table and incapable: 'Do you want me to stay and organise things?'

I didn't expect the answer she gave. 'Oh, Jo, yes please!'

⚜

I met Cathy from the library and we went to register the death.

It was dark. There was a chill in the air, mist coming off the river as we crossed the bridge. The road was sticky with wet and with memories. Cathy took my arm, and there we were again, after all these years, walking arm in arm as we had done after beatings.

'Please wait,' the female registrar instructed with a coolness amounting, in the circumstances of her profession, to callousness. She went off into a room, teetering on high black heels in her tight blue dress. She left the door open and shuffled papers with a sound that seemed to me insolent.

Cathy whispered: 'She's no idea that I know her from school. She was known as the town bike.'

Finally, without moving from her desk, she called us in.

As we sat she kept her eyes on the papers.

'Now.' She dragged her eyes up. 'Name of deceased?'

'Patrick Jackson.'

She dropped her pen along with her jaw. 'No! Not Patrick Jackson?!!'

We nodded.

'Oh *no!!*'

We exchanged our neutral-to-any-observer look.

237

'Oh no!' She was girlish now, and upset, slumping in her blue dress. 'Oh, he was *such* a lovely man! So friendly! And so *generous!*'

The phone started ringing, Masons from all over the country and even from abroad, wanting to know when the funeral was. Even my mother was stunned by their number.

Most of the callers thought I was my mother.

'No, this is his daughter.'

Several replied: 'I didn't know he had a daughter. I thought he only had a son.'

As soon as our father's body had gone from the house, David had gone too, decamped to stay at Janet's until our father's return, and along with him a good deal of the tension.

The morning he was back, our father's body also due, he paced once again.

'If those bastards have smothered him in makeup I'll bloody kill them!' he said more than once as he whirled.

Seeing the arrival of the hearse through the window, he groaned. This time, as I made for the front door, he darted past me. The dog followed him, shot through the front door and, abandoning its customary nervousness, sent a volley of barks at the undertakers getting out of the car. As the coffin emerged it howled.

The men manoeuvred the coffin in through the front porch and the hall, and David followed close, at one point making a lunge for it so they hesitated and exchanged uncomfortable glances. He followed them hard into the dining room, where our mother had decided the coffin should lie. He hung above them as they placed it on the stand.

They straightened up.

'Sir . . .' They waited.

He stood his ground.

'Sir, if you would give us a minute, while we open the coffin.'

I moved in from the doorway. 'Dave . . .'

He glared at me. 'I'm not leaving this room. No one's sending me away from my father's coffin.'

'Dave—'

He squared up to me, and I almost flinched. 'Well, what do they need to do to him that they can't do in my presence?'

I said, 'Straighten him up?' and felt a spurt of hilarity.

At last he let me usher him from the room.

They were done; they opened the door again. He rushed back in. As I moved them away into the hall I glanced back and caught sight of him pulling at the white silk in the coffin, sending ribbons flying.

Once again, in the midst of the crisis, our mother had been forgotten.

❧

The next day, the day before the funeral, in the late afternoon Uncle Gwilym, our mother's brother, and the wife he had belatedly married, arrived.

I hadn't seen them for years.

Llanfair was sadly different once Grampa died: all the places we'd walked with him, secure for once in the sense of being specially loved, the peaceful cow-dung-smelling lanes, the sweeping beach with its banks of round stones, echoed with loss. So as we grew up, Cathy and I went less often, and once we left home hardly at all. Meanwhile David had continued to go every summer with our mother, becoming, it was clear, a great favourite with the childless Gwilym and Renee. I knew that in recent years David and Janet had been to stay with them several times.

I hadn't been to Llanfair for years when, the summer Greg moved in with me and my small children, we took them camping in west Wales. On the way back we decided to make a detour, to go and see Nanny and Gwilym.

As we got near, as we drove between the moss-covered walls, the silky strip of sea opening up ahead, I felt all the old excitement and sense of coming home.

But the elms were all gone, destroyed by Dutch Elm disease, and now a power station loomed above the cornfields and beach; the pink thatched cottage had long been razed to the ground and Nanny rehoused in a new council build. Nanny, bent now and wispy-haired, held up her palms with her old affectionate greeting and cooed over my children, but she quickly tired, and kept looking at the clock for the time that Gwilym would be home from work when we could go and see him.

Gwilym and Renee kept us standing on the doorstep. They were awkward, stiff. Not even very friendly. I realised they were waiting for us to go. We left.

As we drove away I wondered: was it Greg? Were they, like my father, disgusted that Greg was still technically married?

Probably they were. Much later I would think: they were probably party to the dim view of me held by their favourite, David, and adultery would be just one proof of that.

That day, though, I simply felt confounded and hurt. My throat was tight as we drove away, and that night I woke from a grey aching dream of exile and loss.

Ten years had gone by since, in which I'd seen Gwilym and Renee only once, and briefly, at Nanny's funeral.

Now they prised themselves from their car, looking a good deal older, Gwilym stiff in his tweed jacket and like a stouter version of Grampa, the tiny features of the previously skinny Renee lost in the white flatness of a fatter face.

David was in the garage, from which I expected him to emerge straight away.

He didn't appear.

There was no doubt that he'd have heard their car arrive and my mother and me bringing them through the yard right past the stable doors where he was working.

'David's got to finish a job in the garage,' my mother told Gwilym in the kitchen, airy and over-bright in the way that meant she was tense and covering up. 'He'll be here soon, I'm sure!'

'Oh!' said Gwilym in his bouncy way, but he'd clearly seen through it, and looked as if he might pop with embarrassed uncertainty.

Renee was very quiet.

Finally David came in. There was the usual bonhomie, but something was different: it seemed forced. David had a steely air, and Gwilym seemed wondering and increasingly flustered and somehow trapped inside his tweed jacket.

'I'm just about to walk the dog,' David told him. 'Will you come?' There was a domineering edge to his voice.

Gwilym seemed half-relieved but still uncertain.

They put on their coats in a stiff ritual, and went off into the dark with the dog, both looking self-conscious, Gwilym the more so.

When they came back, David seemed pulled tight, moving briskly for the first time since our father had died, his mouth set. He didn't take his coat off, but to my shock left immediately for Janet's, left the aunt and uncle, whose favourite he had been for so many years, to me and my mother for the evening.

There was a tense atmosphere when he'd gone, my mother working hard to act as if nothing was strange, and Gwilym and Renee both subdued.

'What's going on?' I asked my mother as I helped her take the electric blanket off their bed.

'Ssh!!' We were in the bedroom directly above the kitchen, where sound carried down the chimney, and Gwilym and Renee were sitting beside it at the Rayburn.

'Well?'

'Oh, you know!'

'No, I don't!'

'Yes, you *do*! Remember, David couldn't forgive Renee for not looking after Nanny when she was ill before she died.'

More than three years ago now, in the months before Nanny died, Renee had said she was no longer able to look after her, she'd become ill herself with the strain. There had been no option but for Nanny to leave south Wales against her wishes, and brought to Thwaite to die. Away from her home, and feeling abandoned by Renee and Gwilym (the boy, the favourite!), she had thus died unhappy.

And David had been angry with Renee for causing it to happen by giving up her care.

At the time I'd been angry in turn, angry at my father's misogyny replicated in his son – in this day and age! I felt angry again now, and said again in objection what I'd said to my mother then: 'But Renee was ill!'

'Ssh!!'

'And anyway that was more than three years ago now!'

My mother looked stricken. 'Well, he hasn't spoken to Gwilym since.'

'What?!!'

'Yes, it's been awful. Every time Gwilym's rung he's asked to speak to David, but David wouldn't come to the phone.'

'Oh, for god's sake!'

'Jo - please! I don't want them to hear!'

She went on, her voice low: 'I'm hoping David's made it up with Gwilym when they took the dog out.'

I imagined she had begged him beforehand to do so. Though it didn't looked too much as if things *had* been made up between them.

'He was going to explain why he hasn't been coming to the phone.'

'You mean Gwilym didn't *know* why he wasn't?'

I thought about it. I imagined my mother's airy excuses to Gwilym - Oh, David was out cycling, Oh, David *just happened* to be down at Janet's. The excuses she had always used to me ...

I had a rush of hurt resentment. I burst out, I dared to: 'Who the hell does he think he is, making rules for women he wouldn't make for himself!'

She dropped the quilt as if wounded. 'Oh, Jo, how can you say that? He was so good with Nanny when she came here. He sat with her for hours!'

She'd told me that before many times. I would think: easy to sit with someone who's ill when someone else is doing all the running around and caring. Easier still to do it as a sanctimonious show. But I had never dared upset her by saying it.

I felt that old taboo, the taboo against speaking ill of David, rise up around me again now. I struggled against it.

'Well, anyway, if it's Renee he's mad with, why did he stop talking to *Gwilym?*'

'Because Gwilym supported Renee when it happened.'

Of course: according to the Jackson rulebook, Gwilym should have been keeping his woman in line.

By the time he returned from Janet's, Gwilym and Renee had gone to bed.

All evening my mother kept saying hopefully, 'David should be back soon!' but Gwilym looked, actually, as if he were horrified at the prospect, and they went upstairs as soon as they decently could. In any case, he came home late.

As soon as he came in my mother asked, keeping her voice low: 'Well? Did you make it up with Gwilym?'

He threw his keys on the table with crack, in the manner of our father.

He said shortly, 'Well, I told him.'

'Ssh! What did you tell him?'

'I told him what I think. That that bitch killed Nanny.'

'Oh, David, you *didn't!*'

'Why shouldn't I? It's the truth.'

'Oh, shush, David, they'll hear you!'

Before he'd arrived, their murmurs had been filtering down the chimney, but now they had stopped and were probably listening.

'I don't bloody care if they do hear me! Gwilym knows what I think.'

My mother asked faintly: 'What did he say?'

He said in disgust, 'He kept on saying Renee was ill.'

My chest was heaving. I burst out: 'But she *had* been looking after Nanny up to that point! And caring's a stress, it *can* make people ill!'

He blared: 'She didn't even try! She *refused*. And Gwilym's still backing her up! He wouldn't even apologise.'

Apologise. Say sorry to Daddy, say sorry to David. I thought my heart would burst out of my mouth.

He was booming now. 'I want them out of this house the minute the funeral's over!'

My mother looked as if she might faint.

I could feel myself vibrating, throughout my guts and all along my limbs. I cried, 'What if *Mum* doesn't want them out of the house?'

My mother turned on me. 'Oh, both of you, *shush*!'

David moved over to us where we sat by the Rayburn and the sound-carrying chimney. He towered over us and bellowed: 'I'm not having them here in my house another night!'

'*Shut up!*' I cried, the taboo crashing down, though my heart was going like piston with the terror of it. 'Will you *stop* upsetting Mum when her husband's just died!'

He erupted. 'Don't you tell me what to do in my house!'

And he'd gone to bed, slamming the door.

❦

Next morning, the morning of the funeral, David was steely as he came down, but as flowers began to arrive and the golf-club ladies helping out turned up with trays of sandwiches and sausages rolls, bringing with them eddies of cold air, his eyes grew wild.

He went out to patrol the grounds, and our mother said quickly, 'Cathy, Jo, I want you to come with me.'

She led us into the dining room where our father lay in his open coffin.

There was no heating on here, but in front of the tall windows the air simmered in the sun as if alive.

There lay my father in the clothes my mother had picked out from his extensive tailor-made wardrobe: the Masonic black jacket, the pin-striped grey trousers, the tie with the set-square-and-compass symbol. The thug ring with the Star of David was on his finger, and around his neck was the arcane gold pendant with the Star of David in a sunburst.

'Are you sure he should be wearing all these?' I had asked her, helping her to pick them out. 'Is it supposed to be on public show, this Masonic stuff?'

She had hesitated, unsure, but then decided it was what he would want, and I'd thought: too bad then if it wasn't, but it was all too secret for her to know.

David's frantic efforts to pull the white viscose silk from the coffin had failed. It was nailed and glued, and he'd had to push it back and content himself with smoothing out the flounces.

That evening, while David was briefly away at Janet's, Cathy and I had sat beside the coffin. They hadn't made our father up as he'd feared. The colour of his skin was normal, if a bit less tanned-looking. The grim expression on his face was the one he'd so often had in private in life.

'I keep thinking he's going to jump up and grab us,' Cathy said.

She pushed down on a tuck of satin that David had left

bulging. 'Don't tell David I touched it,' she said, grimly ironical, and I snorted. But also I felt annoyed: however ironical she was being, I knew that she meant it. For the sake of peace, for the sake of our mother, she was going along with the family deference to David.

Then, to my shock, she did that thing that people did in books, in films, no doubt in real life: she put her hand on our father's. The hand we had never touched in life, that had never in my memory touched us except to hit us. And then, to my further shock, she stroked his cheek. The cheek that, when we'd been forced to kiss it – *kiss Daddy and say sorry* – had always been bristly and unyielding.

How could she? I wondered, alone beside the coffin when she'd gone.

Touching our father like that had always been entirely out of the question. It seemed now, in his death, a violation. A continuing prohibition.

I felt a sudden urge to resist the prohibition. I reached out – feeling fraudulent already – and touched his cheek as Cathy had done. It felt like marble, no more resistant than it had seemed in life.

Now, as we stood with our mother at the coffin on the day of the funeral, our mother took a deep breath, and we knew right away: an unwelcome announcement was coming. 'Now, you do know, don't you, you girls, that your dad has left all his personal possessions to Dave?'

Cathy's grey-green eyes bulged. We didn't know that.

Later we would discover that along with half the house and his personal possessions, he had left him all his money, of which, spender though he may have been, there turned out to be a fair bit, after all.

Cathy spluttered now: 'But what about *you*, Mum?!'

'Oh, don't start, Cathy – please!'

Cathy shut up.

I looked down at my father. He was starting to thaw: the corners of his mouth had dropped, and he was grinning.

'But I want you two girls to have the jewellery he's wearing.'

Cathy said quickly she'd have the ring, and I stared at her: that ring that could catch you such a vicious blow? Which left me the pendant with its symbol I wasn't meant to know the meaning of, and didn't.

Our father's fingers had shrivelled, the little ears of the chopped digit no longer rosy but bleached, and the ring came off easily. We had to raise his head to get the pendant, a dead weight with which the three of us had to wrestle together, and I suddenly wanted to laugh again.

'No need to mention it to David,' my mother said in warning, and I stopped wanting to laugh.

The hearse had appeared in the gateway, and my mother came to me, puzzled: not one of the Masons for whom she'd taken such care to dress our father's body had turned up to view him in his coffin.

David spiralled in alarm: 'They're not watching my border!' The hearse was turning in the wider space near the gate in order to back towards the front door and coming perilously close to the ankle-high ivy hedge fringing the lawn. He shot out to direct them away from it, but his mad gestures caused them to drive right into it. His agitation spread: as they carried out the coffin, someone stepped on the wreath of pink roses chosen to echo the ones in our mother's wedding bouquet.

We followed the coffin with its half-crushed wreath into the church, Cathy and I behind the chief mourners, our mother and David.

We were met by a wall of deep blackness: the Masons had come after all, a huge company. The church was filled to capacity, so many black-coated men that extra chairs had had to be placed at the back, yet still some were standing.

The service began. The first hymn started up, and the force of the sound, the sound of many men singing, was shocking, so powerful you could feel the vibrations.

Caught in the vortex of sound, I looked around. There, in the pew opposite, was Sandra Suggate. She appeared to be with another, older woman, presumably her mother. She was fatter than she had been, her coat stretched across her belly. Her hair was still lank. She looked guarded and watchful. I turned away.

With so many Masons filing from the church and sharing their condolences, we were late for the crematorium, and the funeral car sped as if our father must be cremated before he escaped. There were five of us in the car, my mother, David, Cathy and me, and Janet, girlfriend of the son and heir. I had always felt as uncomfortable with Janet as I had with Sandra Suggate. On the few occasions when I visited my mother's office, Janet would watch me from under her frizz of black hair with what seemed like sly knowing, making me think of the girls when we were kids, who thought our father liked them better than us.

The hedges batted past. A choking sound made us all jump: Janet starting to cry, loudly, dramatically, a dry, coughing artificial sound. Cathy sent me a meaningful look.

Very few, it turned out, had come to the crematorium,

three miles out of town, yet almost before those who had were assembled, the service had started. Almost before we knew it, the coffin had gone along the rails, an inverse Jack-in-a Box, and the curtain had closed.

We came out into the vista of flat fields, our ballast gone.

Out of all the Masons, only one, and old friend, came back to the house; the rest had dispersed like bluebottles.

The food, meant for their number, was hardly touched.

Cathy put on a tape, *Danny Boy*, which she said our father had listened to a lot in his final years, but then, afraid the Mason wouldn't find it seemly, she switched it off.

It was only as the sound clicked off that it came to me that our father's sister, the gentle ex-nun Aunty Cathy, hadn't come.

That evening the new order – the new-old order – closed round.

Greg and my sons had gone off in the freezing night, back to Manchester and the modern world. Four relatives remained, our mother's sister Molly and her husband, and Gwilym and Renee. David had relented over Gwilym and Renee – no doubt my mother had had to plead – but had warned that he wanted them out next day. It was clear in any case from their subdued manner that they wouldn't want to stay any longer than they had to.

Cathy and I began to clear up the dishes.

'I'll wash,' said Janet, stepping to the sink with a proprietorial air, and Cathy caught my eye.

Janet pulled a fine porcelain plate out of the suds, held it up, demonstrative, and said to my mother: 'I was with you, wasn't I, Gwen, when you went to buy this tea set?'

Cathy smouldered.

Next day when Gwilym and Renee left early, David was nowhere to be seen, and the parting was strained.

He reappeared when they'd gone, striding around the grounds he'd inherited in a flat cap and green wellies. He was beside himself no longer. Indeed, coming upon our mother wiping her eyes on her pinny, he pronounced: 'The time for crying's over.'

That late afternoon, Cathy, back from work, stepped in from the dark yard and asked, aghast: 'What's David doing?'

Our mother and I, sitting in the kitchen, were blank.

'He's in Dad's Masonic den and he's going through his papers! That should be your job, Mum!'

Our mother looked momentarily distressed, then deflated. 'Well, Cathy, you *know* your father left all his personal things to David.'

'But Mum, his *papers!*'

'Oh Cathy, there's nothing I can do about it, leave it, please!'

Cathy subsided, but a moment or two later she gave me a look and the subtlest of nods in the direction of the door. We strolled into the scullery together and then out to the yard.

Frost winked in the light coming from the window of the converted dairy.

Cathy pushed on the door.

David came quickly into the doorway, preventing us from entering. It was hard to see past him: a glimpse of a desk, and a white-and-gold cloth on the altar table. He had a waste bin under his arm, half-full of papers.

'Can we come in?' Cathy was challenging, rhetorical.

'Nope.' Adamant.

'*Why ever not?!!*'

'Dad didn't want anyone except Masons coming in here.'

'You're not a Mason!'

'I am, you know I am.'

This was news to me, though I supposed I shouldn't be surprised.

'But you didn't want to! You stopped going!'

'That's got nothing to do with it. Dad didn't want women in here.'

Fury spurted in my chest and I could sense it spurting in Cathy's.

'What's this?' Cathy snatched a card from the bin.

An air force card with our father's portrait and script in Polish – the Polish squadron he'd been attached to. 'You can't throw that away!'

David snatched it back and dashed it into the bin again. 'I bloody can.' Decisive, iron-hard. And he shut the door, shut us out of our father's private life and history, as our father himself had always done.

That evening our mother discovered that Janet had put her house on the market. That, at the end of the twentieth century, our father had given his son to understand that he and his woman would succeed as heads of the household, the household created with our mother's money and hands-on labour. A house built, a century before, for that very purpose: deposing a wife in favour of a son.

His final trick. His final revenge.

PART SIX

*In which, although the book is written,
further conundrums arise*

PART SIX

In which, although the book is written,
further considerations arise.

DAVID AT THE STATION

'OH, JO,' MY mother said in response to the way I'd portrayed David at the funeral, 'He wasn't himself then!'

I felt bad. Though of course I was annoyed and even resentful. I thought savagely, Oh yeah, save David from his own worst aspects, just as she'd always done with our father.

She didn't say anything about the scene in which David had hit me, just as nothing had been said at the time. What she did say, as the novel led her to reminisce, was: 'Do you remember, when you came to stay with Luke just after he was born, how good David was with him?'

'What?'

'You were so ill and exhausted, and Luke just wouldn't go down. David used to rock him for hours so you could get some sleep. He was so patient with him.'

Was she serious?

'Don't you remember?'

'No.'

She looked disappointed and upset.

I thought: He did it *once* maybe, no doubt pushed into it by her. And it's grown in her memory, to gloss his image, for me, for him, for herself.

But I was thrown, unsure of my own memory. After all, I'd been in such a state at the time, hardly conscious for much of the time, probably even a little insane.

And then I thought of what happened the day I left after the funeral, something I hadn't put in the novel because I didn't understand it.

David came to me that morning as I brought my bag down.

'I'll take you to the station, Jo.' He was stiffly, ebulliently friendly. And he seemed quite genuine, as far as I could tell under no pressure from my mother to make the offer.

The change was so sudden and unexpected, that I hardly knew how to behave towards him.

As he drove me to the station he was bluffly loquacious, chatting about the traffic and the buildings as I imagined he would with strangers, as our father, more naturally and cleverly perhaps, would with strangers.

And a stranger, I thought, was what I was, of course, in so many ways . . .

But why the change in his attitude? I sat beside him frozen with awkwardness, and with growing resentment. Did he think he could just wipe away the past? Did he think I could, would forget that he'd actually once hit me, a new mother?

But then my mother had said he'd lost much of his memory in the subsequent cycling accident . . .

Even so, did he think I could just lay aside all those years of being cold-shouldered?

I expected him to drop me off outside the station, but he parked the car and came with me to the waiting room. I wished he wouldn't; I felt coerced and wanted him gone.

He said, 'You know, you've been great, Jo, doing everything you have, organising it all.'

I went hot. So that was it. Unlike Renee, I had done the female duty expected of me – expected in spite of my years of exile. I'd earned his patriarchal male approval. An approval, I thought bitterly, that no doubt would be quickly withdrawn if I ever put a foot wrong in his eyes again.

I could hardly bring myself to answer. 'It's fine.'

On one wall of the waiting room an old gas fire was popping uneven flames. He said, 'Come nearer the fire, love.'

Love. A term of approval, of belittlement. An expression of power. I could hardly make myself move towards the fire, perform the role he was setting out for me: renegade sister who had earned forgiveness at last and was glad of it.

He said: 'You look great in a beret.'

A demonstration, I thought, that he would deign to notice me now. I could hardly get the thanks past my teeth.

He moved over to the window, wiped away a patch of steam and looked out onto the ploughed field behind the station. 'This is a great place for fieldfares. You can see them down Stenners Lane too.'

He had the tone of instructing the uninitiated in the subject. He had no memory, I supposed, of those walks to school when he held my hand asking me the names of birds.

He went on: 'I often go down Stenners Lane on my bike. It's a great ride. If there's one thing I love it's riding the lanes.'

'Oh yeah?' I forced through my rigid jaw.

He was informing me about himself as he would a new acquaintance. As if choosing to bestow on me the knowledge of him he thought I now at last deserved.

Yet I felt uncertain. There was something eager, too, in his tone, as if, after all these years of not caring about my opinion, or even despising it, he actually wanted to impress me.

It was time for the train.

We stepped out onto the platform. Flakes of snow were

now separating out of the air, whirling every which way as though beside themselves.

He said, 'Do you remember the time we went to Loch Lomond?'

I stopped walking. He remembered *that*, then.

It was when Terry and I were in Glasgow. We had bought our first house, our little townhouse, and had painted it from top to bottom, and I asked my parents to come and visit. I wanted them to see my life, I wanted them to be proud of me. (Of course, as usual, I forgot how it was.) My father didn't come - no surprise there - but David, aged nineteen, drove our mother up and they stayed two nights. I hadn't seen much of David in the years since I'd left home, and although already I had been feeling a distance between us, that time seemed different. We went to Loch Lomond, Terry and I and my mother and David. We wandered on the shore picking driftwood, just as we would once on the beach at Llanfair, and my mother and I and David started singing, our voices looping over the still silky water, the mad Jacksons, *twp*, as we'd have said in Llanfair. There was a sense, with us together and our father absent, of something restored. And as we rocked on the stones, I caught hold of David's arm and tucked it in mine, my little brother restored to me once more.

He said now on the station, his voice fervent: 'It was a wonderful day. I'll never forget it.'

And then the train was roaring in, and to my shock he had flung his arms around me and was hugging me tight.

As the train pulled out he walked beside it, walked until he could keep up no longer, just as he'd run the first day I left for university, running and running that time on his stocky little legs in his baggy khaki shorts until the train had rounded the bend and I was gone from his world altogether.

❧

It was an anomaly, that scene at the station.

For after that I rarely saw David; he seemed to be avoiding me once again.

In fact, my father's specific patriarchal plan for the household failed. Janet didn't move in to become its new mistress because our mother, rising up against our father for once, put her foot down. It turned out that the plan had in any case been balanced on rocky foundations: only one week later, Janet finished with David, thus proving to Cathy her gold-digging intentions, and I briefly felt sorry for David. The week after that David took up with a childhood sweetheart I'd noticed him talking to at the funeral (and I stopped feeling sorry for him). Now, whenever I came he'd be at that girlfriend's just as he used to be at Janet's. In fact, now that he owned half the house, his absence seemed even more pointed.

My father had gone, along with the cigarette smoke and the particular tension he created, and his specific plan may have failed, but the patriarchal order still reigned in the house where David now lived off the money our father had left him, where, amongst the ticking clocks and vast spaces, our mother cooked his meals and ironed his clothes, just as she had for our father.

It was during this time, on one of my visits, that my mother mentioned that my father had once won the pools.

'What!? When?'

'Oh, it was when you were at university. Quite a lot, it was. It was how he could start his business.'

259

Why had I never wondered how he had? It struck me that it was the one thing for which I'd respected my father: the fact that after all, in the end, he'd managed to make good on the strength of his own toil . . .

So his Irish luck had truly come up trumps in the end . . .

'Why didn't we know?'

I thought I knew the answer: my mother would be happy to have me think that, think well of my father . . .

'Your father didn't want you and Cathy to know.'

A ball of shock jammed my throat.

I found my voice: 'So did David know?'

'Oh, yes, well, of course, he was there at home at the time.'

At the time he must have been thirteen or so years old. He must have been in on the fact that Cathy and I weren't to know. At thirteen years old he'd been given the sense of belonging to an inner circle of family to which Cathy and I, irrelevant, excluded, were a threat . . .

My mother didn't seem to have noticed my shock, she was laughing about my father: 'I was surprised that you *didn't* find out, he won enough to get in the papers! Eleven thousand, which was a lot at the time – more than a hundred thousand in present-day money!'

Even more by the time I had written my novel . . .

And yet it wasn't his money that subsequently bought the big house, but my mother's . . .

Now it was explained how our father had managed to spend so much money and still leave David enough to live on . . .

It was in the papers. I would think afterwards: so perhaps the Stanfords had known. No wonder, if they had, they'd been so disgusted that my father didn't want to pay for a wedding . . .

And so taken for granted now was the patriarchy of this household that my mother, who as a young girl had been bent on a career and insisted on her intellectual independence, had told me this simply as a matter of fact.

No, that scene at the station after the funeral simply didn't fit the story.

❧

Despairing about my novel, I went for dinner with my oldest writing friend, Judy, and poured out my woes.

'I must be mad!' I told her. I was on my third wine. 'What am I *doing*? Why am I writing about the kind of patriarchal stuff everyone knows about and no one believes *exists* any more?'

'Because it *does* still exist?' Judy suggested.

I could always count on Judy to support me.

'Not amongst the section of the population that reads novels!' I objected. I could always count on her to take it cheerfully when I threw her support back in her face.

She laughed. I could always count her not to let me depress her.

But since finishing the book, the more I mulled over it, the more the sense grew that there was something I still hadn't grasped.

REMEMBERING AND
FORGETTING

I HAD TRIED consciously to grasp it as I walked along the
river with Cathy the Sunday before the funeral.

We were walking the dog, as David, decamped to Janet's,
wasn't around to do it. Reeds lay broken and tipped in the
slow-moving water, and the copse across the water was a black
tangle. The fat dog lumbered ahead, every so often stopping
and running back a few steps, as if having to remind himself
who we were.

I asked Cathy: 'What do you think was behind it all?'

And there we were, after our lives of college and careers
and marriages, my own years of motherhood and living in
different cities, walking arm in arm just as we did at the
ages of eight and ten, puzzling about the way our father had
treated us.

Was he simply a relic of an outdated social order?
'Patriarchal bastard!' Cathy had answered bitterly. Or was he
a particular aberration? 'Sadist!' she had added.

I said, 'You know, when we were little: I can remember so
much of being beaten, and being frightened of being beaten,
but I can't remember *why* we were beaten, no particular
reason.'

Cathy spat: 'For being children. Just for making a mess
and making mistakes.'

I turned and looked at her. Did she really think that? Was that all it really was, as I'd tried to tell myself when I first met Terry? A different era and a different childcare ideology . . .

Had I been making more of it than it was? *You take things too seriously, Jo . . . !*

But I thought of a tale our mother would tell, of how once when she was a child Grampa tried to beat her for leaving the cover off the drinking-water steen outside the cottage. When he told her off she cheeked him, so he put her over his knee, but he never managed the beating, because every time he raised his hand she shot up her heel and clonked him on the side of the head. Even while laughing, I could never listen to this tale without thinking of the implications: that, unlike our father, Grampa had had no practice at beating; that he let her triumph in a way our father would never brook: such childish subversion would have brought down disaster on the heads of Cathy and me. That, in any case, by the time we were six and four any impulse for subversion had been beaten out of us . . .

'All that beating,' Cathy was saying sourly.

But it wasn't just the beating, I thought. It was the sense that we were treated differently from other children, that we had to be, that we were thought more troublesome, somehow more of a *danger* to things . . .

A feeling that for me had continued into adulthood . . .

Ahead, the dog turned briefly to check on us.

Cathy said, grim, 'Anyway, I *do* remember some of the things we got beaten for when we were little.'

'Like what?'

'Well, what about that time we ripped a page in his Bible?'

And the memory hit me, an incident I'd completely

forgotten, but which came to me now with a jaundiced sepia vividness.

He had a huge antique Bible bound in dark-grey leather and reinforced with ornate brass, with full-colour plates we would beg to be allowed to look at, cross-hatched drawings tinted in russets and eau-de-nile and subtle ochre, each plate protected with tissue paper. He didn't often allow us. When he did he would lay it on the floor in front of us, making us sit back out of the way, and issue strict instructions: we must turn a page by taking the weight with the whole of one arm, and once it was turned, sit back again and keep our hands away.

For most of the year in Easton he was in too bad a temper to ask, but one particular afternoon at last we sat in front of the open volume again. We gazed at the picture of Moses' mother pushing his basket into the rushes of the Nile to save him from the Pharoah. Pleated water, an intricate plaiting of leaves, the neater weave of the basket, fluid but sure lines catching the moment when persecution turned to escape.

Cathy asked me: 'But where's Moses's sister?'

The sister who, in the story, was watching in order to know where to come back and save him.

'She just isn't in the picture.'

'Why not?' Cathy peered at the picture as if she didn't believe it.

'She's further off,' I said, 'outside the frame.' I began to turn the page just as Cathy, still puzzled, put her hand on it to stop me, and the page tore in half.

'See what I mean?' Cathy said now, as we remembered. 'Fancy *letting* two little girls look at something you don't want spoiled.'

It seemed to me far too domestic a gloss on the incident. It wasn't in fact the beating that I remembered. What I remembered, what came back to me now, was the sound of tearing, and along with it the sense of something else, something dark and terrifying, ripping through the acrid-lit spaces of the room.

How could I have forgotten it? I wondered now. Now that I had remembered it, it felt huge. A huge yet mysterious clue . . .

Yet I *had* forgotten it, it had fallen away.

I had stopped on the river path and Cathy had stopped beside me. The dog reeled and turned back to see what was up, and as we started again, yanked himself round and bounded on. When we caught him up he was snuffling down a rabbit hole and looked up as if surprised that his view down the hole hadn't made us disappear.

We sat on a boulder where once we sat as teenagers, and the barrel-shaped dog placed himself between us, looking from one to the other of us, as if sharing the puzzle.

Cathy said, 'Twisted bastard. What about the time in Prestatyn when he went to ring the children's home?'

And that came back too with a thud, another thing I had forgotten, that for years I forgot altogether, and then whenever I remembered repressed quickly again.

I don't know what we had done. Cathy, after all, couldn't say either, that day by the river. We were still in the first flat in Prestatyn; I must have been seven and Cathy five. It had happened finally: Daddy was sending us to the children's home. I swirled in the dip in the stairs begging him not to. 'Please, Daddy, please, please, don't!' He pushed past me and his granite shoulders descended the stairs and he'd gone through the flat door to the phone box.

'Mummy, Mummy!' I ran through to the little kitchen. 'Please stop him!' But my mother couldn't answer, she was slumped at the table weeping.

We waited, petrified. Down below in the building, the outside door slammed: he was coming back. His footsteps approached, rising through the building.

He opened the door. I couldn't speak to ask. I didn't need to: he shot me a look, cold blue stones. 'Pack your case. They're sending a van for you.'

The blue shadows yawned. There was no stopping it now. There it was ahead of us: the men in uniforms knocking, the booming metal doors of the big black van, the high gates clanging behind us in the hills.

My heart was leaking, my legs were dissolving. But my father was telling me: 'Get moving!' and my mother couldn't help, she was still too upset, weeping in the kitchen. We were on our own now. We would be on our own forever more now.

We didn't have a suitcase, I told my father, and he brought us one, a small leather one suitable for children, as if he'd had it ready and waiting for this occasion.

I was punched helpless with grief, but I had to think: what would we need? Socks, spare jumpers, and our pinafore skirts. I took them out of the drawer, the drawer that would no longer be ours. There would be a future in this flat, beginning this moment, when Cathy and I would no longer belong. I took our toothbrushes and facecloths from the bathroom. The spaces where they had been were icy with emptiness. I gasped with grief as I got our nighties from under our pillows. But I had to keep my head, for us both: how many knickers should we take? How many would they let us, those harsh guardians of the children's home, that punishment home? I went through, shuddering, to my mother and when I asked her if we should take them all, she nodded, helpless through her tears. She didn't know, of course; the world that Cathy and I were going to now was unknown to those we would leave behind here.

No one would know about us once we had gone.

And then we were packed. On my bedside table sat a brooch I'd bought for my mother from Woolworth's for Christmas, a ballerina leaping inside a gold circle over flowers made of pink glass, and which I'd guessed she hadn't liked because she'd given it back to me. They would never allow me, I was sure, to have such a thing in the children's home. I took it to my mother. 'Mummy,' I said between gusts of grief, 'I want you to have this to remember me by.'

My mother broke down.

And then we were sitting, as our father had ordered, at the top of the ghost-haunted stairwell, the case between us and our coats on ready, waiting for the men to come with the van, waiting to be nothing but ghosts here ourselves. We had said goodbye to our mother and baby David. He wouldn't remember us now, he would grow up without us (as indeed, in a way, he did).

Our father came back from the living room where he'd been watching through the window. 'They're here.'

My terror ignited. I whirled again. 'Please, Daddy, please – send them away! Daddy, please!'

He said nothing. He brushed past us and went down to meet them.

He came back for us. I collapsed against the bannister.

He said: 'I've sent them away. Next time you won't be so lucky.'

A memory so painful that any time it had surfaced I'd quickly pushed it under again.

I said to Cathy by the river, 'Do you know, it was years before it dawned on me that he never really rang the children's home. Only a couple of years ago, in fact.'

Pushing it under all my life, I had never examined it. And then I had woken one morning from a disturbing dream, a grown woman with teenage children sleeping in their rooms nearby and a meeting at the BBC that day. As I pulled myself out of the dream, that memory came back to me, curling out of the dream world into daylight reality, and I saw it for what it was: my father's cruel bluff. I went hot; I could feel myself going red: all my life, all this way into adulthood, into early middle age, I had gone on being successfully bluffed.

Down by the river Cathy gave a short laugh. She said, with a kind of cynical pity: 'Yeah, you were terribly upset. I knew at the time that he hadn't really rung them.'

I couldn't speak. How could Cathy have known, and I, two years older and supposed to be the clever one, hadn't?

I felt my grasp on reality slipping.

How could I have been so naïve?

Yet, as I pondered it now, as I felt my way back into the memory, I saw and felt again all the things that had convinced me: the granite set of my father's shoulders as he went down the stairs, the cold pebbles of his eyes as he handed me the case, our mother's sweeping grief. And felt again that utter conviction that he wanted to be rid of us, that he wanted to annihilate our existence from his life.

Aged fifteen, I would see it again, out in the garage as I asked him for money.

I would stand outside the closed door beforehand as the bark of his saw came from inside, forcing myself to go through the ordeal. Inside, the fug of blue smoke. His thick body bent away over the workbench, wide trousers flapping as he swayed.

He didn't stop or turn.

I'd have to call over the sound of sawing 'Dad . . . !'

I'd have to call several times.

Finally he'd stop and put the saw down with deliberate slowness.

As he turned towards me, everything about him seemed threatening: his electric hair floating horizontal, his huge nose poked towards me, his big dangerous hands swinging at his sides. Then there would be the petition, and the inevitable insults, his words knocked at me like well-aimed stones.

But what was worse was his eyes when he first looked up, the way he swung them unwillingly towards me, that look of loathing as they met mine.

And the way, as soon as the interview was over – as soon as he'd refused, or insulted me, or kept me on the hook ('You don't bloody deserve it; I'll have to see how you behave') – he'd turn away, back to his sawing, wanting me gone.

It was there, that sense, whenever I found myself alone with him, the day of my wedding, the time I tried to help him creosote the fence; any time he had to drive me anywhere alone. The first time I came back from university.

TROUBLEMAKER

MY TRAIN PULLED in, bringing me back for the first time from university. My mother had said my father would meet me from the station. I expected David to be there, so keen had he been to come to see me off at the start of term, but my father stood alone, away near the exit, solid and stark in his black blazer. He wasn't looking out for me. I had to call him as I approached. He suffered me to kiss him on his stiff-bristled cheek; he took my case but he didn't meet my eye. He didn't ask about my journey, or my time at university. He drove in silence.

I was silent, too, confused (in my life at university, I forgot!). I wondered if he simply didn't know what to ask, the whole notion of university being so alien to him, but as we neared home, I couldn't avoid the feeling that he just didn't want to be alone with me. As soon as we got home he went off out again, as if he couldn't wait to get away.

His car revved off. Cathy wasn't yet home from school, but David was home from his. In the two and a half months I'd been gone he'd grown taller and leaner, his face more angular. I exclaimed in delight and put my arms out to him. He ducked away, avoiding the hug, and went off out to play. I dropped my arms, feeling like a silly over-demonstrative distant aunt. He had hardly acknowledged me. It was almost as if he hardly remembered who I was.

I felt hurt, and then told myself that that was selfish, and silly.

I sat by the electric fire with my mother as she lengthened a pair of his trousers, and told her all about my term at university.

I said, 'I'm going to take my bike back next term. The landlord says I can keep it in the garage.'

My mother stopped sewing in alarm. 'You can't. David's got it now.'

'What?!'

How could they have done that, given it to David without asking me? 'But I still want it . . . !'

How could they have imagined I wouldn't?

My mother had looked so surprised: had they even thought about it, considered me at all? It was as if, gone from the house, I'd been wiped from their minds.

I thought. 'David's *got* a bike!'

'Well, something broke on it. And your dad said he could have yours for the parts.'

'What?!! They've *dismantled* it?!'

Now a different look came on my mother's face. Her look of panicky warning. 'Well, it's done now. So don't go saying anything.'

'But—'

'Jo, please, for my sake!'

Which silenced me, as always.

Into the silence she said, serious and intent: 'Look Jo, I don't want you coming back here and causing trouble.'

And I felt then she had been dreading my arrival.

Indeed, in later years she would admit to me from time to time, with a laugh: 'I was dying for you to go off to university and no longer be clashing with your father.'

Of course it was true that I'd answered back and protested, but when she said it, laughing, as if at the comic antics of a hot-headed teenager and her buffoon of a father, I never failed to feel misrepresented and hurt.

And there came a day when the seriousness I sensed behind her laughter was proved.

It was the day I went to tell her I had finally decided to leave Terry.

She was distraught.

'Don't do it!' she begged. 'For the sake of the children, don't do it!'

I felt momentarily sick and faint. As if I hadn't tried for the sake of my children. As if that wasn't why I had ended the affair.

She was clutching her pinny. 'Jo, I could have left your father. Many times. I thought of it.'

I studied her. She was admitting it now, then, how very bad it had all been.

She said, pleading: 'Jo, there isn't a problem between a husband and wife that can't be fixed between the sheets.'

My throat went dry.

'I've made my mind up, Mum.'

'But how will you manage? How will you *live?*'

Later I would understand what she was thinking: that my father would never help me out financially, though the idea of his doing so hadn't even occurred to me. Looking back on it all now, I thought: no wonder my father had been so positive latterly to Terry; no wonder he had been so angry with me for leaving him.

'I'll find a way,' I told her. 'Terry will pay maintenance for the children.'

'Where will you go?'

'I don't know.' My throat constricted. It was something that kept me awake at night. I had moved away from Manchester to be with Terry, and we'd spent a miserable year in a small North-East town where I was lonelier than ever, more trapped than ever with my two small children. I couldn't stay there as a single parent, even lonelier, even more trapped.

'Go back to Manchester, I suppose.' Though the friends I'd made in Manchester, the colleagues of Terry's and their wives, had moved away too.

My mother looked agonised.

She was silent. Then, plucking up courage to say something she clearly felt she had to: 'I'm sorry, Jo, but I couldn't offer you a home here. The men wouldn't allow it.'

I couldn't answer. It wasn't as if I would want to go back there: heaven forbid, I thought, wild horses couldn't drag me. But my throat was stretched and aching as I remembered that two summers before, when Cathy's first marriage had ended, they had offered her a home, though of course she hadn't accepted. I turned away towards the window, too proud to let my mother see my pain.

Beneath the holly bush outside the window a blackbird was rooting, tossing the leaves like so many rags.

Of course, I told myself, Cathy didn't have children to disrupt the men in their nest, and her husband had left *her*: unlike me, she was not, according to our father's hypocritical code, in the wrong. And yet . . .

It was the way that my mother, agonised as she was, had taken for granted that it was quite beyond question. That I couldn't be, as she put it, *allowed*.

'I couldn't wait for you to leave home,' she would often say laughing. And then one time, growing more serious, she added, 'But I missed you so much after you'd gone, I couldn't eat for a fortnight.'

I was taken aback by this last statement, so used had I become by then to the notion that she had simply wanted me gone. My first reaction was not to believe it. Yet gradually it began to seem truthful. After all, hadn't we been so close when my father wasn't around, in all those story-telling sessions, all those chats as she sewed and baked? Hadn't I been her right-hand girl in all things domestic; hadn't I been more than willing, before I became rebellious, for the closeness it gave me to her?

And then, just before my father's funeral, she said it again.

I was dusting the house for her, in readiness for my father's return in his coffin. Dusting the way she always wanted it doing, the way she'd learnt from her landlady Miss Protheroe during the war and had trained me in the house on the housing estate: taking the duster into every wooden curlicue, into every fold of every china Coalport cottage or shepherdess, along the top of every picture frame, of which there were scores, framed embroidered pictures worked by my mother, prints and water colours and oils.

Along the old servant's corridor was a whole row of black-framed Masonic certificates, honours bestowed on my father from lodges and arcane chapters, each with a blood-red wax seal. One, I noticed with grim irony, giving him the freedom of the City of Dublin as the benefactor of a children's home.

I took the duster, just as my mother would want me to,

round the panels of the door leading to the cellar where she'd said she never went because she'd heard ghosts there.

'What did you hear?' I had asked.

'Laughing,' she said. 'The sound of young girls laughing.' She said she liked to keep the door well locked.

I was in the blue-and-silver dining room now. There were banked silver-framed photos, on the mantelpiece, on sideboards, on little tables covered with hand-made lace cloths. Black-and-white photos of the south-Wales family, of my parents when they were courting, leaning against field gates. A studio shot in which they were handsome young marrieds in Llanfair, with Cathy on our mother's knee a doll-like three-year-old, and me a squinty splay-legged five-year-old on our father's. Our parents in early middle age, in gown and DJ at Masonic and Con Club balls. A tale in pictures of a happy, conventional marriage.

The wedding photo taken in the Methodist Hall, the curtain behind as if about to reveal the real, non-fantasy future that our mother must never have expected that day.

Portraits of David at various ages, and lots of Cathy because every year the library had had staff photos taken, charting her progress from exotically maned twenty-two-year-old, through her mulleted years in the eighties, to her bubble-haired present. Plumper some years, slimmer others, and looking increasingly like our father.

A couple of me as an adult: a colour print of me and Terry cutting the cake at our painful wedding, faded now to smoky blue, and me with our babies when Terry and I were still married.

And on the wall, an oil my mother had had done from photos. In it, Cathy and I, seven and five years old, stand each side of David in his pram which Grampa is pushing. We had been copied from a photo taken beside the cowshed at Llanfair, but here, in this painting, we were transposed to the driveway of Thwaite House, copied from a different photo and made to rise magnificently behind us. Like a flat contradiction of our real-life exile, a different story running in our mother's head . . .

I finished the dusting and stood back and surveyed the room. Huge baroque mirrors at either end of it endlessly, dimly repeated my reflection. I looked like my own ghost, my own various ghosts.

My mother came in. She said, 'Oh, your dad loved this room!'

She stood beside me, and now there were two of us reflected over and over in the deep, dark multiple versions of the room.

She said, 'He so loved this house! Of course, as you know, I wasn't keen. All the renovation it needed . . . Mind you,' – she gave a little laugh – 'I did think one good thing was that no one would hear your father shouting here.' She gazed around. 'But we did get it nice, didn't we? One day when he was in his wheelchair he asked me to wheel him around so he could look at the downstairs rooms. And I said to him, "Well, Patrick, we got a lovely house, didn't we, in the end?" I said to him, "We had a good life in the end, didn't we?"'

I couldn't speak.

She went on: 'I said to him once, "What a shame we didn't get this house with all the grounds until after the girls were grown up and gone. They'd have loved to play out there."'

I glanced back at the painting.

'But he didn't see it, he didn't know what I was talking about.'

I peered at her, unsure I'd heard right, that for once,

276

instead of insisting on the opposite, she was admitting to the fact that our father had discounted me and Cathy.

I said, joking (but not joking), 'Yes, he couldn't wait to get us out of the way,' and then instantly panicked in case I had upset her.

But she was laughing. 'Oh, it was *you* he couldn't wait to get out of the way!'

In spite of myself, in spite of being sure I had come to terms with it long ago, I was stung.

She said, 'Well, you did so quarrel with him.'

I had a surge of anger. *Quarrel.* As if it had been a matter of equity and choice, as if I had had any power . . .

And then she said it. 'Well, neither could I. I was desperate for you to go away and leave us in peace.'

In spite of myself, after all this time, after all my carefully developed cynicism, my lips felt numb.

'But I've told you, once you'd gone I missed you so much I couldn't eat for a fortnight!'

She was suddenly serious. 'I have to say things *did* settle down. We were a much calmer household after you'd gone.'

She saw my expression. 'Well, Jo, your father was afraid of you.'

'What?!' I was outraged now. How could she turn that situation, a girl bullied by her father, into *that*? Its complete opposite!

'Well, you were so clever.'

I thought I might burst. He would punish me for being *clever*? I deserved it for being *clever*?

She was looking suddenly frightened, frightened of my anger, I guessed, as frightened of me as she'd claimed my father had been. She quickly left the room.

I stood at the tall window, furious and shaky.

Sun fell like snow through the glass, turning everything white, bleaching and glistening the beige carpet. Outside the lawn stretched away, yellow in the sun, like another carpet, towards the bushes and the high brick wall secreting the garden away from the world.

One good thing was that no one would hear your father shouting here.

Shame. There had always been shame. How she had panicked about the neighbours when I'd screamed at the beatings; how ashamed I would be, too, afterwards, in case they had heard. How hard we had worked, all of us, to put on the front of a happy family outside the house. And how hard we had wanted and tried to believe it, to imagine ourselves into a different reality.

I turned into the room, to its plush furnishings and glistening ornaments, and what seemed to coat them all with the sun was a film of shame.

No one would hear your father shouting here. I went still.

So he *did* go on bawling then, even when I'd gone . . .

Yet: *We became a much calmer household once you had gone.* She had said it so earnestly, gravely, even.

How did those two things go together?

SECRECY AND SHAME

I WAS SEVEN years old when I became properly, painfully conscious of the need for secrecy.

It was a sequel to the children's home incident - buried, too, for long periods along with it.

A girl in my class had come to tea. We were playing in the living room of the flat, while my mother was in the kitchen preparing the food. We knocked over an ornament, or an ashtray, the white china pieces smashing on the lino and skidding like pieces of ice on a frozen lake.

My friend, Sylvia, said, matter-of-fact: 'We'd better tell your mummy,' and turned away to do it.

I grabbed her. 'No! You can't!'

'Why not?'

'Because we'd get sent to the children's home!'

'Of course you won't!' She looked almost contemptuous at my stupidity.

'We will! We nearly did once!'

'You *didn't!*'

'Yes, we did, we had to pack our case!'

Which convinced her, and she helped to hide the evidence.

A few days later, on the prom after school, my mother turned to me gravely. 'Josie, there's something I want to talk to you about.'

Sylvia, it turned out, had told her mother about the children's home.

'You shouldn't talk to people about such things, Josie. They don't understand.'

And in that moment I knew that my mother had been given a talking-to by Sylvia's mother. By someone who didn't understand, didn't understand that it wasn't my mother's fault, didn't know how upset my mother had been. And there she was now, my mother, publicly, unfairly shamed. There was a notion out there now about our family that we didn't want to be true, that *wasn't* true: for, after all, wasn't the true reality about us the one from Llanfair, before we came here, when we'd been happy, when Daddy wasn't so cross all the time and Cathy and I were good girls? *Your Daddy loves you really* . . .

And I knew I had never to tell anyone anything like that ever again.

❧

One day in the sixth form in Thwaite, in the old Victorian wing where we sixth-formers were housed, four or five of us were having an A-level English tutorial. Our teacher, Rod Haigh, was young, and as a man a rarity in the school. He was an iconoclast: he let us call him by his first name, he played protest songs at the folk club Cathy and I went to on Friday nights. He stood for intellectual freedom and Truth and Inquiry.

We were discussing King Lear and his treatment of Cordelia, and the discussion widened out to the general theme of punishment in parent-child relations.

I had never, ever told anyone that my father hit me, but suddenly, in this open, impartial intellectual context, I felt that I could; I could say it and render it merely academic.

I said it. 'Well, my dad hits me.'

A silence slammed in.

The sun leaned in and lit up the little hairs of my navy-blue serge school skirt. I looked up. The other girls were looking at their laps. Rod Haigh was focussing on the floor, his head cocked, as if deciding how to handle this situation.

Finally he raised his head and glanced at me briefly before looking past me to the window. 'What does he do?'

I was horrified. I had wanted to minimise it, depersonalise it, make it academic, but now it was the focus, magnified and horrifyingly personal. I said unwillingly, roughly, unable to find the words that didn't make it ugly: 'He does this,' and swiped my hand in the air.

Everyone looked even more embarrassed. One girl squirmed in her seat.

Rod Haigh said evenly – my heart bucketed as I detected exasperation – 'I mean, what does he do for a living?'

I felt an utter fool. I said quickly, breathlessly, to cover up, but also with growing horror – this hadn't been meant to be about my father *personally*, I hadn't meant to expose him, to ruin his reputation; and when it wasn't even true any more, he hadn't hit me since I'd started going out with Terry! – 'He's an engineer, a supervisor, he travels.'

Rod Haigh seemed to think about this and nodded inscrutably. Then he turned to the text and asked the group to consider Lear's relationship with Goneril and Regan.

As if nothing had happened.

What *had* happened?

I sat frozen with uncertainty and horror and shame and panic. The only thing I knew was that Rod Haigh had blocked me, failed to accept what I'd said as part of the discussion.

And afterwards no one, not Rod Haigh, not one of the other girls, mentioned it again.

It seemed frighteningly wiped, but – even more frightening – I didn't know if it was.

I lay in bed night after night turning it over. Did Rod Haigh think it didn't matter? Did he think it normal for a father to hit a teenage daughter, and silly of me to make such a self-centred fuss? Was it normal?

But if it was, it clearly wasn't normal to admit it publicly, since everyone had been so embarrassed, and not one of the girls had piped up to corroborate my experience. And now they seemed to be keeping away from me – though it was hard to tell, since out of embarrassment I was keeping away from them. I was keeping away especially from a girl with whom I'd recently become friendly: her father was a headmaster in the neighbouring town, a man who, if he *didn't* regard it as normal and acceptable, had just the kind of status and power to destroy the reputation my father had worked so hard on building for himself . . .

Lying awake, I would run alternative interpretations of the scene. Had the girls squirmed in recognition or shock? Were they keeping away from me now because they had never heard of anything so aberrant and ugly and common, or because of the danger of exposure for themselves? Or: did no one believe me? Because, after all, I was a clever girl, wasn't I, showing all the signs of getting the right encouragement at home, especially good at drama and possessing a confidence gifted to few on the stage (that other world I could escape to, to be other, better people). (And so at odds with my sudden bouts of lack of social confidence.) My mother came to all the school events,

282

sometimes now accompanied by my father looking interested and smart, giving off all the signs of a vibrant, creative and nurturing home. And my mother *had* nurtured me, hadn't she, with all her stories and her life of creativity, encouraging me in creativity of my own and a love of book and stories? Was I being entirely unfair?

I thought of Rod Haigh's exasperation. Had he decided that I was a self-dramatiser (was I?) and a liar?

And I was deeply hurt. Because, after all, it *hadn't* just been an academic point, it *was* personal: I had wanted to understand what it meant, to pocket it away for myself in a social context, and be able to feel all right about it at last.

Instead, I understood far less what it meant, and was far more unsure of what the reality of life with my father was.

There was another, frightening possibility. That Rod Haigh couldn't decide what to think, that he had gone to the staff room and shared it with those gentle spinster teachers – who *would*, I was in no doubt, be horrified – and it would become a scandal, and my father's reputation was about to destruct . . .

I had either demeaned myself or I had seriously risked my family who had to stay on here when I'd be gone to university at the end of the year. Or both.

Panicking, trying not to panic, I tried to bury the whole incident – I stopped going to Rod Haigh's after-school guitar class – burying myself in my books and my daily letters to Terry (my saviour). I pinned my thoughts on the autumn when at last I'd be gone and any rumours about my family attached to me would fade.

In a way, I exiled myself.

And then I did it again, let the damaging truth out.

I was in my final year at university. It was the first time in my life I had a proper circle of friends. I was sitting with them cross-legged on the floor of a room in our hall of residence.

They had begun talking about their families – academically, as something long in the past now that we were leading our distant, adult, academic lives. And I found myself able to say it: 'My dad used to hit me.' Past tense, safely in the past – it was almost two years now since the Easter he'd beaten me in front of Terry.

The others looked baffled.

Someone said, 'Oh,' and I couldn't detect the tone of it.

I couldn't tell what they were thinking. What *would* they think, the daughters of a vicar, a teacher and an orthopaedic surgeon? What would it *mean* to them? What would they imagine? A judicious tap once or twice, a basically caring fatherly corrective? After all, I thought, in the grand scheme of things, perhaps it hadn't been much . . . What on earth was I doing, twenty years old and still harping back to my childhood when the whole point had been to leave it behind?

Yet a panicky jabbing had started up beneath my ribs: I had the sense of having punched an ugly hole in the surface of my new life.

I changed the subject quickly. I got drunk. I got so drunk I started weeping.

They put me to bed with a solicitousness I found frightening: it meant that they'd taken it seriously, they were shocked. I lay alone in my room and imagined them discussing it in my absence, shocked at the ways of the lower classes, the free and ironical persona I'd built for myself here at university shattered, replaced by the demeaning status of victim.

I'd have given anything not to have said it. I was glad when no one mentioned it afterwards, though once again I was afraid it meant rather that their shock was so great that the subject was taboo . . .

I vowed then and there never to tell anyone again. The real solution, I decided, would be to make it so that I wouldn't even *think* of telling anyone again.

To make it not the point about myself.

∞

I broke my vow in the end.

While I was writing the novel, I went for a drink with an actress who'd been in one of my plays, and the subject came up, and I told her. It still had the feeling of breaking through a barrier, but I could be calm about it now, ironic and matter of fact.

She said, 'My god! I'd never have known!'

And I felt proud.

But also, as the moments ticked by, I felt fraudulent, as though I'd cheated myself. As though I hadn't told the truth. Those words *My father hit me* didn't scratch at the truth. For it wasn't just the beating, it was something else I had never grasped.

And going home on the bus afterwards I remembered with a drop of the stomach that it wasn't after all the first time I'd broken my vow.

It was the night before I was due to travel to my father's deathbed. My writing friend Judy had come over for dinner. We hadn't known each all that long, but we were editing the literary magazine together, and she'd come to discuss it.

I decided, consciously and deliberately, to tell her, to see if, after all this long time, now that my father's life was at an end, I could do it without a lurch of the stomach. I said it: 'He used to hit me.'

She said, 'I know, you told me.'

My stomach turned right over then. I had no memory whatsoever of telling her previously. How could I have done so, and not remember?

It was as though I had no control of it, this history that slipped out of my mouth and my memory without me.

And going home on the bus from the meeting with the actress, through an unfolding telescope of remembering, I thought of yet another time I'd told someone.

The wife of a colleague of Terry's. Housebound with toddlers, we'd spend occasional afternoons together, and one afternoon I went with her to visit her parents.

They lived in a Manchester terrace so strikingly like the one not so far off where we'd had one of our worst times with my father that, in spite of our two toddlers playing on the floor between us in the sun-pooled back room, I was plunged unnervingly back there.

Her parents, a shrewy little woman and a stocky, blustery man went out, and I asked her: 'Did your father ever hit you when you were a girl? Mine did.'

I found the blood was pounding in my head.

'Oh god, yeah!'

Her tone was matter-of-fact, cynical. I was taken aback.

'What . . . often?'

'Sure!'

'What . . . even when you were a teenager?'

She snorted. 'God, more often when I was a teenager.'

I felt a surge of grateful recognition. 'Yes, when you got to answer back!'

She looked amused. 'When I got to be sexual, you mean.'

'What . . . ?'

'Well, it's obvious, isn't it? There *has* to be a sexual element when a grown man beats his sexually burgeoning daughter!'

'What . . . what makes you think that?'

'Well, the *way* he hit me.' She said it as if it was obvious. 'Too much relish. And especially the way he grovelled afterwards, wanting me to forgive him. The way he stroked me better . . .'

I racked my own memories of being beaten, and I simply couldn't relate to this. There was nothing of *desire*. The opposite. He would beat me in a frenzy of resentment, as if he wanted to obliterate me.

I couldn't encompass it with my mind. I let it go. I had my child to think of, my marriage with Terry and my interrupted career. And with it that memory of telling slipped away, and, along with the subsequent tellings, would go on slipping away.

THE CHINA DRESSING-
TABLE SET

I COULDN'T TRUST my memory.

Yet it was the very memories I found it hard to hold onto that reverberated the most strongly once they returned, making my blood thump.

I was alone in my mother's bedroom, waiting to help her choose the clothes for my father's coffin, when one of them surfaced.

I stood looking around the room. Purple and green and white, the colours in which my mother had decorated their bedrooms ever since we lived in the North West. Purple-and-green-and-white William Morris lily design on the walls, deep-green velvet curtains she had made herself, a neat little Georgian chair covered in needlepoint in matching hues, embroidered cushions backed in purple and green velvets, the fine white lace bedspread she had started crocheting in north Wales. Suffragette colours, I thought, for a temple to domestic slavery. All that work, all those years of neat, fine, beautiful work to cover up the emotional tangle of the household.

I took in the layering of smells, as I would when a small child wondering about the riddles of pattern on the furniture, or as a teenager sent to dust it. The catchy fragrance of my mother's face powder, the dusty-sweet scent of the furnishings, and in the old days the dusky burnt-tobacco smell and the flat fungusy odour of my father's feet, those last now gone since for weeks he'd been sleeping downstairs. Still there was that air of everything in the room somehow crouching, holding back. Holding something back.

My eye moved over the tiny cast-iron fireplace and up to its mantelpiece. And hit on the china that dictated the colours of the room, that for years had dictated the décor of their room wherever we lived: a white Victorian dressing-table set, hand-painted with violets. And the memory connected with it surged back to me.

It was the year we lived in Easton in the Midlands. We were going to buy the china dressing-table set, our mother and me and Cathy and little David. Our mother couldn't really afford it, but she'd seen it in a junk shop and had fallen in love with it, and had it put aside until she got her Co-op divi. And now we were going to get it.

She had been excited about the china, I remembered, but there were things in the memory cutting across this notion. The rain slicing on the bus windows, the lights of the town shimmering like grease in the bowl of the darkening winter afternoon. And a troubling picture in my head of our father at home: the acid light of the room he sat in, and the darkness yawning at the big windows, even though I knew that in reality he'd close the curtains. And something odd about my mother. She wasn't talking; sitting across from me and Cathy, with David on her knee, she seemed cut off.

The memory coalesced around me: the steep road from the bus down to the junk shop, slicked with a sheet of running water as we ran with the pushchair, and my fear that we would slip. The dirt-caked grille across the junk shop window, the cold dark interior, the musty smell. The woman bringing the pieces of china, cold blue-white and cold purple, and wrapping them in old dank newspaper. Handing them over, significant and precious, unyielding and dead.

On the bus going home I held them in the carrier as once again my mother had David in her lap. The feel of them through the thin canvas, cold and ungiving.

And my mother opposite, still not saying a thing.

Always afterwards those images and feelings were in the sight and texture of the china: the slippy road in its smooth cold surface, the sadness and puzzlement knotted in the rough bruise-coloured violets.

Until I forgot it again.

What, I wondered now, was going on that day?

My mother was approaching up the stairs, but I knew I couldn't ask her. I knew what she'd say if I did: she'd relate it as an amusing little adventure – How wet we got! How hard she'd had to save up! – and if I challenged that she'd just laugh: *Oh, Jo, you take things too seriously!*

Also: I was stopped by that old sense of something vulnerable that would crack . . .

She came into the room. She opened up my father's tallboy.

'Most of these are bespoke, you know,' she told me, fond and proud, indicating the crammed contents: suits in various fabrics and colours, grey, black, navy-blue; plain and pinstriped and checked. As if, I thought, she had never complained about his extravagance.

She riffled through them and the arms of the jackets juddered, like a row of different, shifting men, standing one behind the other.

'Oh, he did look smart,' she said, picking out the Masonic

clothes, 'going off to all those meetings,' a musing half-smile on her face.

As if, I thought, she had never suffered from his desire to be gone from his family and responsibility, leaving her to carry all the burdens.

She laughed. 'And he did love to spend money!'

She looked up from laying the clothes out and saw my face. Serious now, almost earnest, she said what she'd so often said to me laughing: 'Well, he needed plenty of rope, your dad.'

She paused. 'And I always gave it to him.' There was something of defiance in the way she said it this time. I guessed she knew what I was thinking: that she'd rewarded his extravagance and irresponsibility.

And then, ironic and triumphant, she said: 'But I always pulled him back on it again!'

She snapped the tallboy door shut and the veneered pattern closed back on the contents. She turned back into the room, and noticed that the lacy bedspread was slightly off true. She straightened it, counting the squares, and it lay perfectly parallel, like a flat denial of any mystery.

THE SECRET ROOM

WHEN TERRY AND I were newly-married students, we rented half of a stone house, out beyond the jute mills, above Dundee. The house was big and detached, colonial in style, partitioned in two straight down the middle by the widow now renting it out. We had the grand staircase on our side, dark-wood-panelled, but it stopped short at the bottom just in front of a new wall and led at the top to a high-ceilinged and once spacious but now truncated landing. Our bedroom was one half of a once-huge master bedroom, the main entrance to which was now lost beyond the new wall on the landing, and to get to it we went along a low narrow servant's corridor to what was once a second entrance.

I was uneasy in that house – its giddying heights and yet suffocating cut-off lengths, the brooding baronial wooden panels, the fact that I knew that when we were out our landlady, a tall mournful-looking woman in an old-fashioned duster coat, let herself in – I'd caught her once or twice – and went around touching the faded regal furnishings, sadly dreamy and clearly grieving. I felt we were living in someone else's faded dreams.

I half-knew I was depressed but I didn't want to believe it. I was newly married after all; I had achieved my desire, escape with Terry . . . I told myself it was the move to a colder climate, to shorter winter days and a town of grey stone. Or the teaching practice, the gaunt school run by nuns, the bare walls of the classrooms, the kids blank or defiant and impossible to control, the nuns constantly flailing the vicious leather tawse. As I stepped in the mornings through the big iron gates of that school and I made my way through the dirty mounds of melted and re-frozen snow, I had to battle the same phobia with which I'd stepped into the playground of our school in Easton at the age of nine.

But also: I had a feeling, clinging like a mist and impossible to bat away, like longing, like loss. Like homesickness. How *could* it be that, when all I had ever wanted was escape . . . ?

I had a thing in particular about the tiny corridor to our bedroom. Like the stairs, it was panelled in dark wood, but so narrow that your shoulders almost touched each side and the ceiling so low that Terry – taller than me but not a tall man – had to bend his head. There was no light there and if the bedroom door was shut and there was no light on the landing, you'd be in pitch darkness. I'd have a feeling of claustrophobia whenever I passed through there, and I'd squeeze my mind and rush, just as I'd once rushed across the ghost-haunted stairs in Prestatyn.

One spring afternoon, when we'd been living there six months, in the light coming from the bedroom we noticed that one of the lower panels in the corridor wasn't flush with the rest. We felt around it and it gave, slipped slightly sideways. We pushed and it slid across the next panel, revealing a square-shaped hole. Beyond the hole was the bottom of a flight of steep little wooden stairs, lit by daylight filtering from above.

We ducked into the entrance and crept up the steps.

A proper room. A long low empty room with half-panelled walls, and above the panels on one side a row of windows we hadn't even noticed from outside, tucked as it must be behind a pitch of the roof. It was still and warm, warmer than the house below. Just then the sun came out and the room was filled with honey-coloured light.

'Wow!' we said. 'Who'd have known?'

'We should have a party up here,' I said, and Terry agreed.

We never did. We pushed back the panel and didn't go up there again more than once or twice. But all the time it glowed in my head with a meaning I couldn't identify, that mysterious room with its atmosphere of secret happiness locked away.

And with the panel closed tight again, I went on holding my breath and squeezing my mind as I passed, as quickly as I could, along the corridor.

For years after that I had a recurring dream of having to squeeze through a subterranean tunnel hardly wide enough for my body, to escape, or get home, or to save someone or something – it varied or, rather, it was all of those things at the same time. There was always some kind of fairground, or an arcade with bright lights and neon colours, but I'd have to leave, through an old familiar and secret entrance, a tiny hole at the bottom of a wall, hold my breath and close my eyes and squeeze myself in, and I'd wake up, stuck in the tunnel and gasping for breath.

I had other recurring bad dreams. I'd be entering the hall of a grand mansion for a celebration, a ball; chandeliers and gold-and-crimson colours, an elegant mezzanine gallery all around. And then a great bellow would come from above, and swinging down from the attic would come a monstrous grey devil, roaring and looping above me. I would wake, sweating with terror, my heart hammering, as Terry lay peacefully beside me, my babies asleep in their beds. And I knew it meant that something was unresolved, something I couldn't identify, out of my reach.

Even after I was settled with Greg in our tumbling sun-filled terrace, my children grown into their teens, I would dream of a house I had left and tried to go back to but couldn't, a different house every time but always looming in the dusk, down lonely streets or between black trees.

I was still dreaming this dream, in fact, when I was pondering my failed novel.

I happened to tell my mother about it.

She said, 'Oh, so do I! That's exactly *my* recurring dream!'

There was one dream about a house, or a building, that was different from the rest. It was the dream I had the night Greg and I had been snubbed by Gwilym and Renee at Llanfair.

There was a building, a wooden building with verandas and a little bell tower, on a green in the centre of a village. All was dark and abandoned, the grasses long and swishing, a lone bird circling mournfully.

It had a strange, Eastern-European feel. It wasn't I who had left it, yet in the dream I felt I knew it, in some way I couldn't fathom.

I woke. Greg breathed steadily beside me. My house was still, the boys asleep in their rooms.

A dream of abandonment and exile, I thought. Obviously because of what had just happened with Gwilym and Renee, I thought.

But I felt strangely moved. As if in my sleep I had touched something I had known long ago, in another time, or another world or dimension, buried deep in the coils of my brain.

PART SEVEN

In which I conduct some research

UNANSWERED QUESTIONS

I T ALL WENT on bugging me.

I tried not to let it, to concentrate on my own, present-day life. I put aside the novel and went back to writing plays and the gregarious business of having them produced.

But those dreams about houses went on, and in the corner of the room, the box into which I'd shoved the typescript sat like a slightly resentful yet patient pet.

In the end I opened it up again.

And now, as I skimmed the typescript, and as its contents, and my past, came flooding back again, things made even less sense than ever.

I read the bit I'd written about our move from the first flat in Prestatyn to another around the corner, and although it made sense on the page, I felt I no longer knew why we had to do it.

I ought to: my mother had explained often enough. How in that holiday town in the autumn the policies failed and my father kept losing his commission. How he'd decided he was on a hide to nowhere, so he went back to being an agent, and because the flat had come with the inspector's job, we'd had to leave.

The truth was, though, that whenever my mother gave this explanation, I would always glaze. The cheerful way she would tell it cut across the darkness of my memory, and my mind would rebel, and I'd shut off.

I quizzed her again now. 'You *know* why we moved!' she exclaimed, amazed that I needed to ask again, and went through the explanation once more.

And then she added something I'd never caught before: 'And the worst thing was, he was still having to pay off the book in south Wales as well!'

'What do you mean?'

'Well, when the agents started, they had to buy their books of policies from the firm. It was a kind of franchise. And in south Wales your father had a thriving book – well, you know your dad, able to charm the birds from the trees . . . But when we left south Wales he had to sell that book on, and the man who bought it turned out to be hopeless and lost a lot of the policies your dad had sold. And the awful thing was, if the policy folded it was the agent who'd sold the policies in the first place who was responsible for paying back the commission to the firm. So in Prestatyn your dad was paying back commission on two books of policies! We went on paying it back for years, actually. It was why I couldn't afford to go to Gwilym and Renee's wedding, I couldn't even afford the train fare.'

I remembered that now; it was when we were living in the grim terrace beside the Mersey. I remembered how upset Cathy and I had been that we hadn't been able to go . . .

My mother was going on: 'And, actually, we had borrowed money from Nanny and Grampa to buy the book in south Wales in the first place, and we still owed them that too.'

On top of the debt for the furniture and the bed-and-breakfast equipment and god knows what else . . . She had definitely never told me that. I could tell from the tone of her voice that she hadn't. Covering the shame of it, I guessed, the extent of our father's fecklessness.

There was something else I'd been wondering about.

'Why did we take that terraced house when it was so awful?'

'You *know* why! Because we had no choice, we were desperate, we had to get out of the house in Easton so quickly. Remember, the owners came back from Canada and demanded we get out! And after we were going to buy it, remember?!'

'But why *that* place, when it was disgusting . . . ?'

'Well, your father had already taken it. We'd been going to buy a house over there, of course, and we'd found one, remember? But then it turned out to be due for demolition.'

'You were going to *buy* a house there?!'

'Yes, you know that! Turned out it was in the way of a new road they were building. And by the time we found out, there was no time left, we just had to get somewhere to rent very quickly.'

'But that filthy house . . . ?' I remembered them quarrelling about it in the car on the way home from seeing it.

'Well, your father didn't have time to look around. He was doing all that travelling on top of his work, and worn out with it all.'

I thought about the new piece of information, the fact that they had been going to buy. 'So why didn't you look for another after we'd moved? Why did we end up spending three years in that rented terrace?'

'Well, you know what your father was like when we lived there. He was very depressed. But if you remember, he got himself together towards the end of that time, and we did find another house to buy.'

301

I didn't know that, either.

'But before it could all go through he got promotion and we moved here.'

It was only after I put the phone down that it would come to me to wonder: but if at the start we'd been well enough off to buy a house there, why were we then so desperately short of money?

And the picture she was painting, of a couple in a position to buy a house – a really nice semi-detached, painted white, she had said – a family equipped to move into the new, respectable, middle class of that time, was so at odds with my own memory of us as atavistic, aberrant and shameful.

I thought of our time in that grim terrace with its dark-blue-painted internal walls. I thought of my mother recalling Aunty Cathy's visits there, laughing about her convent-induced naivety.

'When she wrote to us from the punishment house,' she had said recently, 'she thought we could easily visit her – she had no idea of geography! She was in Preston! She had no idea that in Easton we were on the other side of the country!'

And yet . . . It occurred to me now: hadn't my father been working near Preston at the time?

Please visit me, my mother had told me she had written, *I am feeling desperate.*

Although he was working nearby, he hadn't. When she came to us the following year, when it was unavoidable, he had played the caring brother, but that year of her torture, the year of her desperate plea, he had turned a cold shoulder.

Why? Was it callousness – the callousness I so often felt in him and that made me shrink in dismay? Or inability? An emotional inability induced, as my mother had explained, by the work and the constant travel that year?

Or maybe a deeper, more long-seated inability . . .

What was it behind those black brooding moods and those violent eruptions of anger? Surely more, I thought now, than his belief in my mother's long-ago sexual betrayal . . .

Something perhaps in that shrouded Irish past . . . The religious conflict, the hard cold mother, the exile . . . I thought of that other, divorcing sister who had cold-shouldered *him* . . .

I thought again of the puzzle of what had happened to the fortune of his aunt in Australia and another odd thing occurred to me. One or more of the cousins in Birkenhead had gone over to investigate, my mother had always told me. But Aunt Lizzie was his aunt on his father's side, and weren't the people in Birkenhead his mother's relatives? And of course it was my father who had been supposed to inherit . . .

I asked my mother: 'Why them, and not Dad?'

'Well, your father couldn't have afforded the fare.'

'But it's still strange that he didn't have anything to do with it . . .'

'Oh, well, I don't know.'

She wasn't even interested. It was odd, I thought, how uninterested she was in Aunt Lizzie now, in view of the relish with which she had always told us the tale of our father's visit to Sydney.

But then she had never really been interested in our father's family, she had shut her mind to them . . .

I knew that if I wanted to explore it, if I wanted to discover what was behind my father's difficult, complex character and its fallout through our lives, I'd have to do it myself.

I'd have to do what he once forbade.

303

THE JACKSONS AND
THE KELLYS

I STOOD WITH Greg at the lonely crossroad and stared at the little stone house in which my father had been born.

It was one of a pair set back from the road. I stared at the spot in front, now tarmacked over, where my father had once stood barefoot in the dirt, quizzed by the schoolmaster.

There were trees, which I had somehow never imagined, and the cottage, clearly, had long ago been renovated, the yew hedge in which my father had left his boyhood treasures long gone. But beyond the cottage rose the bare moorland I'd always seen in my mind's eye, where my father trudged to the lake to fish, or ran, slipping school, to swim.

We got back in the car and drove into the town. Here was the hill he had sped down standing on the saddle, the pastel-painted terraces I'd always pictured. And there at the bottom the garage where he wiped his hands and vowed to come back driving a Rolls, still in business but with its corrugated roof now rusting and slumped.

No way of knowing in which of the three streets my father had lived with his grandfather.

In the churchyard of the gaunt Catholic church on the wide road between the cottage and the town, we looked for my father's parents', my grandparents', graves. When he first came into money, when he'd got his business going, my father had bought and arranged a headstone for their grave. I was away in Scotland at the time, but I knew all about it: he had wanted the best, the best marble, extra care over the inscription; he spared no expense.

We took a long time to find it. In the years since, the grave had sunk and the ground above it cracked, and the headstone was half-hidden by brambles. I prised the brambles away.

The inscription, over which my father had taken such care, was gold-painted still, but stark in its simplicity: *John and Teresa Jackson*, and below it: *Their beloved son Joseph* – my father's brother who'd had polio and who died not long after them. That was all. No ages and no dates.

I got Greg to take a photo of the headstone while I held back the brambles, and then let the branches fall back again.

In Dublin Central Library, the genealogy assistant, a plump breezy woman, came bustling towards me. 'What have you already?'

'Just this.' I handed her my father's birth certificate, which, kept in a bureau in our mother's lounge, had escaped David's post-funeral purge and appropriation. I didn't have the photo my father had once shown me of his ancestors; my mother had searched and searched but there had been no sign of it.

The assistant read out the surname of my father's father and the maiden name of his mother.

'Jackson and Kelly. Right, what we'll do: we have on computer the 1845 valuation of properties. We'll look there for Jacksons and Kellys in the townland where your father was born.' She led me briskly over to a bank of computers where middle-aged and elderly couples were bent at screens searching for romantic Irish pasts. That morning in the hotel one such

American couple had leaned over from their table and their full Irish breakfast and said, 'We found *our* relatives, and we wish we hadn't! They turned out to be so poor, and lived in such terrible conditions!'

The assistant twinkled as she typed in *Jackson*. 'We should find both families in the area,' adding with the air of a practised entertainer: 'Cupid didn't travel very far!'

Nothing came up for Jackson.

'Oh!' she said in surprise.

She quickly typed in *Kelly*.

A reel of Kellys came up on the screen and she pointed in triumph: 'Look, holdings! Quite big ones! Fields! This one had outbuildings and four acres! Looks like the Kellys were a big farming family in that area!' She turned to me beaming, one of the lucky ones for whom she had found an ancestry worth claiming.

I said, 'It's the Jacksons I'm most interested in tracing. There's a suggestion they may have been Jewish. Maybe that's why they weren't there then . . .'

'Oh, I should forget about *that*! Do you know the Christian name of your father's paternal grandfather?'

The grandfather he went to live with. No, I didn't . . .

'Well then, where you need to start is the dates on your grandparent's graves.'

But of course there were none. My father had wanted no expense spared when it came to the stone; he'd wanted, as always, ostentation, but it seemed that his constitutional urge not to leave too many traces had triumphed.

'Right so, you'll need to go and look for your grandparents' marriage certificate. What place was your father in the family?'

'The eldest . . .'

'Then look out for a *Patrick* Jackson,' she told me firmly. 'Naming the eldest son after the paternal grandfather is an Irish Catholic tradition.'

At half-eight next morning I was at the register office before it opened.

A long queue had formed already to the right of the door, snaking around the building. To the left of the door was a sign saying FAMILY HISTORY RESEARCH: QUEUE ON LEFT, and I went and stood beside it.

The sign was angled away from those queueing on the right, and they couldn't see it. They became ruffled; a subtle shifting and muttering started up, and they darted me looks of resentment and accusation.

'Family History,' I told them uncomfortably, pointing up to the sign. 'Different queue.'

They went silent and looked away. After a moment one man stepped forward and looked at the sign and stepped back with an air of not believing it.

They were weary, passive; they had glazed eyes and high colour, the signs of having spent a long night in the presence of birth or death.

I went up the steps – making them tut and gasp – through the open door towards a bright-cheeked man with his feet on the desk and his hands behind his head. 'Can this be right?' I asked him. 'Family History Research in a different queue?'

He jumped up. 'It is indeed, my darlin'. Now don't you be letting them bully you.' And he followed me out and addressed the queue: 'Now this young lady has come home to research her family history, so she'll be going in first.'

The queue subsided, submitting to the creed I knew so

well, putting the rest of the world before your own and romantic pretensions over real, searing life.

When nine o'clock arrived he came out again and, ostentatiously, his hand up to stop the other queue moving forward, waved me in with the ten or so other researchers who had now fetched up behind me, a gaggle of English and American accents and Burberry checks and glittery jumpers.

The research room was like a subversive schoolroom. There were plain wooden tables and a counter at the back where assistants heaved over huge books of records as they were ordered, slapping them down regardless of the danger to corners and spines. You were meant to pay each time you ordered one, but the assistants had no change; they said you could owe them or they would owe you and then they forgot. The rules pinned on the wall stated that a book must not be passed on between researchers without due process, but everyone did it and the assistants themselves suggested it. You were supposed to use only pencils, pens were forbidden, but no one bothered, and the pages of the books were covered in biro dots. Beneath a sign saying NO FOOD OR DRINK ALLOWED, a jolly group of professional researchers now arrived passed round a packet of mints and drank from cola cans.

Every rule was a joke. Nothing meant what it said. The whole setup seemed designed to let things slip away. I had a vision of my father watching and sniggering, it was beginning to seem like one of his tricks.

I searched all day for the marriage certificate of my father's parents and drew a blank.

In the evening I rang my mother and told her.

She said: 'Oh – ! Oh no, Jo, you *won't* find a record of

their marriage in Ireland! I remember your father said they got married in Birkenhead.'

So at the time they had been living in Birkenhead, alongside her sisters . . .

Another thing I hadn't known.

'Christ,' I said to Greg at dinner that evening, 'fancy her letting me get here and spend two days researching before telling me. She obviously didn't think about it. She just isn't that interested . . .'

Next day, our last full day in Dublin, we sat before two boxes of papers in the National Archives, census returns for the townland in which my father was born.

I opened the box for 1901.

The papers were greasy with handling, transparent as rice paper, each one listing the members of a household in careful copperplate pen and ink.

Almost straightaway, as in the library, I came up against Kellys: my father's mother Teresa, aged thirteen, living in 1901 with her parents and her two elder sisters according to the Kellys' relatively affluent tradition, in a good-sized house with land.

I had to riffle for the Jacksons.

Then there they were.

James and Mary Jackson, in 1901 living with three children – my father's father John, his Aunt Lizzie, and another son I'd never even heard of – in a tiny one-room house in the town, the house, presumably, where my father had gone to live at the age of ten.

There was a grandmother then. *Mary*. She must have died by the time my father went to live there.

'*James*,' read Greg, pointing to the name of the Head of Household, my father's grandfather. Contrary to the genealogy assistant's prediction, my father had not been named (by his devout Catholic mother) after his paternal grandfather in the Irish Catholic tradition.

I looked back at the return for the Kellys. *Head of household: Patrick Kelly.*

For some reason my father had been named after his mother's father instead.

Could it be because his paternal grandfather, as my father had always claimed, wasn't part of that Catholic Irish tradition?

Yet in the column for *Religion*, beside every name of the Jackson household, including that of James, was written *Roman Catholic*.

I turned to the box for 1911. Ten years on, the three Kelly sisters are alone in the house, their parents presumably dead, though some time not long afterwards they must have gone to Birkenhead. By this time James Jackson, my father's grandfather, was living alone as he was when my father later went to live with him, presumably widowed and the children flown.

'I'll get these photocopied,' I said and stood.

And as I did so, I had a kind of vision.

Ahead, in an angle of the air, I seemed to see a ranked band of stolid Kellys, my grandmother at the front, a stocky girl with arms stonily folded. And half-hidden behind them, a little man, moustachioed, in a black coat and beret, was turning quickly away, his coat flapping, and then gone.

It was in a kind of dream then that I went instead back towards the shelf of ranked census boxes and picked one up at random.

A box for an entirely different townland some distance off. I opened it up. 'Good god.'

Right on top was an entry for 1911: *Head of Household: Mary Jackson.* My father's grandmother, Mary Jackson, living with her two sons.

At lunch I puzzled over it.

Why, in 1911, in a time and a culture where the separation of married couples was nigh-on unheard of, was the grandmother my father had never mentioned living with her sons more than ten miles off, leaving her husband James Jackson all alone?

'Could it have been some kind of covered-up scandal? Another reason for my father not to be named for James Jackson . . . ?'

Greg shrugged, pouring water. 'It's impossible to know.'

What was the story of my father's separated grandparents, my great-grandparents?

'The disappearing Jacksons . . .'

I pondered. 'And remember, there were no Jacksons at all in the area in 1845 . . .'

That afternoon, in the Valuation Office, we heaved our way through great tomes, the housing records for subsequent years, looking for the time when they did appear.

A long search before we found it: the first appearance of any Jacksons in the whole area was James and Mary moving into the little house in the town in 1885.

I stroked my hand across the page. 'Well, my father did say that they came from Dublin . . .'

311

Next day we were leaving in the afternoon, but there was just time to return to the register office and look for the marriage of James and Mary Jackson.

We searched all morning and found nothing.

Beneath the SILENCE sign I got talking to a professional researcher, a man in a bright-red jumper.

'The more I've found out, the less I've found out,' I told him.

'Well,' he said, 'if they *were* Jews that would figure. Looks like they weren't married in Ireland. And arriving around 1885 . . . And Jackson's a Dublin Jewish name.'

'They were listed as Roman Catholic . . .'

Right under the SILENCE sign, he let out a loud laugh. 'They would be! Good god, they'd have got straight off the boat and gone to the first mass! They'd have to in this god-dammed country.'

There was one more thing we could try, though we had very little time left: we could look for the birth certificates of their children. It was almost time to go when I found one. A child John.

Greg said, 'Your father's father.'

'No . . . no, this child was born earlier. I suppose he died, and they named their later child after him . . . Look at the date: 1885. The year they first appear in the housing records . . . And look, the birth is registered by someone else they were obviously staying with.'

Everything seemed to point to their being newcomers, outsiders, as my father had always said . . .

And yet. There in black and white was the maiden name of the wife, my father's grandmother Mary: *Mullen*. Not a Jewish name at all.

I went on the train to return my father's birth certificate to my mother.

It was December again. I came through the big gates and the side wall of Thwaite House loomed before me in the darkening early afternoon.

I was struck, for the first time ever, by the oddness of the angle. Coming through the gate you approached the house side on, though this was not, I realised, how you'd have approached it in the early nineteenth century. Then, a road connected it to the manor to which it was the dower house, sweeping across what was now the house garden and down the slope of what was now the town park. As you came up towards it from the manor, your view would have been of the long elegant frontage with its tall windows, now hidden from any visitor standing at the gate. Sometime in the nineteenth century a new road had been built past the side of the house and the old road discontinued, its ghostly remains the gravel drive that curved from the gate round to the front of the house out of sight.

A house turning away to the past, away from the world and in on itself.

'The more I found out in Ireland,' I remarked to my mother, 'the more the mystery deepened.'

She said, 'Well, I rang Aunty Cathy last night.'

In spite of her lack of interest in my father's other relations, she'd kept up with Aunty Cathy, and she was curious about the question of Jewishness.

'I reminded Aunty Cathy about your dad's grandfather being Jewish. She had no memory of it!'

'She quickly suppressed it, I suppose.'

'Yes, but what she said then was: "Well, I did always wonder, when I was a girl, why our grandfather was buried in the Protestant churchyard."'

'Good lord!'

You get off the boat, you go straight to Mass, you claim to be Roman Catholic when the census man comes knocking, but the Catholics won't have you in the end . . .

But then my father's grandmother Mary Mullen hadn't come off the boat at all . . .

My mother broke into my thoughts. 'By the way, when I was searching for that photo of your dad's ancestors I found a photo of his Aunt Lizzie in Australia. It was in a box that he kept in our dressing room, separate from his other papers. I'd never seen it before, he never showed it to me. Come and see.'

She led me through to the long sitting room, flitting ahead like a little bird, in her seventies now though you wouldn't know it. She took an inlaid box from the bureau and opened it and handed me the black and white photo.

My father's Aunt Lizzie was a jolly-looking middle-aged woman in round specs, her black hair in a low bun, standing in front of a suburban art deco fireplace. She was plainer and more homely than I had always imagined.

I turned the photo over. 'What's this?' On the back was a pencilled message.

'Oh, I didn't see that!'

It read: *Taken at Gran's birthday party. She was 95 on 18/5/49. See her photo on the wall (aged about 88).*

I turned the photo back over. Above the mantelpiece behind Aunt Lizzie was a framed photo of a white-haired woman in a shawl.

'"Gran!" That must her mother . . . Mary Mullen, *Dad's* gran!'

The gran he'd never mentioned, who had lived separately from his grandfather . . .

My mother said in vague surprise, 'Oh, I suppose it must be . . .'

'By the look of it, she ended up in Australia with Aunt Lizzie . . .'

My mother looked blankly amazed.

I looked again at the pencilled message. 'And in 1949 she was still alive.'

The year Cathy was born.

I peered more closely into the picture on the wall in the photograph. The old woman, Mary Mullen, was sitting over a cloth she was embroidering on a hoop.

1949. The year Aunt Lizzie sent those strange embroidered baby bags.

'Do you think it must have been Dad's grandmother who embroidered those bags?'

'I suppose it could have been . . .'

I remembered the obstruction of the little blue forget-me-knots under my fingers, that niggling sense of something unresolved . . .

'And you had no idea she was there?'

'No . . . Well, I told you, your dad showed me hardly any of Lizzie's letters . . .'

'But he didn't even *mention* it?'

'No.'

My mother was looking a little odd. She said quietly: 'Well, there were a lot of things your father didn't think worth mentioning.'

'Like what?'

She opened her mouth and then shut it. Then opened it again: 'Well, for instance, I didn't know until we cycled from Shropshire to visit his Birkenhead cousins that his father was a gambler.'

'A gambler?! You never told me that!'

'Well, I don't think your father ever knew that I knew. One of his girl cousins told me. She said that her own mother had to send half a crown a week to his mother because his father was always gambling all his wages away.'

'So *that's* why they were so poor . . .'

'I never mentioned it to your dad because he hadn't mentioned it himself. He was obviously ashamed.'

'No wonder he didn't want me to do family history research. A gambling father, a runaway grandmother . . .'

There was a pause in which my mother looked strangely uncomfortable.

Then she said with an air of finality, 'You can have the photo, I don't want it.' All her old disinterest seemed to return, and she seemed to be ending the conversation.

But my thoughts had not stopped running. 'Can you believe it, though? Dad not even mentioning to you that his grandmother was in Australia! Expecting you to go there without telling you anything about it!'

'Well, that's it exactly.' She took a breath, and then she told me something else she'd never told me before.

❧

She never really thought about Australia, she said, when she learned that my father had expected her to go there. She just knew she didn't want to go and made that clear, and took no more interest. But when the tickets for our passage came, along with the news that Aunt Lizzie had set us up with a bungalow and a garage for my father to run, she was shocked into thinking about its reality.

She wondered: how had Aunt Lizzie, a girl from a poor background in Ireland, managed to be given such a fortune by a famous man?

One evening, as she put a plate of herrings in front of my father, she asked: 'So Aunt Lizzie met that matinee idol in London, did she?'

My father nodded, unwilling and hostile: my mother had already made him return the tickets.

'Were they courting?'

He grunted tense assent and asked was there any more bread for god's sake.

She went to get it, but when she came back persisted. 'I read that he was married.'

'Don't be so bloody stupid.'

'Yes, he was, to a famous actress. Happily married, from very early on.'

He had no answer. He stared at his plate, doggedly eating.

'So he palmed Lizzie off on the other side of the world, well away from the wife . . .'

He was beginning to look furious.

'I wonder why he needed to do that?'

My father didn't answer.

'He must have really loved her . . .'

My father nodded, tense.

'Unless, that is, he had to pay her off. And such a lot . . . Maybe she had something on him.'

He growled: 'What's going on in your twisted Methodist mind?'

'Well, how did they meet?' A famous matinee idol and a girl from her background whose most likely occupation would have been maid. Or . . .

'She was a prostitute, wasn't she?'

'Wash your bloody mouth out, woman!'

'And these businesses of hers. They're brothels, aren't they?'

He stood roughly, knocking the chair over behind him. 'You filthy-minded Welsh witch!'

And he left the room and was gone from the house.

'And these were the businesses he was expecting to inherit,' my mother said to me now.

'Are you *sure*?'

I looked again at the photo of Aunt Lizzie, plain and homely and standing in front of the photo of her mother from whom, surely, she'd have had to hide or gloss the truth of such a profession. The woman who had begged my father to rush and save his sister from divorce, to save her immortal soul . . .

'Well, he didn't deny it. I'd asked him about the businesses before, and he'd always been vague. And of course, I'd never really been interested.'

She laughed. 'And that's a joke, the Catholic church getting the proceeds of a string of brothels . . .'

It could explain why my father had kept his head down, affected not to be involved, when it came to sorting out Aunt Lizzie's affairs in which the other relatives were naturally showing an interest. Left the more distant relations to come up against a mystery, or maybe uncover the truth and hush it up . . .

I said, 'But even if they *were* brothels, maybe Dad didn't realise, until you pointed it out to him? And then he felt a fool . . .'

My mother gave an uncharacteristic cynical snort. 'Your father was never that naïve.'

I was taken aback. All the times she had portrayed him as exactly that, naïve – the foolish decisions he made, the trusting word-of-mouth deals, the sucker he made himself for others . . .

I said, 'But he was going to take you out there . . . He must have known how you'd feel about *that!*'

'Well, once he got me out there . . .' She paused. 'I don't think he cared.'

I stared at my mother who had always so conscientiously promoted the notion that deep down my father *cared*.

'But what about Aunt Lizzie? He was always such a moralist when it came to women!'

'Well, your father could always do doublethink when it suited him.' She was cynical, grim.

I was amazed, even dismayed, by this jaundiced view of my father from the woman who had always defended him from my similar criticism.

We were back in the kitchen now. Seeming to change the subject, she pushed the copies of the census papers I'd brought back across the kitchen table. 'Take them back, I don't want them.' She had moved them away almost with aversion.

'Aren't you interested?'

'No, I'm not.'

'Why not?'

'I'm just not.'

She seemed distracted, even troubled.

I gave up. I slipped the papers back in my bag. It was time for me to leave for my train.

When I unlocked the door at home the phone was ringing. It was my mother.

'Jo, I can't bear it, seeing you struggle like this.'

'What do you mean?'

'Struggling to understand. You'll never be able to, unless I tell you the truth about your father.'

PART EIGHT

In which my mother makes an even more stunning revelation

SOMETHING UNSUSPECTED

'**P**EOPLE WARNED ME not to marry him,' she said. She had always said that, but never without a little light laugh, as if to say that ultimately they'd been wrong.

She was more serious now.

She told me: she was coming out of chapel the year of her engagement to my father when her old school friend Delyth Reece fell in beside her and asked, 'Is Patrick coming down this weekend?'

She'd stopped walking so my mother had to stop too.

Delyth Reece was oddly earnest. 'Don't marry him, Gwen.'

My mother was shocked and annoyed, but (according to her constitutional habit) she laughed. Obviously, she thought, Delyth was judging Patrick by his outward appearance, his cocky grin and daredevil ways.

Delyth persisted. 'He's not a man to spend your life with. He's a liar.'

'How do *you* know?' my mother demanded, letting her annoyance show now.

Delyth had no answer. She looked at the ground – ashamed, my mother decided. And so she should be, she thought: Patrick was right, there was a lack of heart in too many of these chapel people.

But then another friend, Enyd Jones, said the same: 'Don't marry him.'

Enyd was in the ATS and stationed near Cardiff, and liked to think of herself as a woman of the world. She was sitting in the village café, wearing civvies when she should have been in uniform, a little pillbox hat and bright red nails. She flicked her cigarette and said down her nose, pouring smoke: 'He's not to be trusted.'

My mother refused to pay this the respect of an answer.

Enyd shrugged her padded shoulders. 'Well, you have to admit he's very secretive. You can't get a thing out of him about his background, for instance.'

This did strike a chord with my mother. She knew the few things he'd told her and her sister Molly when he'd first met them, the things she would eventually pass on to us, but very little more: whenever she questioned him now, he clammed up. But she knew also that Patrick was ashamed of his poverty-stricken background. And, after all, it was wartime: people were being ripped away from their pasts; they were living in the moment and not looking back. And hadn't Patrick, long before that, wiping his hands in the Ballymoyne garage, vowed not to look back?

My mother decided: Enyd Jones might think of herself as a woman of the world, but she was as infected as the rest with the small-mindedness of chapel.

Glyn Evans, a pleasant chap, had none of their suspicions. He liked Patrick. 'He was down last weekend, wasn't he?' he said to my mother, meeting her in the road. 'I saw him in the village on Sunday when I was on the way to my mother's.' Usually after chapel on Sundays Glyn went to visit his bed-ridden mother.

'You must have been late, then,' my mother remarked. 'Patrick was at Mass up at the camp until one.'

'No . . . No, I came more or less straight from chapel and met him in the village.'

My mother thought of my father the previous Sunday, swinging down the hill in a rush, arriving at the cottage at ten past one saying Mass had run over.

Next time he was on leave she challenged him. 'So you didn't go to Mass last time?'

'Of course I did,' he said cheerily.

He looked up and saw her face and looked away quickly.

Which was the first time she knew he was capable of lying to her.

It was a trivial lie, though, she decided. She married him.

And then, two weeks after their wedding, he knocked her into a hedge for dancing with a pilot officer and refused afterwards to speak to her.

The quote from the Bible came to her then: *Beware of false prophets which come to you in sheeps' clothing, but inwardly they are ravening wolves.*

But she had made her vow, she decided, *for better or for worse.*

And she knew, from the way he had cried when she'd said she wasn't sure she could marry him, that he was suffering some deep unarticulated pain. She was the strong one, she decided. And she was Christian: she could turn the other cheek.

He went on refusing to speak to her, turning his back to her in bed at Miss Protheroe's. But she went on being loving, and in the end he melted.

I remembered what she had said to me: *Jo, there's no problem between a husband and wife that can't be solved between the sheets.*

Yet she went on being shocked by my father; he went on revealing sides of himself she had never suspected. The squandering of money, the almost criminal blitheness, she said, with which he took part in black market scams. The way he kept things from her until he pulled them from his hat. The fact of Australia and the RAF commission were shocking enough, but the business of Miss Protheroe, she said, she found more deeply disturbing.

The morning after Miss Protheroe offered him the money to set up a garage in her orchard, they were late getting up: they'd been awake for most of the night arguing about it. They were still dressing when Miss Protheroe knocked on their door. Gwen was still rolling up a stocking and called, 'Just a minute!' but the door opened.

Shockingly, Miss Protheroe – the prim, correct Miss Protheroe – was only half-dressed, in a skirt and petticoat, her grey hair loose down her long straight back. She smirked and threw Patrick a look that mocked my mother's prudery. It was a look of conspiracy and – there was no doubt about it – a look that was sexual.

She said to my mother: 'I'm seventy-two, Gwen, and I can still do that, put my stockings on standing on one leg.'

She was sarcastic, almost triumphant.

My mother turned to see my father's reaction, but he'd turned away, busying himself with his cuff buttons.

Miss Protheroe went on: 'I came to say I've overslept and I'm behind.' My mother could imagine why: she'd been awake all night too, listening to them rowing. 'So will you put the eggs on, Gwen, before you go for the milk?'

The strap of her petticoat fell off her scrawny shoulder,

and she left it, seeming even to preen. And then, not looking at my mother, but with her eyes on my father, she said, 'If I were twenty years younger, Gwen, I'd give you a run for your money.' And she turned from the room and was gone.

My mother was aghast. How could she have been so outrageous? Why did she not think that my father wouldn't be outraged on my mother's behalf?

She turned to look at him. He was sniggering slyly. And then she knew: he'd been deliberately egging Miss Protheroe on for what he could get out of her.

There was another day round about that time, she said, when she realised that my father wasn't simply secretive, but was hooked on the very idea of secrecy.

She still had her bike, and they were out on a bike ride, spinning along the lanes. He was leading and she was following. He was looking for something, some kind of stately home.

'It's here!' He pulled on his brakes in front of huge iron gates with parkland beyond. The gates were open and they cycled in and between rocky knolls crested with trees.

'There!' he cried as an ugly obelisk hove into view. He threw down his bike and circled it, running his hand on its surface.

My mother couldn't see the attraction, just some aristocrat's ugly folly.

My father told her eagerly: 'There are secret caves under these outcrops. And each cave is dedicated to a particular ancient mystery.'

'What do you mean? What kind of mystery?'

He didn't answer. His face was a secretive half-smile.

'What mysteries?'

'I told you, ancient ones.'

'*How* ancient? To do with what?'

Again he didn't answer. And his face closed.

She understood then: he relished the keeping of the secret. Relished keeping it from *her*.

She clung to the truth of their sex life, she told me, through all the surprises, the secret appropriation of her money, the terrible unjustified jealousies, the vicious knocks he'd give her that could pass for accidents, the swiped plates and objects which couldn't, the night he chased her round the kitchen with the gun.

I cried: 'He was *violent* with you?'

There was a silence. I could sense her shock at the way I had framed it.

'Well . . . yes.'

'When?'

I thought of her falling in the mud running back to Nanny and Grampa. It was violence she had been running from . . .

'Well . . . always.'

'*Always?* What – even when we kids were older?'

Another short silence. Then: 'Yes.'

I had never guessed. I had thought the physical violence was only directed at me and Cathy, and especially at me.

'Whenever he got in a temper about anything, I got it in the neck.'

Don't make him angry. For my sake.

I had never guessed, in spite of the time he threw the teapot and it hit her head . . .

He had been so careful with us girls not to bruise us where it would show; why would he not do the same with her? Leave no sign, no mark to give it away . . .

328

And she herself had hidden it so well.

I thought of her crumpled and weeping in the kitchen, unable to protest and protect us, as he made us pack to go to the children's home. It came to me: we were a sideshow in a wider drama: he had probably beaten her.

She was saying: 'People warned me before I married him. And I always wondered afterwards what they meant. What they knew.'

She was no longer talking about the violence. She meant something else.

⚜

'Your father was never faithful to me, Jo.'

'What!?'

I had always thought the affair with Sandra Suggate a one-off midlife crisis. Down the years I had written stories with uncommunicative and absent fathers like my own, and because they were stories and needed an ending and an explanation, the fathers had sometimes turned out to be secret philanderers (though often drunkards or spies), but I'd never been sure they were convincing. It didn't feel like the truth about my own father.

And what she told me next had never even entered my head.

It was the time he wasn't sleeping with her, the time just before we left Llanfair.

She was pregnant with David, the baby she had conceived the one night he relented.

Our father was out. He was always out, she said: he did

329

things to avoid her. He'd do his insurance rounds in the evenings; he'd joined the Special Police Force and was on evening duty. She had just put Cathy and me to bed – that dreamy time in which a lonely wife and mother can take comfort, in which, years later, I would take comfort myself: the yeasty small limbs and sweet talcum smell, the rocking rhythm of the bedtime story.

The peace of the house was broken by an urgent banging on the front door.

My father had already had the two accidents on his motorbike, and her heart must have been drumming against the baby in her belly.

A man stood on the doorstep, slim, small-featured (clearly, these details were ingrained in her mind forever), and was steely with fury and grave with import.

'Is this where Patrick Jackson lives?'

'Yes—'

'Is he in?'

'No, he's out on an insurance round . . .'

'Then I'll wait.'

She didn't want to ask him in, she didn't want to let in whatever trouble he had brought, but of course she felt obliged. 'Won't you come in?'

He thought for a second, and then nodded grimly and stepped in.

'You are . . . ?' she asked.

'It doesn't matter.'

'Is it about an insurance policy?'

He looked at the floor. 'I'd rather not say.'

'You're one of Patrick's clients?'

He gave a twitch of his head, admitting that he was, and

then shook it as if denying the admission.

He wouldn't have a cup of tea. He was all refusal. He wouldn't meet her eye. Was there somewhere he could wait? he asked, and he meant alone.

She led him into the front room. 'I'll be fine here,' he said, dismissing her.

She pottered in the kitchen, wondering and worrying, until at last my father's motorbike turned into the drive. He came in through the back door, his face closed to her as usual.

'Patrick, there's a man here to see you, he wouldn't say who he was.'

Alarm flared in his face, quickly wiped.

'He's in the front room.'

If he knew who it was he wasn't saying, and without a word he'd gone and the front room door was closing behind him.

At first the voices were low, and then both of them were shouting behind the closed door. She couldn't hear what they were saying; perhaps, she said to me now, she didn't want to.

The door burst open and the man strode out. He stopped at the front entrance and called back to my father: 'If you ever come near my son again, I promise you, you'll end up in jail!' and the front door slammed.

'What was that all about?' she asked my father who was hanging on the front-room door jamb. He looked unperturbed. He gave a chagrined grin.

It was the first time in two years he had smiled at her, and her chest leapt with joy.

He said, 'Stupid bastard. I sold his son an insurance policy.'

His grin faded and he grew contemptuous, then rueful. 'As if it isn't hard enough selling policies in the first place, without the bloody relations coming and complaining.'

For the first time in two years he was appealing to her over a problem, and all she felt was gratitude and relief.

And almost immediately we left, moved to north Wales.

She said to me now: 'I don't think he could get out of there fast enough.' (Although his book was thriving.)

She said her father, Grampa, begged her not to go with him – in spite of the fact that separation and single mother-hood in those days were shameful. He knew that my father hit her; after all, she'd gone running to him and Nanny those times with the pram. Years later, she said, her father would tell her about the night he and the other men, Gwilym and our mother's cousins, taking pity on our father because he was so depressed at the time, gave him a gun and took him with them to shoot ducks on the marshes. They were lying in the grass in the dusk waiting for the ducks to fly in, and without any warning, my father took a shot into the air, a practical joke that terrified them out of their skins. As they made their way back up the road with empty bags (the ducks would never fly in after that shot), our father in the rear, another shot rang out behind them. They turned: he was lowering his gun and a dark shape lay in the road: the neighbourhood owl. Grampa was furious, she said. 'Never fire a gun without warning!' he told him. *Trigger-happy bastard*, he said he told him he was.

So he knew our father was irresponsible, dangerous even. In later years, though, my mother said, she would wonder what else her father, an ex-World-War-One sailor, knew about Patrick, or at least guessed.

But of course she went with him. *She* hadn't guessed, or rather, joyful that he'd turned to her at last, wanting to believe him, she'd suppressed any awakening awareness.

And he'd so dramatically put her off the scent: half the work in the Special Police Force was catching men down lanes together in cars . . . And the disgusted, vicious way he spoke of them: *poofters* and *pansies* . . . You could always tell them, he said in contempt, because they had *sheep's eyes*.

And she loved him. She couldn't bear the thought of being without him. That night when she'd first found him lying on the floor deep in his meditation and thought he was dead, she had fainted, her own spirit giving up.

He still wasn't sleeping with her, but she thought her constancy would melt him once more. The move to Prestatyn would be a new start.

⁂

May. She lay in a sun-filled bedroom in the flat in north Wales, the new baby in the cot beside her. I remembered running in and seeing the baby drowning in sunshine before Aunty Molly, who'd come to help, pulled the curtain to shield him.

My father was not around. 'A boy,' the midwife had told my father, my mother now told me. She held the baby out for him to see, but he'd turned away, she said, without even looking.

The end of July. Sports day at my school in Prestatyn.

My mother was standing alone at the side of the track, two-month-old David in her arms and four-year-old Cathy at her side. There was a gaggle of mothers a little distance off. She knew them all to speak to, but not enough to move along and join them. In any case, they were in an impenetrable

333

huddle, failing to watch the race and discussing something intently. Occasionally one of them would lift her head in my mother's direction and she came to realise it was her they were discussing.

A new race began, and some of them turned to watch it and cheer, but one of them, a little woman with corkscrew curls, broke from the group and sidled towards my mother. My mother thought she must be coming to ask her to join them, but as she neared she saw that her expression wasn't friendly. The race was over, and the woman looked back at the others, who were now watching her expectantly, then turned to my mother and said: 'We want you know that none of us wants your husband coming round to our houses selling insurance.'

'Why ever not?' exclaimed my mother in shock.

'We don't want someone like that coming into our homes.'

'What on earth do you mean?'

'A homosexual.'

She had never heard the word before, my mother said.

I had never heard the word homosexual until I was twenty-nine years old.

I remembered the way she had said it when my father had refused to go to the play at my school. The way she kept her head down, kept stirring the stew. And the way my father had reacted as soon as he knew who the play was by. The denial. The way that, in denial, and I supposed now in terror, he had gone from the room.

I thought of my mother standing there on the sports field in Prestatyn, the new baby in her arms, hearing the word for the first time ever, the meaning of it dropping into her brain, hearing it applied to my manly father and not just the effeminate men he called *poofters*. Struggling with the contradictions.

Absorbing the implications. *Stay away from my son or you'll end up in jail*, the man in Llanfair had called. Patrick could go to jail.

I thought of her standing there, the baby in her arms, the seagulls crying the word overhead, *jail . . . jail . . .*

She told me now that she would always wonder, after this, about the accident on his motorbike when he went through a plate-glass window. He had been on his way to the county court to testify against one of the men he and his fellow Special Force officer had picked up for cottaging. She had always wondered if, riding towards possible exposure, he'd come off his bike on purpose.

I thought of the night he came back from the hospital, and the desolate, glittering look in his eyes that had made me, five years old, flee in dismay . . .

We don't want your husband coming round to our houses selling insurance.

He had to get out of the insurance, she had always told us. *The policies were failing.*

Those staring women had dropped their policies.

And those women could send him to jail.

For safety's sake, to prevent us all being destroyed, it had to be denied. It had to be buried.

And so my mother buried it, and worked against my father's growing bad temper to create a cohesive family that couldn't be destroyed. Making a point of singing after every row with him (and irritating him all the more: he took it as an insolent challenge, I knew), sending us girls to say sorry (and making him feel even more pestered). Swept by fear at any censure of the family, at my courting scrutiny by letting slip that we'd 'nearly' been sent to a children's home.

I *never heard the word homosexual until I was twenty-nine years old.* She would say it to me and Cathy when we were adult, and we'd exchange knowing glances at her old-fashioned naivety, and no doubt she felt her job was well done.

The following spring, she said, it seemed that her persistence and efforts were rewarded. His moods were better. He took us out for drives on Sunday afternoons, he even deigned to carry David.

That August he drove us all back down to Llanfair for a fortnights' holiday. He couldn't stay, he had to work. As soon as he got back to Prestatyn he wrote my mother a long letter describing his meandering journey back through the Welsh borders, and his lonely return to the flat.

It was among the bundle of his letters she would eventually give me, written in the copperplate hand he'd learnt in the church school:

> *You should have seen the behaviour of the kitten when I got back. He nearly went mad with excitement, but he cried like hell when he saw that I didn't have any of you with me, and he's been crying ever since. He goes into our room looking for you, smells the bed, looks under it, round the wardrobe and tallboy, and then repeats the process in the girls' room.*
>
> *Yesterday I ran out of sugar and had to drink my tea*

without it, but I've got some today. I haven't done any
housework yet, but I'll have a good old turnout before I
come to get you.

Last night I slept in the children's bed, as I couldn't
sleep in our bed without you, and I was frozen as hell,
there aren't enough blankets on that bed for those kids.

I tipped a cup of tea over myself at teatime tonight,
but all's well that ends well.

She took it as an expression of commitment, proof that he
had come back to her.

At the end of the fortnight he came and drove us back to
north Wales. He seemed relieved to be having us back again,
my mother said, and on the return journey we all sang.

She walked into their bedroom to unpack and a stark black
shape smacked her vision.

A man's black shirt hanging over the back of the bedside
chair. Not the kind of shirt men wore in those days, mid-
night-coloured and sheeny, slithery-looking.

'What's this?'

He came up behind her. 'I bought it.' He sounded tetchy.

'You bought *that?*' (And when they were so short of
money.) 'Where on earth would you wear a shirt like that?'

And yet it had clearly been recently worn. The sleeves were
plumped and creased at the inner elbows.

He said irritably, 'All the men at weightlifting wear shirts
like that.'

His cheek was beginning to work. A row was brewing. Any
moment now he'd be dangerous. She turned to leave the room,
to dispel the tension, and a sight hit her eye that nearly broke
her: on the other side of the bed in which he'd said he'd been

337

unable to seep without her, which he'd said the kitten, pining for her, had sniffed, lay an empty cigarette packet, a brand she knew Patrick would never buy.

And the shirt hung there beside the bed, a sleek corrupt presence.

There could be no challenging him about it, she said, or indeed about anything, ever. As soon as she asked even tentative questions, he'd close up, lose his temper, 'You suspicious-minded bitch!', twisting it always so the fault was hers.

Push was *pull*. Left was right. Black was white. It was she who was in the wrong.

And then he would begin his recriminations, his long-held grudge: she was a tart, an adulterous bitch; and if she protested, she got thumped.

Besides, she had no words for that particular challenge, no words she could ever use, certainly not that frightening one hissed at her on the sports field that day. And even if there had been, there was no concept in her head to form them around, no concept that she wanted there, no truth of that sort that she wanted to face or believe.

Without words to catch it, the truth can slip away, black can become white, and part of her wanted it to anyway . . .

Above all she was working to avoid challenges and rows – not of course that she succeeded – in order to hide it from us girls, and also because whenever there was tension, the baby, David, had one of his turns.

He was punishing her, she felt. Which meant, she decided, that whatever he got up to she was still important to him, and she clung to that fact.

She still had the little leather Bible that Arnold Hitchins

had given her before he went away and promptly ditched her. (At least Arnold had been honest with her, she thought now grimly.) She had kept it as a reminder of the good things that had happened between them, an impulse that now became her determined policy: to look for the good things where she could.

She kept the little silk ribbon marking John 14:1: *Let not your heart be troubled . . . in my Father's house are many mansions.*

I thought of her quoting it to me when I was a girl, and my angry unsuspecting interpretation.

My mother thought it fanciful when my father said he practised astral travel. Your spirit climbed out of your body, he said and flew. But she clung to the image, she said, because that's how she saw his betrayals: as a fanciful flight from which he needed to return, down the rope, to solid ground and reality and her.

I always gave him plenty of rope, but I always pulled him back on it again.

And yes, after a year or so, he came back to her. And he took to religion, the Jewish religion, made friends with the Jewish carpet-dealing family over the road, bought her the Jewish cookbook. As he handed the cookbook over he said, carefully, meaningfully, 'I've given up the weightlifting, Gwen,' and that was the real gift, she knew.

He wrote excitedly from his new job in the Midlands describing the house he'd found and the efforts he'd made to clean the floors ready and get us girls into a good school.

The letter goes on:

I must say, my Darling, that for the first time in my life I'm looking forward to it all. Do you recall, my Darling, how I used to make plans, have wild dreams and ambitions, but could somehow never put them into practice and was frustrated at every turn, getting deeper and deeper into debt? And now my luck has changed and things have started going right again, and I have started making more sensible plans, and sacrifices.

It's sobering to realise that one's prayers get answered, for the changes in our fortunes took place when I started praying and studying Judaism. I saw the error of my ways then. As someone once said, my Darling, there's none so pure as the purified!

Well, I'd better wrap this talk up or you'll think I've gone crackers. Please don't worry, Dearest, about the £3.00 you've had to borrow from the girls' savings, we're going to be much better off here. Now that I've been made foreman you should have a tenner clear for your housekeeping, and I'll be able to take care of the rent from now on.

My Darling, I can't wait.

Good night and God bless to you and the kids.

I remain as ever,

Your loving husband,

Patrick. xxxxxxxxxxxxxxxxxxxxxxxxxxxx

With what relief and hope and energy she polished the big modern house in Easton, giving the green kitchen floor tiles a diamond sheen, buffing up the picture windows in the lounge where light came pouring through and anyone could see in.

They could be open now, she thought. Here, in this new place, she could be proud.

And, unlike in Prestatyn, they made friends, and straight away: a young workmate of Patrick's and his heavily pregnant wife, the Ellises – a couple of whom I had no memory – so taken with my father's charm, my mother said, that they'd already asked him to be godfather to the coming baby. Two weeks after we arrived in late November, she said, she and my father went to the christening.

Then one afternoon she went to buy the china dressing-table set with violets.

Saturday afternoon, late January, just beginning to rain as she turned out of the gate with us children. All of a sudden my father's van appeared at the top of the hill – unexpected, as he'd been meant to be working all afternoon.

Perhaps now he'd be able to take us . . .

He pulled up at the kerb beside us. He was cheery. 'We finished the job, so I let the men go. Have you got any cake in the tin, Ken Ellis is coming round.'

'Oh, yes, but Patrick, I'm just off to buy the dressing-tale set! You knew, I told you!'

'Doesn't matter, you go, it's just Ken, Alice isn't coming. He's just coming to watch the football on TV.'

And he took his foot off the brake, and rolled on, grinning.

The rain came on suddenly, battering the pushchair cover. It was odd, she thought, as she made her way with us up the hill. Patrick didn't have the slightest interest in football beyond doing the pools, in fact he pretty much hated it. It was the one subject on which he couldn't converse with other men.

She thought of his odd animation as he slid away from her.

The street lights came on, switching the grey afternoon to navy blue, and in that instant she knew what it was: sexual anticipation.

I remembered again her silence as we sat on the bus, the lights of the town trembling like water running away. The coldness of the china as I held it.

When she'd seen it in the junk shop, she told me now, it had made her think of the day she was eight years old. She was recovering from chicken pox, and bored because at eight years old she still couldn't read and was consequently thought, in comparison to Molly, to be stupid. It was March, and her mother, Nanny, said, 'Well, why don't you go up the cemetery and see if the violets are out?' And she did, and they were, though she had to part the long grass to find them, the heart-shapes of sudden purple and stark white. She went home with a bunch of them, and that afternoon she sat down with her book of fairytales and found that she could read after all, a talent as hidden as the violets, and as striking once it was revealed.

She had to have that china set. It would be a symbol for her hidden talent in bringing Patrick back to her, a symbol for their arrival in a lighter, safer life.

She knew now that there was no safety and no arrival. Patrick had tried so hard to reform, but now she knew: he was in the grip of something that none of his efforts or good intentions could end or control.

She travelled back with us, hardly daring to, fearful of what she might find. Once off the bus, she dragged her feet, although the rain was still pelting and we kids in our home-made tweed coats were sodden, and already on the bus David's face had become pale and clammy.

Thankfully, when she reached the top of the road there was no sign of Ken Ellis's car at the bottom.

'Has he gone?' She kept her voice as light as she could.

The TV was switched off, and Patrick was at the table, hunched over his paper. He grunted assent. He didn't look up.

'Did you watch the football?'

'No, he couldn't stay after all.'

She studied the set of his shoulders: slumped yet tense. The lines of rejection. And fear. He had been rejected. He had risked too much, exposed himself to danger.

The following week he got himself sent on a job back over the Pennines.

And, god-parentage notwithstanding, they never heard from the Ellises again.

'Did he guess that you guessed?' I asked her.

It was hard to know, she said. What she did know was that he denied it to himself much of the time.

She was all alone now with the care of the children in a place she was new to and where, since the Ellises had defected, she knew no one. She was finding it harder and harder to deal with me and Cathy, she said, miserable as we were and whiney. And, contrary to all our father's promises beforehand, there was less money than ever, as of course I was fully aware at the time.

This time he didn't write. When he came home at weekends it was clear he just didn't want to be there. He'd arrive smouldering and glaring, and if she greeted him with her problems and asked for help with us girls, he would beat us too hard – unless, of course, he had his workmate Mick Daly with him.

Mick Daly seemed particularly fond of my mother, she said. He was young, in his twenties, another Irishman far from home. He would stand in the doorway when he arrived, his ruddy fuzzy features brimming with some emotion that she took to be that of a young man in need of mothering. And so she did, mothered him, with cups of tea and biscuits and cake. One day he brought her a present, a brass poker he made himself, for her specially, and then he made her two brass ashtrays with fluted rims. When the engineering firm sent him on a foreign trip he brought her back a tooled jewellery box.

'Mick, it's beautiful!' she cried, turning it around and admiring the work.

His face smeared with shy pleasure. He looked across at Patrick, and Patrick, she saw, looked away quickly before standing to get his fags from the table. Mick's eyes followed him: like everyone else, he idolised Patrick.

Her stomach dropped.

Mick looked back at her, his pupils dark, his eyes wet-looking, and Patrick's phrase knocked at her skull: *sheep's eyes*.

Was this why there was suddenly not enough housekeeping again, she wondered, and no explanation whenever she asked, only terrible rows ending in another clout? Was he spending money on another life elsewhere, a life with Mick Daly?

Was this why, once more, he no longer wanted sex with her?

Now she hated Mick Daly coming. And Patrick knew it, and by the time Mick had gone, Patrick would be a wound-up spring and he'd pounce, calling her an antisocial bitch. Once we kids were in bed there'd be a full-blown row, a push-me-pull-you skirmish around the issue that neither could or would voice.

One weekend when Patrick was in bed before her, she found him sitting up against the pillows smoking again.

'Patrick, you know you're risking falling asleep and burning a hole in the sheets again! And you know I can't stand sleeping with the smell of your smoke in the bed.'

He scowled. 'You're as bad as Mick, he says that.'

He went very still, a man who'd given himself away. He resumed puffing with careful carelessness, trying to pull back the drawbridge he'd inadvertently dropped.

She steeled herself to say it: 'Why on earth would Mick Daly say *that?*'

He said, nonchalant, though not so nonchalant, 'You *know* we have to share a bed.'

'You *share a bed?* Why in god's name would you need to do that?'

'You bloody *know* why!' The old accusing tone. 'I told you how hard it was to get digs. It was all we could get.'

He flicked off the lamp and turned his back on her with such a convincing show of irritation at senseless probing, that she wondered if senseless probing was all that it was.

She lay awake for hours, she said, questioning the evidence of her senses, trying to doubt her suspicions.

I imagined his shape beside her, a black mountain against the moonlight coming through a gap in the curtains. Finally he would turn on his back and start snoring and in his sleep fling a heavy muscular leg across her, in the way she always laughingly complained that he did, pinning her down.

Another weekend she picked up a pair of trousers he'd left flung across the bed. She checked the pockets for his keys before hanging them up and a paper flicked against her hand.

A handwritten envelope addressed to Patrick's digs.

Such a cliché. But not such a cliché. This was not a letter from another woman, but from Mick Daly who'd been sent to Newcastle for a fortnight.

My Dearest Patrick, it began. He was writing in the middle of the night, he wrote, because he couldn't sleep, which was a joke, he said, because the site foreman was a tartar and worked them into the ground. But he couldn't sleep without Patrick, for missing Patrick, just as he couldn't, he said, when they had to spend weekends apart. He longed for the job to be over and to be back with Patrick again.

She put the letter back quickly and shut the wardrobe fast.

But she couldn't shut away the thought of it. That evening, desperate to know yet no doubt desperate not to, terrified of having the thing spoken and realised, she asked my father: 'What was that letter you got from Mick Daly?'

There was alarm in his face, she said – terrifying proof – which turned immediately to anger. 'Have you been going through my pockets? What right have you?' He was bawling, his fists were clenched.

She lied quickly. 'It fell out of your trousers when I picked them off the bed.'

For a moment he had no answer.

'What was it, Patrick? What's it all about?'

He'd recovered. He said, sour and dismissive: 'The bastard's mad. He's weird.'

Then, regaining his anger: 'You've still no right to go through my things!'

And having efficiently pushed her into the wrong, he switched on the wireless and tuned into that screechy wall of sound, looking for foreign stations.

Patrick had successfully deflected her challenge; she would challenge Mick Daly, she decided.

One Friday night when Mick Daly was there, Patrick nipped out for fags.

She took her chance.

She didn't mention the letter over which she'd been put in the wrong, but as she offered Mick another biscuit she said carefully, 'Patrick tells me that you and he share a bed in your digs.'

He looked her straight in the eye. He nodded sheepishly. Apologetically.

And it came to her: those gifts had been an apology.

His face was brimming. He said sadly, but also with a kind of matter-of-fact resignation: 'Don't think anything of it, Gwen. It's you Patrick *loves*.'

Don't think anything of it.

She was supposed to accept it, she realised, this thing between men, some men, like Patrick and Mick Daly. It couldn't be objected to because, secret as it was, illegal, it was hardly acknowledged by the men themselves. She was supposed to accept her role in the scheme of things devised by them without her knowing, the woman at home excluded from companionship and passion, who must be content with *love*. By which they meant *need*. Because, she thought, how could Patrick love her, to treat her as he did?

Don't think anything of it. The implication closed around her: it was a way of life, which must be adjusted to. It was the way of life that lay ahead of her. This was all there was for

347

her and the children in a life with him: a life of not-loving.

She felt finally defeated. She wrote in defeat, she said, to the council in south Wales and asked for a council house for herself and the children. She wrote telling her parents, Nanny and Grampa, that she was doing so, that her relationship with Patrick had finally broken down.

She didn't tell our father, no point in sparking one of those terrible rows before it was all arranged. Just as well: defeat, it turned out, was not an option. A letter came back from the south Wales council: because she didn't currently live there, her name was so far down the waiting list it would be years, if ever, before she got housed.

I could have left your father, she had said to me when I was planning to leave Terry.

She had no option but to carry on.

She turned to her little Bible, to Corinthians 12:9: *My strength is made perfect in weakness.*

She buried herself in domesticity, fulfilling Patrick's need of her, pursuing the only way open to her of bringing order and wholesomeness to our family. She took pride in scraping together enough to make dungarees for David and skirts for us girls. She took refuge in her embroidery, the stash of jewelled silks and patterns she'd saved up for in the past, calming herself with the rhythm of the needle and the neatness of the stitches.

She had to watch every halfpenny. In the bundle of papers she gave me was a little accounts book she kept at the time:

Groceries £3.12s.7d / Meat 10s.91/2d / Veg 11d / Fuel, 5cwt coal £4.19s.1d / Repayment Mam and Dad Nil.

It was a conscious illustration to my father, she said, of where his money and his affections ought to be going. And, I imagined, a perverse comfort to herself, the neatness of the columns and the way the figures tallied in the bottom right-hand corner giving her some sense of control.

But of course my father, his head turned elsewhere, wouldn't even look at it, as he hardly noticed the letter from his sister from the punishment house in Preston, and her pitiful plea.

Don't think anything of it, Mick Daly had said, as if it were nothing, but also with sadness and resignation, and, sure enough, that December Patrick got different digs and appeared to have dropped Mick Daly.

But she couldn't this time take comfort. Mick Daly had shown her that it was a way of life. And this time Patrick didn't come back to her; he stayed shut off. He wouldn't get involved when the owners of the house reneged on the deal and came bullying her, and while she was battling with them all alone, he threw it all in the air by accepting a permanent job across the Pennines. This time he had no interest in the move. This time he made no exploratory visits to schools, and was so far from making domestic preparations that he rented a house that turned out to have human shit on the walls.

No, this time he didn't even try to reform.

So when did she get proof that it was happening again?

She found it hard to remember, she said. It was the time that she had buried deepest.

February, that was the time of year, of that she was certain. There had been clues, his late homecomings to the blackened terrace above the tannery, the excuses that the jobs had run over, yet the absence of any overtime pay. The itchy discharge she developed after the one time he gave in and had sex with her. And now he'd begun to come in very late and go straight upstairs without her and climb into bed fully dressed, stinking of oil and male sweat, as if deliberately trying to repulse her.

One night as she was undressing, she said, she caught his eye and it was icy, cruel. The words of Peter 5:8 echoed in her head: *Be sombre, be vigilant, for your adversary comes as a roaring lion, seeking whom he may devour.*

And yet she knew he was suffering. She knew that a man who refused to go to a play written by a homosexual was frightened of himself.

And the day came when she knew for sure it was happening again.

She was late leaving the house to meet Cathy from school. She turned into the road beside the tannery, and a bus, which she'd never needed to use before, came along. She lifted David up and clambered on.

To her slight consternation, at the top of the road, just before the school, the bus turned sharp right, making a detour around the rows of little terraced houses above the glittering water. At last it turned back towards the main road and she stood with David, ready to alight.

And saw this sight: my father's navy-blue van parked outside one of the little terraces, and in the upstairs windows of the house the curtains tightly closed.

She was a madwoman then, she said. Hardly aware of her surroundings, in automatic response to Cathy's plea for sweets, she turned into the newsagents' near the school.

And a Valentine card on the stand leapt out at her, seeming planted there specially.

As soon as she mentioned it, I remembered it, the Valentine card she had once sent my father, and which she'd laughed about ruefully down the years. He hadn't liked it, I'd always thought because of the shape of the lovelorn creature it featured, barrel-shaped as my father was becoming at that time, and the fact that the creature was an alien, a sly reference of my mother's, I'd always thought, to his shut-off broodiness and bad temper.

It was in the bundle she would give me, a thick card that unfolded out into several pages, telling a story. On the first page the creature, lime-green, alien yet cuddly, stands looking sad while a crowd of uncaring colourless earthlings passes by in the background. On its head is a bright-red antenna shaped like a cross between the male and female symbols. On the second page, the antenna lights up as another, identical antenna pokes up out of the crowd. Next, the second antenna comes alive too, responding over the heads to the first. Finally, in a triumphant double-page spread, the two identical alien creatures, relieved and delirious, embrace.

She picked it up, that perfect allegory of bisexuality and its social status at that time. It was Valentine's Day the next day. She had stamps in her purse. She bought the card. Disguising her handwriting, at the end of the final page she wrote *Guess who?* and slipped it in the post box on the way home.

Next morning she heard it bullet through the letterbox in the cold front room. She took it to him, affecting innocence, though no doubt with a stone ricocheting beneath her ribs.

He went green with shock (green like the alien), she said.

Bull's eye: he thought it had come from someone else.

She knew for sure now.

'Who on earth could have sent you *that*?' she asked, popping it on the shelf above the kitchen range, watching his teeth start to grind and his shock turn to fury, at someone else beside her for once.

The card sat on the shelf for days. 'What the bloody hell have you put that up there for?' he growled, and she knew he wanted to swipe it away but dared not give it that much importance.

That week he was home early every day. The scare, it seemed, had brought him back to her.

But he was obsessed with it, and in the end he said to her, genuinely distressed: 'I've asked around, and none of the men say they sent it as a joke.'

It was clear to her then: the person he'd thought had sent it had denied it. And it wasn't so much that he was afraid of losing her, which his early homecomings had made her think, but that he was afraid he was being blackmailed. He was terrified of public exposure.

She was dismayed for herself, but also for him: she had to put him out of his misery. She confessed.

And that, it turned out, was the afternoon he threw a teapot and knocked her out.

He came back at midnight, she said. Walked straight past her without a word, making for the stairs.

She tried to speak to him, but the look he gave her, she said, was pure hatred.

And so, in the next days, it went on. It seemed he hated her now.

No life could be worse, she decided, than the one she was now leading with Patrick hating her. She would have to leave. She wrote to the manager of the Manor House at Llanfair, asking if she could have the flat in the outbuildings for her and her children, in return for domestic service.

I could have left your father.

The reply came back by return of post: regrettably, the executors were not letting the flat at that time.

There was no way out. One night, she said, after he'd gone up to bed without speaking, she turned on the oven tap and lay down and put her head inside.

'What?! You really did put your head in the oven?'

There was something she had said down the years, laughing grimly: *Oh, it was so bad at that time that I nearly put my head in the oven!* Well, that was what I heard; perhaps what she'd actually said was I *tried to put my head in the oven.*

I'd resent it: the way she laughed, and the hyperbole of it, when Cathy and I had lived in fear of it as a real possibility . . .

She told me now: my father, awake in the bed upstairs with the gas fire on, my father who could sense the tiniest change in an engine, heard the pressure drop in the fire and knew straight away, and was bounding down the stairs, turning off the tap and pulling my mother, already unconscious, from the oven.

She nearly died. She could have died.

I thought of myself frozen in fear at the sight of those tangled cooker taps, running in terror from the science lab and the hissing gas. Knowing yet not knowing, in the cells of my skin, the future that lay in wait in that kitchen.

They never discussed it afterwards, she said. He pulled her from the oven, flung the kitchen door open, slapped her face and brought her round. He lifted her up and carried her upstairs. But they didn't talk about why it happened, and they never referred to it afterwards.

She knew, though, that that night my father came to a realisation and a decision. He didn't want to lose her and he ended his affair.

But actually, she said, he *had* lost part of her. Coming to on the floor, with my father leaning over her, terrified and panicking, she suddenly saw him for what he was: pathetic. Cruel in his pathos, but pathetic. Sly and selfish and uncontrolled and needy as a child. And for the first time ever, she felt contempt for him.

He didn't respect her, she decided, and she would no longer disrespect herself by colluding with that. She hardened towards him.

I thought of their early rows about torque: *No object can exert a force on another without having the other exert a force on it in turn.*

She said: although he would kick against it forever afterwards, and use it as justification for however he chose to behave, there was something in him that was forever afterwards cowed.

There was a sequel to that episode that she didn't tell me right away: it was too hard for her to exhume.

Not long afterwards, only an hour or after he'd gone to work the van pulled up in the yard again. He came up the back steps and into the door looking pale and strained.

'We've been laid off,' he told her.

'Why?'

He couldn't meet her eyes. She could see he was steeling himself to be calm. 'One of the lads from McKenzie's. He's committed suicide. Thrown himself off the bridge.'

The bridge that hung like a scaffold over our playground, that soared above the terraces and my father's van as my mother swung by on the bus, towered over the implacability of my father ending an affair, that no besotted young man could have been prepared for . . .

My father was devastated, my mother could see, as he sat white-faced at the kitchen table. But she saw him with a clear eye, and knew that, grief-filled as he may be, his prime concern was for himself. There would be an inquest. He would be frightened of what might come out. She knew he was relieved the day the local paper reported the inquest without any suggestion of a cause for the suicide.

My father went to the funeral, she said, as the representative of his firm, his big hand trembling as he put his fags in his pocket before leaving. He came back clearly having gone through an ordeal.

That night, as they were getting into bed, she said, marvelling at the calm tone of her voice: 'You were close to that young man, weren't you?'

He didn't answer, but she didn't need him to. It was a statement rather than a question: that she'd got the measure of him now. And that she wasn't going to let him destroy her; that in the battle for self-respect it was she who would win.

As she lay there awake beside him that night she thought: if she had killed herself, she would have let him off the hook. She would have allowed him to abdicate responsibility altogether for the children whom her parents would have quickly taken in.

And if she'd left him . . . It was difficult enough as things were to get money out of him: she knew she'd have got nothing. She would have doomed her children to a life of stigma and poverty with a single working mother, their prospects damaged. (*Don't leave Terry*, she had begged me. *For the sake of the children.*)

It's you he loves, Mick Daly had told her, by which he meant *needs*. She could count on that need, she thought, hardened. She could use it.

She would stay, and make our father face up to his responsibilities.

But also, she said, she didn't want to hate him. She didn't want all the love and effort she'd expended to shrivel into hatred. She wouldn't allow hatred to be the air her children would breathe.

And she was strong enough to prevent it, she thought.

She thought she had succeeded. Our father clearly stopped his particular kind of straying, although she didn't flatter herself, she said, that he'd done so out of anything but fright or necessity. She saw with clarity that though the death had touched him – indeed, because it had so deeply touched him – he then put it quickly out of his mind, and any guilt he felt he quickly wiped. She saw this with contempt, but also relief. It was best for us children, she thought, if the reality slipped away.

And when we moved to Yorkshire, back over the mountains, to that brand-new house beside the fields and a decent white-collar job for Patrick at long last, it was as if nothing had ever happened.

Apart from the problem with me, she said.

'With me?'

'Jo, he thought you knew!'

'What?'

'You were so clever . . . And you were always watching and listening, and challenging and asking pertinent questions . . . You obviously sensed something.'

Something. Looked for it, sensed it, everywhere: despair seeping in the lights of the amusement arcades, squalor in the cracks of the cobbled lane to school, fear and premonition hissing in the gas pipes and arcing with the bridge girders. Writing a novel in which, in the afterlife, my father meets a man of whom he's instantly suspicious, who has something on him . . .

'Mum, I *didn't* know!'

'I know you didn't.' (So perfectly had she managed to make sure I didn't.) 'But he thought you did.'

I thought of all the times my father had avoided being alone with me, how uncomfortable he'd been when he couldn't avoid it . . .

'Why didn't you tell him I didn't?'

'I told you, we never spoke about it. We never once acknowledged it. But I knew he thought you had guessed.'

He was afraid of you, she had said.

I was the challenger, the speaker out, the one who spilled the beans and put us all in danger, letting out about the children's home, who snarled with fine irony as he beat me *How come you know so much about immorality?* The one who would later seem to prove she saw right through him by writing a

story that mirrored his secret adultery with Sandra Suggate
. . .

I could see now that when he slung his pebble eyes at me, there was fear in his hostility. He didn't want me near him, challenging and probing. He wanted me gone.

My mother was saying: 'And, Jo, I was afraid you *would* guess. And I was frightened of what would happen if you did and you and your father started rowing. I've told you, I couldn't wait for you to go and leave home. But of course, once you'd gone I missed you so much I couldn't eat for a fortnight.'

So that's what she'd meant: once I'd gone she'd had more peace of mind. And though she'd missed me so much, she was anxious whenever I returned, which could potentially *cause trouble.*

My very presence had created tension in the house. My very presence, as I'd always sensed, had made my father bad-tempered.

But then: *At least in Thwaite House no one would hear him bawling.*

What about the fact that in Thwaite House, long after I'd gone, he went on being bad-tempered?

'He was *never* faithful to me, Jo. He then started having affairs with women.'

PUNISHMENT AND
RESTORATION

T HE FIRST TIME she knew it, a year or so after I left
home, he had taken her on one of his work trips.

They stopped off at a pub she knew he called at often.

She was well accustomed, of course, to people lighting up
whenever my father entered a room, but this landlady behind
the bar, she said, practically gave off a neon glow. My mother
knew straight away there was something between them.

She went to the lavatory. When she came back through the
lounge door, my father and the landlady were leaning across
the bar towards each other.

They were holding hands.

They drew apart, the landlady quickly, but my father's
response was slower.

He was smirking. He had wanted her to see. It was a
demonstration.

He was punishing her, she said.

He never stopped punishing her for hardening towards
him that night in the gas-filled kitchen.

At Masons' Ladies' Nights the wives fluttered around
him. A coiffured woman from London, where he went often
for Masonic meetings, kept touching his arm in a lewd and
seemingly meaningful way, as if for my mother's benefit. The
woman said, for my mother's benefit, her hand proprietary on

my father's arm: 'Oh, we always have such a great time at my spiritualist meetings, don't we, Patrick?'

'*Spiritualist* meetings!?' cried my shocked mother.

'Oh, didn't you know?' the woman crowed.

My father's face was closed to my mother, but a little smile played on his lips.

Some of the wives, my mother discovered, knew the meanings of the Masonic symbols, whereas according to my father they were a male secret to be closely guarded against women, against my mother.

Once, on a visit from Scotland, I came upon her embroidering a symbol onto a Masonic shawl of my father's. 'What does it mean?' I asked.

'Oh, I don't know,' she replied airily.

'Oh right,' I said hotly (I was in my passionately feminist phase). 'So you'll service an organisation that keeps you out!'

'Oh Jo,' she cried, airily derisive, as if it were all simply harmless and uninteresting: 'I don't *want* to know!'

She told me now: she wouldn't let him have the power to taunt her with withheld knowledge. She would deprive him of that power by not wanting to know.

She said she developed the trick of shutting down her mind.

She didn't let herself think about the implication when he went on giving Sandra Suggate gifts although she was growing up and no longer his caddy. She wouldn't let herself ponder too much the fact that he took Sandra's parents, the kind of people that as a rule he'd run a mile from, for slap-up meals at the country club, where their manners and rough voices drew shocked and curious attention.

It struck me that perhaps he thought my mother's youthful

beauty put people off the scent; he was *using* it, using her.

She didn't let herself dwell on his intentions, she said, when he offered Sandra a job well before she was due to leave school at sixteen. They were still running the business from the house on the housing estate then, and he became anxious they'd lose her if they didn't get office premises in time. My mother didn't let herself think too much about that, or the fact that when things did work out, he promptly appointed Sandra, a girl with five O-levels, his personal PA with a top salary.

She didn't let herself fret about the fact that Sandra very quickly got herself a flat near the premises in town, or that when Sandra and my father were meant to be working late together, my mother would ring the office and there'd be no reply.

When he stopped wanting sex with her altogether she blamed the change.

Then one day she stepped into the doorway of my father's office and to the sight of the nineteen-year-old Sandra Suggate and my rotund fifty-six-year-old father clamped in each other's arms and kissing.

She stepped back quickly behind the door frame. She wouldn't give it the oxygen of acknowledgement. She would leave them in the airlessness of subterfuge, which she hoped would eventually snuff it out.

She turned to her little Bible again, to James: *Let patience have her perfect work.*

One day though, she said, she couldn't resist. Sandra was standing by her desk telling her about a problem that she, Sandra, and my father were having over an order. She was describing it, my mother said, as if to an outsider, and my mother felt intensely riled. She said pointedly, meaningfully,

'You and Patrick are very close, aren't you?'

She'd meant to indicate that they needn't think she was fooled, she was onto them, because it was par for the course. That Sandra Suggate needn't think that this was a situation any different from any other, my father would come back to my mother in the end.

But Sandra didn't get it. Her features settled into an expression of smug, superior satisfaction. She had taken my mother's rhetorical question as an admission of defeat. And, I imagined, as licence.

But it didn't blow over.

One night my father said to my mother: 'I'm thinking of buying Sandra a pair of earrings, and I need you to help me choose some.'

She couldn't help herself: in danger of acknowledging what she'd vowed not to, she cried: 'You're buying Sandra earrings?! What on earth for?'

He was instantly tetchy. 'A reward for the extra work she put in on those orders, of course!'

He was scowling. Next thing he'd be calling her a mean-minded Welsh bitch and he'd thump her . . .

She shut up, she went with him to the jewellers where he simply stood by, leaving it up to her to choose his love gift for another . . .

He brought Sandra everywhere. When they went to dinner she had to come too, like an adjunct to their marriage, a dull monosyllabic girl whose chief response to being addressed was a sly, secretive smile. Often, for appearances' sake, her parents came too.

He decided he wanted Sandra to join the golf club and

put her name forward, and was furious and upset when she was rejected as an 'unsuitable type'. He solved the problem by getting on the committee and bribing the rest to accept her in return for a freezer for the club. He bought her all the equipment and clothes. And insisted, for appearances' sake, that my mother take her up the golf course every Saturday to practise.

And there was my mother acceding, enabling and colluding in her own adulterous betrayal, for the sake of appearances, of course, but also for the sake of refusing to acknowledge it, to allow it reality.

Then one Ladies' Day at the golf club, my mother and her partner were looking for a ball in the rough when her partner said, 'I don't know how you can do it, Gwen, play golf with Sandra Suggate like that, when she and Patrick are doing what they are to you. We all think it's disgusting, carrying on right under your nose. I really don't know how you can stand it.'

My mother was stunned. So everyone knew, when she thought she had managed to keep it secret. Others were openly acknowledging it, when she and Patrick hadn't even acknowledged it between themselves.

Shaken, my mother replied, 'Oh, it's because I know it'll soon fizzle out.'

It didn't fizzle out.

My father gave Sandra Suggate's father a job in the workshop. One afternoon my mother stepped out into the office corridor where they hung the coats, and found Sandra Suggate's weasly little father going through my father's overcoat pockets. He didn't notice her at first, and when he did he jumped and withdrew his hand sharply, caught in the act. And then that man who was supposed to be their friend, whom they taken out to dinner countless times, sidled away without a word.

She told my father.

He didn't believe her.

Didn't he see what was going on, she insisted, the Suggates were taking him for a ride?

She was a suspicious-minded bitch . . . He was starting to bellow . . .

It came to her: Ernie Suggate knew that Patrick wouldn't believe her. That look that passed between them before he sidled off . . . He'd known he didn't even need to excuse himself to her. He didn't even need to pay her the respect of speaking to her. He knew the state of play between her and Patrick.

It dawned on my mother: they were all in it together. The Suggates knew very well what was going on between Patrick and their daughter, and it suited them fine.

I thought of my mother, my once-innocent, chapel-or-gan-playing mother, flooded with the sense she'd been trying so hard and for so long to keep at bay: the sense of a sleazy world of grubby manipulative underhand sex and malice and greed.

Then all of a sudden Sandra Suggate met a pimply youth, and within weeks they were engaged, and in another couple of months married.

My father, my mother said, was devastated.

He wouldn't go to the office; he sat in a slump at home on the housing estate. He refused to go the wedding until, in the end, my mother persuaded him, for appearances' sake. He hung back miserably at the edge of the wedding crowd. The Suggates called him over for a special photo: the bride and groom, the bride's parents and Patrick. Not my mother.

She swallowed it all smiling, she said, because she just kept thinking the whole episode would be behind them now.

A couple of months later my father came into her office with a little velvet box. He opened it up and held it out to her. 'What do you think?'

A pair of earrings, antique garnet drops in filigree rose gold.

He was saying sorry, she thought. Making amends.

'Oh, Patrick, they're beautiful! Thank you!'

He was contemptuous. 'They're not for you. They're for Sandra.'

Only two months after her wedding Sandra Suggate was making it known that her marriage was over, that she was sleeping on the couch in the flat. Before long her husband had moved out, and my mother knew that things between my father and Sandra Suggate had reverted to their former state.

And then, that hot July evening, he tried to run away with her.

They never spoke about that either, she said. Indeed, between them they never once acknowledged the affair with Sandra Suggate.

But after that she knew that the affair had begun to go wrong. Running away had been one thing, but my father would never after all want to face the scandal of leaving my mother to commit himself to Sandra Suggate while staying in that town. She could hear them rowing behind my father's closed office door. He took to drink, she said, in a big way: it was a standing joke at the country club that his car knew its own way home, and woe betide you if you got in his way when he came rolling in.

But they bought the big house, which – although she wasn't keen on it, although he went behind her back, with her money, and signed the papers in his name alone – she took as a commitment, a good sign. And she did what she'd always done: put her energies into it, into creating a home where they could settle down together happily at last.

At the same time, she shouldered the business. As his relationship with Sandra floundered, their rows lasting for days, he kept away from the office, nursing his hangovers, taking refuge in Masonic trips and purportedly working on the big house.

David was already working at the house. He'd begun going out on site, but the chemicals and fuels had brought back his allergies, yet she didn't want him back in the offices. As far as she could tell, she had prevented him from knowing about the affair, but under the circumstances, working in the office again he'd surely find out, so she paid him instead to tile the bathrooms in the house. When she went up there at the end of the day, there they would be, the father and the son he'd once ignored and refused to own, sitting at the table with cups of tea, companionable, companions at last.

There was a drawback to that, though. David was now Patrick's ally in sneering and complaining if the meal was late or if she dropped a plate or put the wrong sauce bottle out. And she had to ignore it. She had always found it hard to take David to task, she confessed, the son so sickly from birth and ignored by his father. And now any attempt to pull David up would arouse Patrick's wrath.

Not that he didn't hit David at that time, she said.

'He hit David too?'

'Oh, yes, we were both in for it if he'd had a row with Sandra. And poor old Cathy would come in for a good bellow if she parked her car too near the ivy border, or braked too hard on the gravel. He would watch her parking from the kitchen window and then storm out shouting his head off and saying he would ban her from the house . . .'

'Wait a minute . . . You were already living in Thwaite House?'

'Oh yes.'

'So how long did the affair last . . . ?'

'For a couple of years at least after we moved here. More . . . But as I say, it was going wrong all the time.'

They had been in the house only two years when I broke up with Terry . . .

No wonder she hadn't wanted me there then . . .

I thought of the day, before that, when my father banned me from Thwaite House for my adultery. Coming in the night before, he must have come from Sandra Suggate's . . . The following day, having issued his ban, he would have driven straight to his adulterous lover at the office . . .

I thought of my mother then, leaning against the sink and looking faint as, unaware of quite how close I was to the truth, I snarled: *One rule for him and another for us women.*

One autumn Saturday morning, she said, she was playing golf with Sandra Suggate. My father had stopped playing golf, due to the scandal my mother assumed, but he still insisted on this duty of my mother's.

Sandra stopped beside a chestnut tree. 'Let's look for conkers,' she said. She abandoned the game and started looking in the grass, twenty-six years old and the long-time mistress of a middle-aged married man, excited as a child.

She found a conker and straightened up. She said, 'Gwen, I don't want to play golf any more.'

'You don't?'

'No, it's all old fogeys here.'

One morning the following week Sandra came into the office and announced that she'd sold all the clubs and equipment my father had bought her. He happened to be in the office, and he was dismayed and enraged. My mother heard them rowing about it behind his closed door.

A month or so later, my mother and Janet were having a coffee break when Sandra came in and announced to them: 'I'm going on a singles' weekend.'

'Oh, really?' I could imagine my mother, cheery-all-girls-together, still refusing to give the affair - the dying affair - the respect of acknowledgement.

'Yes, I've decided I need to meet some young people.'

My mother knew what she was saying: *He's wasted my youth.*

Sandra Suggate at my father's funeral . . . I remembered the way she sat there, watchful and guarded but somehow expectant. Did she think she was owed for the loss of her youth? The way her mother sat beside her . . . Watchful also, alert. Proprietorial, the both of them. What, I wondered, had my father promised Sandra before it all went wrong and he turned on her his vicious anger?

And then, my mother said, it was over.

After that my father fell into a slump. He stopped going to the office altogether. Sandra's singles' weekends became a regular thing. She would return on Monday mornings looking gaunt, dark rings under her eyes.

'What on earth have you been up to?' my mother asked her jovially one Monday.

'It's group sex,' she said flatly.

'And drugs,' she added.

Which was the moment my mother saw, she said, that my father had ruined Sandra Suggate's life, and why always afterwards she would feel sorry for her.

My father, she said, was now broken. Overnight he became an old man, static, sitting at the table for hours, perking up only for the occasional Masonic meeting.

One day, a year after my mother finally wound up the business, he was sitting lost in thought, his notebooks unattended, when he said to my mother abruptly, out of the silence: 'It was my fault the business failed. I neglected it. It's my fault that David's been left with nothing.'

The first time he had ever admitted fault over anything.

He picked up his cigarettes slowly and stood with great effort before going out to join David in the garage, the first time she'd seen him weighed down with guilt.

Such a shock, though, she said, the way he assuaged it: going behind her back and leaving everything to David, all the assets left over from the business she'd worked so hard on, all of his money and personal possessions, and the home she'd spent her life creating in order to bring him back to her.

And then finally she laughed and told me this:

July, the year before he became ill. She was weeding in the garden, those luminous lawns stretching off into the glowing shadows beneath the trees. Through the open kitchen window came the sound of the vacuum cleaner: in that final year before his illness my father had taken to running it over for her. She heard the phone ring and the vacuum cleaner stop. My father's telephone tones came towards her ('Yeah . . . yeah, yeah . . .'), strangely stiff and subdued. She heard him ring off.

And then he was standing in the yard gateway looking blasted.

'Who was that on the phone?'

'Mick Daly.'

'Mick Daly?'

'He's over from Ireland. He wants to drop in. He's just got married and his wife's with him. They're on their way.'

His arms hung helpless. His face was white.

He was pale, utterly unnerved, as that ghost from the past, Mick Daly, settled in one of the kitchen easy chairs. Though actually, Mick Daly didn't look exactly ghostly. They took a picture that day, the wife took it; it was in the bundle my mother gave me. Mick Daly stands between my mother and my unnerved-looking father, surprisingly young-looking still, though he must have been in his sixties by then, not even grey, though ruddier and fuzzier than ever. And fatter: a little rotund man.

The wife, a dumpy Irishwoman in her forties, was watchful and quiet, my mother said. My mother could tell: she knew. Mick had come clean about his past, about his history with my father, and the wife had come to see for herself.

And what did she see? An old feller, scared out of his skin, a once-talkative charmer with nothing whatever to say for himself: my father was more or less speechless, my mother said.

It was Mick and my mother who did the talking. It was Mick and my mother, after all, who had once come to a frank understanding. They chatted, inconsequentially, but a current of understanding ran under everything they said.

Until Mick asked my mother suddenly: 'I made you a poker once, Gwen, do you remember?'

'Of course!'

She had buried so much, but she had kept that poker. 'It's in the sitting room.' She went through and brought it back.

'And these,' she said, taking down the two fluted brass ashtrays that had been propped on her mantelpieces ever since.

The wife's black eyes slithered over them, the phallic poker and the yonic ashtrays.

My father's face, she said, was a parchment sheet.

'And do you remember the jewellery box you brought me back from abroad?' She went and got that too, and laid it with the other things on the table.

'I'd forgotten how intricate it was,' said Mick Daly, running his hands over the inlay.

She looked him in the eye, challenging and meaningful: 'Do you want it back?'

'No – no!' His eyes slid with panic.

And then, ending her story on a note of hilarity, she told me she said: 'Because you can't have it anyway!'

She got my father back in the end, broken and tamed like Jane Eyre's Mr Rochester.

I always gave him plenty of rope, but I pulled him back on it in the end.

PART NINE

In which everything is thrown in the air

CRYING

WHEN SHE TOLD me I cried.

Of course, the whole story came piecemeal as over the next days and weeks I sat hunched by the kitchen window with the phone at my ear. But when she first revealed the secret, I began weeping and couldn't stop.

'Jo? Jo?' she was panicking at the other end of the phone. 'Jo?'

I couldn't answer, gusts of grief sweeping my chest and my throat.

'Oh, Jo, I knew I shouldn't have told you!'

I couldn't even say *Of course you should have told me*, I couldn't speak.

'Oh no, I didn't want you to hate your father for it . . .'

I managed to get out, 'Of course I don't hate him . . . Not for *that* . . .'

'So why are you crying?'

I couldn't say. I didn't know what I was feeling, beyond this flooding wordless grief.

Tears and snot ran down the coat I'd still had on when I'd rushed in and answered the phone. The cat, disturbed, came and sat before me, wide-eyed and staring. Greg came home and stood in the doorway, alarmed. The waves of grief went on washing me.

Next day she begged me: 'Promise me you won't tell Cathy. I don't want Cathy to hate your father.'

She was so distressed, I had to promise. But how could I not tell Cathy? The one person on earth who had shared the complex experience of my childhood, the baffling consequence of this secret . . . If I spoke to her I would have to tell her.

The only way I could succeed in not doing so was to keep away from her. I stopped ringing her; when she suggested coming over I made an excuse.

It made me unhappy. In the end I told my mother: 'I can't do it. I won't tell her, but I just can't have this between me and Cathy. You have to tell her yourself.'

Yet she still hadn't told her when Cathy insisted in a way I couldn't counter on coming over, and brought our mother with her.

We went for lunch in the Italian restaurant. I was tense and miserable with the deceit. My mother was consciously, airily bright.

Cathy must have sensed it. The conversation turned, as it so often did, to our father's bad temper, our mother ruefully laughing, and Cathy said, oddly careful: 'Well, you know, there must have been something troubling him to make him like that.'

There was a silence. I looked hard at my mother, urging her.

Cathy looked from one to the other.

My mother put down her fork and took a breath. 'Cathy, I'm going to tell you something now. Your father had affairs with men.'

The pause was only short before Cathy answered: 'Well, it isn't as if I hadn't always guessed.'

'How did you guess?' I asked her when we were next alone together.

She shrugged. 'I just guessed.'

'Well, *when?*'

'Dunno. When I was about eleven.'

All I could do was stare. I didn't say *Why didn't you say anything to me?* I couldn't ask it. I thought of her getting off the bus from her streetwise school, stalking up the road ahead of me in her hitched-up skirt, unspeaking, clamped down on that suspicion, that knowledge, clamped away from her insistently but naively protective elder sister . . .

She said now: 'Well, even before that I knew there was something going on.'

And then she told me this:

It was a day when we were living in the end terrace near the tannery. A warm Saturday in May. I wasn't there, I had gone for the day to the house of a girl in my class at grammar school, a friendship that didn't last since the way things were in our house I couldn't reciprocate. My father came back from driving me and disappeared into the garage across the cinder yard.

He came out with two fishing nets on long canes he'd made, handed one each to Cathy and David, and took them in the van to a place where he said there were newts.

It was like an old abandoned quarry, she said. A shallow pool in the centre, and all around high sandstone rocks glowing red in the sun.

'Right, go and look for newts,' our father told Cathy and

David, and went and sat against a pile of boulders with his cigarette.

They couldn't see any newts. She turned to tell our father. He looked small, she said, lying back against the boulders, the arena of red rocks stretching around him, which somehow she found upsetting. He realised she was looking and started, and something bright flickered on his face. He was crying.

'What's the matter, Daddy?' she cried, running back to him.

He scowled (of course) as she approached, but he didn't tell her off. 'Nothing,' he said shortly, and tried to hide the fact that he'd been crying.

She said to me now: 'I knew then that something separate, something not to do with us, was going on his life.'

She was ten at the most.

She went on: 'It wasn't the only time I saw him crying. Remember that time he took us to Aunty Cathy's?'

It was the one and only time we ever went: not long after we'd moved to Thwaite, and not long after Aunty Cathy's wedding, Cathy and I, twelve and fourteen years old, went to stay for a week, and our father drove us.

'Don't you remember,' Cathy said, 'you were car sick?'

'I don't remember being car sick, but I do remember we nearly had a collision with a lorry.'

'That was *why* you were sick, he was driving like a maniac. You kept saying, "Dad, I feel sick," and asking him stop but he wouldn't. He kept saying, "You don't feel sick!" You kept on, and in the end he was reaching back and hitting you over and over while he was driving. And then you vomited, all over his arm and shoulder and all over the car seats. So he did have to stop, and wipe up the mess. He was furious, but also I could

378

see he was crying. I guess you didn't see, you were too busy being sick and upset.'

She said: 'I knew then he was in despair. That he just wanted not to be there, ferrying us. That he just couldn't do it: be a father, a family man.'

She was twelve years old.

She said, 'I'll never forget it. We stopped by this field gate, and there were moles, dead moles, nailed all along the top of the gate, their little legs all splayed out. Really spooky. Like sacrifices . . .'

She paused, thoughtful. 'No, it wasn't us. But he took it out on us, the bastard. And I *do* hate him for that.'

'I didn't want you to hate him, Cathy,' our mother had said in the restaurant, explaining why she'd sworn me to secrecy.

Later I heard from each of them separately about the conversation they'd had going back on the train:

'I didn't want you to hate him,' our mother said again.

'I don't hate him – not for *that*! For God's sake, Mother, it's the twenty-first century! It's the way he treated us I blame him for.'

'Well, I didn't want to upset you. It upset Jo terribly. She cried and cried.'

'Well, that's Jo. She *cries*.'

Why was I crying?

As the story unfolded in the days that followed my mother's revelation, I would weep again, for all of it, for all of us caught in the trap of a forbidden sexuality.

For the stress my father must have suffered, which seeped to engulf us all. The fear of discovery and blackmail, the watching over your shoulder, watching out for the looks of those who *know*, the RAF man in the sentry box, the fellow leaning on your car as you come down steps in the dusk in post-war London, the man in the transport caff passing the sugar and raising his bushy eyebrows. (*Who is that man in the afterlife in your novel?* my mother had asked me.)

The man who can walk off with the garage business you've paid for, because of what he's got on you . . .

Ghostly footsteps on a staircase in Prestatyn, threatening exposure, and the consequent demand for money . . .

'Give us a scratch,' he'd say if he were lying on his face on the floor in Prestatyn and we were playing nearby. The more scary he got, the more I hated doing it. 'Up . . . down,' he would demand, 'bit further to the left', on and on, and my arm would ache, and I'd dread having to go near the hole in his shoulder, deep-shadowed with sharp damage.

In the last few days my mother had told me: the boat on which he visited his Aunt Lizzie in Australia was picking up and delivering volunteers to the Spanish Civil War. When they got back as far as Spain, she said, he left the ship and had to travel back alone through the country at war, because he'd had a fight with the ship's cook. The hole in his back, she said, was where the cook had attacked him with a meat hook.

The terrible jealousy of men trapped together for weeks on end on a boat . . .

The suspicious ex-navy father-in-law of your daughter, uncharacteristically twisting your arm for money . . . I wondered now what it was that Terry's prejudiced, Methodist father thought he was protecting me from . . .

The self-loathing. The self-denial. The projection. The threat you posed to others who denied it to themselves, and their consequent loathing . . . The man your innocent ex-nun sister brings to the house, watching you through glasses that magnify his sliding sheep's eyes . . .

My father's doomed attempts to prove to himself otherwise: my mother, a tomboy the night that he met her, seeming to be his salvation. Until he came to believe she had betrayed him, betrayed him back to the impulse he thought he'd overcome. And years later, when my mother had shut a part of herself away from him forever, another boy-girl lifting a club on a golf course and resurrecting that old promise . . .

The momentary urge, on the way to the county court and possible exposure, to end it all . . .

I cried for my own half-understanding. I cried for myself, for the memory of standing in the garden as Mrs McGowan told my mother that *all sorts had been going on in there*, something black, a black flag, flapping in my mind.

I cried for my alert father's sense of my half-apprehension. I cried for his fear of it, which had so confused me.

I cried for my mother's pain, and her lifelong effort to create another reality for us to live in.

And for the images and stories that now bloomed in my head.

ANOTHER HISTORY

A BOY RUNNING wild on the moor, dark-skinned, his feet bare, his long white-blond hair flying, a boy with senses alert, who knows something is lost, though he doesn't know what. Something hidden, slipped away between the leafy shadows at the house at the crossroads, sunk into the bog beyond, the echo of it only fizzing in the peat as he lies in his truckle bed beside the fire. He seeks it in the wind across the moor, in the glint of fish darting in the stream, in the gloomy sun-streaked depths of the lake where he swims. He catches a glimpse in the will o' the wisp before it's snatched away, and the banshee at night seems to mourn its loss.

Words. Is it cradled in words, caught in the net of his father's easy banter, or is it hammocked in his mother's silences?

A mother made bitter by poverty and a wastrel husband, handing words to her son as a precious currency, tickets to a better life, to be presented to the master coming down the road. He will be a priest, she tells him, and in her voice is the sound of relief, and of something once lost now found.

But the thing that he is seeking is nowhere to be sensed in the schoolroom or in the incense-filled gloom of the church, and the Latin words of the Mass seem like an icy wall blocking it away. The boy prefers the wild moor, or speeding down the lanes on the bicycle he 'borrowed', and the words he prefers are the words he can ride like his bike, easy and athletic, like his father, making everyone laugh and feel good.

Disappointment clouds his mother's eyes, and the fear that he's too much his father's son. And once the little house becomes too full of girls, it is to her husband's father's house that, against her will, she must send him.

A grandfather who up until now has been a shadowy figure to the boy, who lives alone, two miles off in the village. A man who, because he lives alone, cooks, and who calls the potato cakes he cooks *latkes*. Who tells the boy he came as a small child on a ship with his parents from a country called Silesia, because people there were stoning the houses and setting fire to them.

He doesn't need to tell the boy that he mustn't tell anyone. The boy understands: this is the thing that has been hidden. A secret so heavy that not even the boy's father, his grandfather's son, has spoken of it ever. Because everyone says that the Jews killed Christ, and when the Jewish pedlar comes to town people throw stones.

He asks his mother if she knew. She wants to know what nonsense he's talking. 'He's *not* Jewish!' she snaps. 'He converted, so he did. So let's not be having you say such things.'

And that's that, the boy isn't to speak of it again. Now, more than ever, he has to prove he's a good Catholic boy.

But the boy is implicated now. His mother's words, the official, Church-sanctioned words, are powerless against the secret ones his grandfather gives him. *Menorah*, the candlestick with eight candles which his grandfather tells him the family lit on Friday evenings in Dublin when he was a boy, on the eve of the Sabbath which wasn't a Sunday as the boy has always known it, but the Irish day of carousing, a holy day after all. *Matzoh*: unleavened bread to be eaten at Passover – *Passach* – to commemorate the flight of the Jews from Egypt, when they couldn't wait for the dough to rise. Jews always fleeing, or, like the boy's grandfather, going into hiding.

The boy is shocked, upset, unbalanced, but also thrilled by this apprehension of a secret, parallel world. Yet of course it isn't his world, or even his grandfather's any longer either. His grandfather takes him to the synagogue in Dublin, but although people nod, no one actually knows him, and when the chanting begins and pours with an ache of longing down the carved wooden panels, the boy knows it's the sound of the loss he's always been trying to identify. And when they get home his grandfather gives him, into his safekeeping, a photo of his own parents, standing in their Dublin backyard.

The world the boy has thought his own, the clearer, firmer, world of his parents and the Church, is no longer his either. He is exiled from it by his own dismay, by his mother's disappointment and suspicion, which rub off on the eldest of his sisters so that years later, when he visits her in England, she will cut him dead. *It's most certainly none of your business . . .*

He is a boy with two homes but he feels homeless. A boy torn between worlds, in each of which he has to cut the other off, but in neither of which he truly belongs. His refuge in the end is himself: his good looks, his athletic ability, his easy manner and his role as a daredevil, which make everyone want to know him and be his friend.

By the age of sixteen, he is a boy steeped in secret languages, schooled in the subterfuge of the IRA, and the unspoken code of a sexuality that isn't even supposed to exist.

At the age of sixteen, he is on the boat from Dublin, fled like a Jew.

Sixteen years earlier, a young couple sail in the opposite direction, from Liverpool to Dublin, their first child, my father, already sparking in the young woman's womb, sailing towards a life with a secret at its heart. A secret of which the young woman, with her years in Birkenhead, is perhaps not yet fully aware . . .

Fifty years before them, another couple with a small child, my father's grandfather, sail into the same harbour, fled from a land of breaking glass and fire, a landlocked village where a single bird now circles above an abandoned bell tower. Red petals of sunlight dancing on the water ahead . . .

That same child a grown young man, fleeing Dublin with his Irish sweetheart, prevented from marriage by parents of two religions, making for the succour of her Irish cousins in the green depths of the countryside, a child already pulsing in her womb. Making for a life of pretence, the strains of which would pull them apart in the end . . .

I thought of David destroying the evidence left of the past, shut in our father's hermetic den with his confusing legacy of homophobia and exclusive brotherhood, frost breathing outside and long-gone histories winking out of the sky. Half shutting his eyes, his mind perhaps, afraid of what he might find.

His struggles with memory. The things he claimed were knocked away one night on a frosty road, the things he actively suppressed – *You didn't want to join the Masons,* Cathy had cried – that made him flip at the thought of our father smeared with makeup in his coffin, and send ribbons of satin flying high . . .

385

The confusing memories that nevertheless spilled from the half-closed mouth of the past: a day when his sister Jo, whom he considers he hardly knows, who always caused all the trouble, rocked with him arm-in-arm on the stones beside the smooth silver water of Loch Lomond, and the sense he had then of something restored . . .

I thought of my mother – a story she had told us – standing in the garden of the pink thatched cottage in 1932, the year my father left Ireland. She is eight years old with a pudding-bowl haircut, wearing hob-nailed boots and a cotton smock with a yoke to protect her dress. A group of trippers comes down the road, off the train from Cardiff and walking to the beach, passing right by the cottage. Four of them today, young adults, society people, in the smartest, most fashionable clothes, carrying a wicker hamper and chatting loudly in the way the locals never would, unaware of the intrusion their voices make into the cottage as they pass. Noisy, glamorous and cheerful, they strike my mother as like a circus parade. The women especially, in their suits with wide trousers, like pyjamas, in fluttering bright-patterned fabric, their hair cut short and plastered to their heads in Marcel waves. They flail cigarette holders as they chatter, and their heeled buttoned shoes clatter on the road.

My mother runs to the wall to watch until they turn the bend by the cowshed and are gone.

There is a world out there, she thinks, a world of glamour and excitement, where you can be a different kind of creature. She stands on the high-banked garden and vows that one day she'll join that world. She sees her future ahead: tall rooms with parquet floors like those in the Manor where you go at

Christmas to be given a sixpence, drenched in the light from chandeliers, and herself in the centre, capable of anything, ready to take on anything.

I cried for all the lost moments of hope and possibility, the things that, as my mother complained, I'd left out of my novel:

Waiting, less than two years old, in the garden of the cottage opposite the garage in south Wales, for my father to come for lunch. Flowers each side, some taller than me, the sun shining through their red and blue petals. The huge doors slide, and there he is in his brown boiler suit, grinning and waving. He steps down the slope into the road and disappears, reappearing like a Jack-in-a-box on the steep garden path, and sweeps me up, high above his head, in a cloud of petrol smell that I will consequently love, like a drug, for years.

A day when I am sitting waiting in the car, drinking that smell in. I am four years old. I have come with my father on his insurance rounds. We've stopped for petrol and my father has wandered off whistling, hands in trouser pockets, jacket bunched back. Rainbow patterns curl across a puddle below the car window; a ginger cat sits blinking on top of a petrol pump. My father comes back. 'Put that in your pipe and smoke it,' he tells me, and drops into my lap a slim soft-backed book: *Hansel and Gretel*.

And we're off, beneath the flickering trees, and he's tapping a fag on the steering wheel, driving one-handed, and saying, 'Hold onto your belly!' as we hit the next bridge, and I hold tight to my book, a tale of children once loved but abandoned and having to find their own way home.

The books he bought us, the gift of words.

And the lesson, too, of the things beyond words:

The nights in Prestatyn when he came home and woke us and took us out in our nighties to see the lights on the prom, or, one night, eerie shifting sparks at the edge of the sea. 'What is it?' we cried in awe, watching the myriad luminous bubbles forming and reforming as the gentle waves broke on the black sand.

He didn't answer straight away, wanting us to know the mystery, the wonder – luminous streaks forming and dying, like thoughts you can't pin down – before he gave us the word, *plankton*, and explained.

The times he reached out: handed me a gift for safekeeping, the sight of the photo of his ancestors, the books with pictures that showed where the prejudice that had blighted his life could lead . . .

❧

Once, when I was visiting, not long before he became ill, my father, scribbling as usual in a notebook at the kitchen table, suddenly pushed the notebook towards me. I was shocked and embarrassed, just as I had been when he'd shown me the photo. There was a look on his face I couldn't make out: proud? Expectant? Bashful, even? Or taunting me somehow (you and your know-all education), triumphant that I wouldn't understand whatever he was writing in his cabbalistic code, his male secret? It was an address he was composing for some Rosicrucian meeting and its subject was the six-pointed star, the same star, I guessed, as the Star of David. I felt too uncomfortable under his scrutiny to read it properly, some cod-philosophical, quasi-religious stuff about opposites and unity. I handed it back with a vague polite murmur, and his face shut down and he went back to his scribbling.

I have read about it since. David destroyed his papers, and to my mother's distress, the Masons descended and demanded his Masonic books, raiding his shelves, but they left one or two behind.

THE SIX-POINTED STAR

Consider that which is above and that which is below, and that whatever is below is that which is above. This is a truth fulfilled by the Six-Pointed Star. It is a unity of opposites, the upright triangle and the inverted, the alchemical symbols for fire and water, and for man and woman. Seperato et non seperato, separation leading to unification. This is the Philosopher's goal, the Philosopher's egg, the true gold, the essence, the elixir of life.

I thought of my mother's thwarted dreams, of her choice to give up her dreams, to help him in his quest to turn the lead of his life into gold. All his life he must have been looking for some kind of unity, some kind of resolution. Perhaps, in showing me the piece he was writing, he was showing me that.

I thought of his hand twitching towards me on his deathbed.

And I cried for that.

❧

Finally, I thought of a tale my mother told me, a tale Nanny told her:

Nanny was newly married. She and Grampa had just

389

moved into the pink thatched cottage. She was twenty-six years old.

One hot summer evening she was alone, cooking at the range, when she heard a strange sound. Like a bird, but not any bird she knew, and she knew them all: a clear, mellow, haunting sound, coming from just outside the door.

Like a signal.

She stood stock-still.

She wiped her hands on her pinny and crept quietly to the door.

She eased it open.

The sound stopped.

She could see nothing. She stared at the garden wall where she thought the sound had been coming from: nothing but lichen baking in the sun.

A beige flicker on the wall caught her eye, which she thought at first must be a lizard. It came into focus: a huge cricket, the biggest she'd ever seen, poised on the top of the wall.

It seemed to watch her a moment, then turned and hopped away down into the road.

She guessed where it had come from: the next cottage up the hill. Her cousin had been living there with his wife and two children but, two months before, his wife had died of consumption, and just two days ago he'd moved out, unable to bear being there alone. They'd always been plagued by crickets living in the warmth behind their stove, but for two days now the stove had been cold.

Next morning she knew that the cricket's song had indeed been a signal, but not to her. Overnight the crickets had moved out too, poured down the hill and under the door and through cracks she didn't know they had, and that was why ever since there had been crickets behind the range.

They always called them a curse. You couldn't hang up anything made of silk to dry by the fire, they'd eat it right through.

But Nanny remembered the stillness of the air that day, that lone defiant cricket watching and waiting, and that beautiful song, a song of hope and salvation, and when she did, she said, she thought of it as a blessing.

&

I stopped weeping. I dried my eyes and picked up my pen and, including everything my mother had told me, I wrote the novel again.

CONSEQUENCE

CATHY SAID, 'YOU can't publish it!'
She had just collected me from the station and we were sitting in the station car park. Our mother no longer lived within walking distance of the station. At long last she and David had sold up the big house with its rotting roof, its hard-to-heat rooms, and the huge garden that right to the bitter end, in her eighties, she still struggled to maintain, weeding on her hands and knees. At last David had a place of his own, and our mother had bought a house on a modern bijou estate on the edge of town.

I swallowed. I watched a woman crossing with a pushchair through the bright day like someone on a screen, someone in a life, in some kind of narrative, where things were simple.

Cathy went on: 'Think of David. He doesn't know.'

'Are you sure?'

Once they'd left the big house, David had surprised me by taking to coming over whenever I visited, at first self-consciously positive, as he'd been that day at the station after the funeral, but growing increasingly relaxed.

'Are you sure he won't have guessed? The way he was about Dad's coffin . . .'

'Quite. He went berserk. He'd go berserk. He couldn't deal with it.'

I stared at her profile, her nose small like our mother's but shaped like our father's. 'You're not subscribing to the old family philosophy of protecting the men?'

She turned to me. The sunlight caught the grey amongst her black curls. 'It's Mum I'm protecting. He wouldn't *want* to believe it. He would deny it. He would think Mum was lying. It would destroy their relationship.'

My hands felt liquid in my lap. I swallowed again.

She started the car.

'But it's just a *novel!*' my mother said to Cathy in her new, cosy, antique-crockery-filled kitchen. 'If it's a novel no one can ever know if it's true!'

Cathy looked hard at my mother, instructive: 'But people always wonder if they are. They think no smoke without fire . . .'

My limbs turned to water.

'Well, change the details,' said my mother, turning to me, urgent. 'The hair colours and things. Change the names and the places.'

I changed the details. I spent the summer on Google Street View and setting incidents and scenes in parts the country far from the ones where we'd lived. I turned the river into a canal, I put the big house on top of a hill, I gave Cathy and my mother light-brown hair.

At the end of the summer I sent the new draft off to Cathy.

'It's no good,' she told me, wretched, when we met again. 'It still rings too true.'

Though, for me, with its fake, forced details, it had become artificial and dead.

She went on: 'It's not just what Dad got up to outside the house. It's everything, the bad temper and the beatings.

393

He had such a different reputation. It would create such a scandal, whatever Mum thinks. She underestimates how upset she would be: you know what she's like about keeping up appearances. And you know she gets ill when she's upset. And if David decided she'd been lying . . . Well . . .'

The old taboo closed around.

I was shocked. I had written a whole novel about it all, I had spent years doing it, thinking deeply about it, but it seemed I'd understood nothing. I'd failed to guess that Cathy would be the one who would feel the need to silence me.

'Why didn't you say when I started writing it?!'

She didn't answer, and I guessed: she knew I didn't have the crucial clue, and wouldn't succeed.

She said, 'I'm sorry.'

Her voice seemed to wobble, but when I looked up her expression was impassive.

And then she slumped. She said, 'Well, look.' Her voice cracked again. 'The thing is, if it all came out, if people asked me about it, I wouldn't be able to deny it. I wouldn't be able not to cry.'

She wasn't a person who cried. In this small town, like our father, she was a cheerful charmer, refusing the role of victim. She was living a different story, a different reality she couldn't deal with having destroyed.

She said, her voice really wobbling now: 'And the thing is, if I started crying I'd never be able to stop.'

❧

We didn't mention the novel again. That autumn it became another taboo subject.

In any case, I'd lost faith in it: I hadn't understood anything.

I was done, I thought, as a writer. That autumn and winter I didn't write a thing. I drank too much. I didn't sleep very well.

When I lay on my left side at night I could feel something hard pressing low in my belly, a dragging ache I had to lie on my stomach to ease.

The doctor referred me to the hospital.

The sonographer showed me the scan. 'You have a cyst, here on your right ovary.'

'But the pain is on the left.'

The sonographer shrugged.

The consultant told me: 'It's a follicle that never got released. We need to check that it's not malignant.'

That night my mother rang me. 'Cathy's in hospital.'

Her heart had started beating like a bird trapped in a chimney.

I waited three weeks for an MRI scan and then another three for the result. I slept less. I tried, for the sake of my health, my aberrant stopped-up ovary, not to drink. I drank even more.

The cyst turned out not to be malignant, and once they'd told me, the sensation in my belly disappeared altogether.

The left ovary, the letter had said.

'Hm,' the consultant said, scanning the conflicting reports. 'It's probably a computer interface problem. It's how you read it. But it doesn't really matter since it's benign.'

It's how you read it: left is right. Black is white.

Cathy recovered. Her heart was quite healthy, they told her; just overactive electrodes sending it into overdrive.

On one of my visits to Thwaite David was due to go on holiday, leaving from Manchester airport. I found myself saying, 'Stay the night, if you like.'

He was pleased. 'Thanks, I will!'

The night he stayed we went with Greg to the pub.

He said, 'We've never really known each other, have we, you and I?'

He was tentative, slightly awkward.

I said carefully, 'Why was that, do you think?'

'I don't know.' He looked wondering.

'Well, I did leave home when you were only twelve . . .'

'Yeah . . .' He tapped his glass.

In the final two years of their time in Thwaite House he had developed cancer of the throat, a disease of passive smokers, but had survived. His hair was now white-grey. He still looked like our father, a leaner, rangier version.

He said, 'God, I was glad to leave that big house. That bloody roof . . .'

'Dad's dream house.'

'Yeah, bloody millstone. All those outhouses, the garages, the old dairy, they all needed re-roofing. But that was Dad. Always loved somewhere to tinker. He had something like that when they lived in London after the war, didn't he?'

'It was his own business,' I told him. 'Or it was supposed to be. He was starting it up with a workmate, but the workmate went behind his back and changed the locks. And Dad went round and he shut the door in his face.'

To my shock, David laughed. 'That's not the story I heard from Dad!'

He said: 'It wasn't a proper business, they were just doing stuff on the side. The guy was diddling him over the invoices, and when Dad found out he had to disappear, because Dad would have killed him.'

It hit me in the gut: yes, he could have been blackmailed, but he *wouldn't* take it lying down . . .

David went on: 'He'd have waited for him down a dark alley with a plank with a nail in it. He did that in the RAF once, he told me: it was how he got his own back on the officer who put him in yankers or whatever they call it.'

He'd stopped laughing. 'That's what he always told me when I was growing up. If anyone does you down that's what you do, wait for them in the dark with a plank with a nail and then scarper.'

He shook his head in rueful disgust.

I thought of him, scared sensitive child that he had been, trying to force himself towards a macho ideal, to please the father who had ignored him for so long.

I wondered if one day he would tell me the thing I was forbidden to tell him.

'See, what can you believe?' Cathy said when I told her what David had told me. 'Maybe all of it's lies.'

I couldn't help laughing.

And I imagined my father in the afterlife, so many of his secrets, in spite of my mother's revelations, still intact.

I saw him thrown from the car in the afterlife forest, picking himself up, leaning on the bonnet and seeing his own reflection: his own wild hair, his own birds'-nest eyebrows.

And I let him go, get in, turn the key and drive off, out of the trees towards the moor and the curved horizon, to whatever lay beyond.